Titus Mooney Merriman

**The Pilgrims**

Puritans and Roger Williams Vindicated

Titus Mooney Merriman

**The Pilgrims**
*Puritans and Roger Williams Vindicated*

ISBN/EAN: 9783337293482

Printed in Europe, USA, Canada, Australia, Japan

Cover: Foto ©Lupo / pixelio.de

More available books at **www.hansebooks.com**

# THE
# PILGRIMS, PURITANS,
## AND
# ROGER WILLIAMS,

## VINDICATED:

### AND

## HIS SENTENCE OF BANISHMENT,

#### OUGHT TO BE

## REVOKED.

BY

REV. T. M. MERRIMAN, A.M.

AUTHOR OF THE "TRAIL OF HISTORY;" AND "WILLIAM, PRINCE OF ORANGE."

BOSTON:
BRADLEY & WOODRUFF,
1892.

# To Posterity.

## HO EVERY ONE — ALL PEOPLE — AND NATIONS!

PROVIDENCE — Charity — Reason — Probability — Possibility — and things Written — compose the World's Great Sanhedrim — whose Judgment, must be consulted, considered, allowed, and adopted — in all our inductions, opinions, conclusions, Constitutions, and Actions. Prejudice, and bribes, to be always Ruled Out.

If this; and this only — be the royal Highway to the just appreciation of the motives, measures, and fruit-bearing; of all noble endeavor; let Posterity therein abound.

Under such scrutiny as this — Posterity will find the Pilgrims, Puritans, and Roger Williams — Vindicated.

Wherefore — "Let there be for them a name, and an Honorable place, among the Benefactors of Mankind."

T. M. MERRIMAN.

SEPTEMBER 15, 1891.

# PREFATORY.

THE Story of JESUS — is the fittest Story, to be told to every creature in all the world.  Next to this, is the Story of Abraham — of Joseph — of Moses — of Daniel — of Apostles — of Martyrs — of Williams — and of Missionaries.

All these belong to the one Story of Love Divine — all interlinked by sweetest bonds of mutual attraction — Stories that are for heart-uplifting, and soul-aspiring, which can never lose their charm.  Every recital makes them more thrilling; every pen that writes them; every tongue, that utters them; every heart that cherishes them; enwreaths them, with the eloquence of the Ages — they ornament the stairway, in Jacob's vision: between Earth and the Heavenly Mansion, whither pass to and fro — the celestial Messengers.

The story of love about the NAZARENE and His friends, is so vast, the Universe is too limited for its expansion — so deep no measuring-line can fathom it — so pure, so constant and constraining, that human reason fails to comprehend it.

Nor has all the world's rhetoric — all speech, gathered up from the Ocean of profuse Oratory — all the sublime conceptions of poetry, and romance; ever been able to portray the Divine, celestial beauty, and sweetness, of that love.

SUCH — was the *sentiment* — that aroused the dauntless *conscientious* souls, of the Pilgrims — the Puritans, and Roger Williams — as profoundly as men's souls were ever stirred. These were exiles, for conscience' sake — and adventurers for righteousness' sake; on a diviner basis, than ever was attempted by the Founders of any Nation, before or since, in all the World.

The story of the Forefathers exhumed from the hoary past — is ever NEW — and the oftener it is repeated, the more it increases in grandeur, and beauty — as do the richest pearls, bro't from the deepest seas — appear best when displayed by the skilful artist — in the *clearest* sunlight.

In PART FIRST of this writing — we have purposely left out all matter of the Early History of N. E. — which does not necessarily belong to this search — so as to keep the special struggle for Religious Liberty — and the parties therein engaged — *sharply* in *view*, to the end.

In PART SECOND — We have briefly recapitulated the Points taken — wise or otherwise — by the actors in the struggle; as they pressed forward to the grand issue before them — and Noting the *one thing* — DONE by the Forefathers; which remains for Posterity to UNDO.

In this endeavor — we have followed no other trail — and no preconceived issue — than to trace the History of Religious Liberty, thro' its Epoch; in New England. To this end, the planting of Plymouth Bay — Massachusetts Bay — and Narragansett Bay Colonies; have furnished our material.

In this Search we have Evolved two Conclusions — and they concern the Ecclesiastical World.

1. That the Standard Ecclesiastical History of New England — *has not yet*, been written.

2. That such a most desirable, and invaluable Church History, *can never be* written; until the Cases of the Pilgrims — Puritans — and of Roger Williams — are *correctly apprehended, and unhesitatingly adopted.* Without unswerving *Justice*, there can be no *Righteousness*.

As in the presence of the JUDGE of the Universe — the following Historical observations, and conclusions — are prayerfully submitted, to whom it may concern.

And as we are taught by the CHRIST — say — " Thy Kingdom come."

T. M. M.

BOSTON, October 19, 1891.

# CONTENTS.

## PART FIRST.

RELIGIOUS LIBERTY — IN NEW ENGLAND, AS IT WAS DEVELOPED, BY THE PILGRIMS — PURITANS — AND ROGER WILLIAMS.

### CHAPTER I.

ORIGIN OF THE PLYMOUTH PILGRIMS . . . . . 1

Section 1. — Their Forerunners. Section 2. — The Separatists. Section 3. — The Exiles. Section 4. — The Pilgrims. Section 5. — The Landing of the Pilgrims.

### CHAPTER II.

SETTLEMENT OF THE PILGRIMS AT PLYMOUTH . . . . 23

Section 1. — Peace with the Indians — Sickness and Want. Section 2. — The Lyford Case. Section 3. — The Pilgrims Independents.

### CHAPTER III.

THE SALEM PURITANS . . . . . . . . 35

Section 1. — They leave England. Section 2. — First Church formed. Section 3. — The Brownes shipped Home. Section 4. — Unabated Zeal.

### CHAPTER IV.

THE BOSTON PURITANS . . . . . . . . 45

Section 1. — Their Charter. Section 2. — Their Theocratic Basis.

## CHAPTER V.

CHARTER OF GOVERNOR AND COMPANY OF MASSACHUSETTS BAY ANNULLED . . . . . . . . . 55

Section 1. — The Right to annul the Charter reserved. Section 2. — The Puritans careless about losing Their Charter. Section 3. — Matters grew worse.

## CHAPTER VI.

ROGER WILLIAMS ARRIVES IN BOSTON . . . . . 67

Section 1. — His Early History. Section 2. — He was called to the First Church in Boston — goes to Salem. Section 3. — He is called to Plymouth. Section 4. — He is re-called to Salem. Section 5. — He is opposed by the Magistrates. Section 6. — He is ordained Pastor of the Church in Salem. Section 7. — His Trial. Section 8. — He is banished.

## CHAPTER VII.

SOUL LIBERTY IN PROVIDENCE, RHODE ISLAND . . . 106

Section 1. — Roger Williams Ostracized, leaves Massachusetts Bay. Section 2. — He settles in Providence, Rhode Island. Section 3. — Providence Plantations Prosper. Section 4. — He founds the First Baptist Church. Section 5. — The Puritans rise to explain.

## CHAPTER VIII.

RELIGIOUS TOLERANCE AND THEOCRATIC ARROGANCE . . 143

Section 1. — Tolerance and Arrogance meet. Section 2. — The Lynn Episode. Section 3. — Roger Williams and John Clarke go to England. Section 4. — The Government of Rhode Island strengthened. Section 5. — The Public Conscience, and Court Conscience.

## CHAPTER IX.

THEOCRACY OF MASSACHUSETTS BAY, UNDER CHARLES II., AND JAMES II. . . . . . . . . . . 164

Section 1. — Theocracy revolutionized. Section 2. — More Synodical Work. Section 3. — Religious Liberty thrives.

Section 4. — First Baptist Church of Boston. Section 5. — Unhappy Strifes. Section 6. — Edicts and Public Opinion. Section 7. — The 5th New England Synod. Section 8. — First Baptist Meeting House in Boston. Section 9. — The Sixth and last New England Synod. Section 10. — Death of Roger Williams. Section 11. — Downfall of Theocracy. Section 12. — The New Charter. Section 13. — The Last Gun.

### CHAPTER X.

TRIUMPH OF RELIGIOUS LIBERTY . . . . . . 198

Section 1. — The Puritans advocate Toleration. Section 2. — Synods declared illegal. Section 3. — The Ecclesiastical Taxes remitted. Section 4. — The "Hollis" Ministerial Fund. Section 5. — Religious and Civil Liberty related. Section 6. — The End of Theocracy. Section 7. — Justice to Roger Williams yet to be done. Section 8. — The True Succession.

## PART SECOND.

REASONS WHY THE SENTENCE OF BANISHMENT PASSED AGAINST ROGER WILLIAMS SHOULD BE REVOKED.

### CHAPTER I.

JESUS CHRIST, AND HIS APOSTLES, TAUGHT THE DOCTRINE OF RELIGIOUS LIBERTY — WHICH ROGER WILLIAMS MAINTAINED — THEREFORE, THAT SENTENCE OF BANISHMENT PASSED AGAINST HIM OUGHT TO BE REVOKED    214

1. Christ's Fundamental Instructions on the Subject of Separation of Church and State. 2. Christ in His instruction to His Disciples discouraged political ambition. 3. Christ's Apostles reproduced His Doctrine of Religious Liberty, in their teachings. 4. Christ's Church for more than 1,000 years, was dandled in the lap of the State Church of Constantine — but Ever, the Fire of Apostolic Zeal — continued to burn on the Altars of Religious Liberty.

## CHAPTER II.

ROGER WILLIAMS, AND THE PURITANS, HAD EQUAL RIGHTS — TO LIFE, LIBERTY, AND THE PURSUIT OF HAPPINESS, IN MASSACHUSETTS BAY — THEREFORE — THEIR SENTENCE OF BANISHMENT AGAINST HIM, OUGHT TO BE REVOKED . . . 223

1. Let us sum up the Cause of Religious Liberty between the Puritans, and Roger Williams — as Plaintiffs, and Defendant. 2. Roger Williams — and the Puritans were Mutually Cordial — holding each other in High Esteem — for Christ's sake. 3. Let Posterity assume towards Roger Williams and the Puritans the most Liberal and Cordial Use of the "Olive Branch and Mantle of Charity."

## CHAPTER III.

THE DOCTRINE OF RELIGIOUS LIBERTY AS ADVOCATED BY ROGER WILLIAMS, SURVIVES : — WHILE THE THEOCRATIC SYSTEM OF THE PURITANS HAS DISSOLVED AWAY — THEREFORE, THEIR SENTENCE OF BANISHMENT AGAINST HIM — OUGHT TO BE REVOKED . . . . . . . 255

A. Theocracy declined, through its own Mistakes. B. Remarkable Stages, of the *Decrease* of Theocracy — and Increase of Religious Liberty — *Before* ; Roger Williams' Banishment. C. Continued Decline of Theocracy *After;* his Banishment. D. The Continued, and *Demolishing Blows* that fell upon Theocracy, after Roger Williams' Death. E. That *Sentence*, should be REVOKED; though Theocracy is gone. F. "Let Roger Williams have some Distinguished Mark of Esteem, in Boston."

# THE PILGRIMS, PURITANS, AND ROGER WILLIAMS, VINDICATED.

## CHAPTER I.

*ORIGIN OF THE PLYMOUTH PILGRIMS*

### SECTION I.—THEIR FORERUNNERS.

"Rise O my Soul, pursue the path
By ancient Worthies trod."

"BEHOLD I send my Messenger before thy face, who shall prepare thy way before thee." "So shall My Word be; it shall accomplish that which I please; it shall prosper whereto I send it." Such words are suggestive of the glowing discoveries, we hope to make in our search for the *paths* of the *messengers;* and what the "Head of the Church," has accomplished through them, by HIS WORD.

A remnant of this long line of ancient "Worthies," is most familiarly known to us by the name of "Waldenses." Of them Dr. Mosheim says: "Their true Origin is hid in the remotest depths of antiquity: they are the seed of the "PRIMITIVE CHURCHES"—first planted by CHRIST, and His APOSTLES. Their existence, spirit, and zeal in the Dark Ages, engendered the important changes, which prepared the way for the Reformation;

which has proved to be the forerunner of the light and liberty of this Nineteenth Century.

Three Hundred years, previous to the coming of the Pilgrim Fathers, to America; the papal church, held a "Reign of Terror" over the nominal Christian World. Kings submitted their *necks* to the *foot* of the Pope; and the Waldenses were scattered as "partridges on the mountains," obliged to "hide themselves in the dens and caves of the earth," or fall a prey to those, who "went about, seeking whom they might devour."

But scattered here and there, was a Prince; whom God raised up, moved with compassion, for the oppressed Waldenses; who extended the arm of civil protection over a few men of learning, and piety, through whose labors the "day-star of freedom" from popish tyranny arose, and the light of the glorious Gospel of Christ, again dawned upon the world.

Such was the important service rendered by the Duke of Lancaster, England, who protected John Wickliffe in making the First Translation of the Bible into English, in 1380; which gave irrepressible impulse to the Reformation. Wickliffe was Born 1344; Died 1384. His followers were called Lollards, so nearly did his sentiments correspond to those of Walter Lollard; an eminent Waldensian "bard," who formerly visited England, and won many converts. Wickliffe's Doctrines, of the Sufficiency of the Bible, as a rule of Faith and Practice; and the Separation, and Independence of churches of Christ, from all hierarchical domination; continued to leaven the intelligence, and consciences of the nation, until the rise of the Pilgrims.

Early in the 15th Century, John Huss, was Chaplain

to the Queen of Bohemia and also Rector of the University of Prague. While in this position, an officer from Oxford University, conveyed to him the writings of Wickliffe. These he read with avidity, and disseminated them by pulpit and pen, until his influence was feared by the Pope. Huss was summoned to the popish Council of Constance, where he would not have ventured, but for the *assurance* of a " safe-conduct ;" from Emperor Sigismund — but — he was betrayed — doomed by the Council, and burnt at the stake, in 1415. This outrage the Bohemians resented, by repudiating popery. They gained "Freedom of Worship," under the intrepid Ziska ; and Bohemia became a stronghold of the Reformation. They "threw off a yoke they were not able to bear ;" the same was done by the Pilgrim Fathers.

William Tyndale, was Born 1477 ; Died 1536.

In the fore part of the 16th Century, Frederick the Wise promoted Martin Luther to be Doctor of Divinity in the University of Wittenberg, and protected him, in his vehement attacks upon the flagrancies of the popedom. Many learned and zealous men espoused the cause of Reform ; and sad to say differences arose among the Reformers — as, about the Lord's Supper. Luther, rejected the popish tenet of *tran*-substantiation, but held to *con*-substantiation. Carolstadt, and the Swiss Reformers, maintained the Supper to be merely *symbolical*.

This freedom of Thought, spread among all classes, and aroused a strong determination to maintain freedom against all oppression. In 1524, broke out the "War of the Peasants" — of which Frederick said ; "Perhaps the cause of these commotions, is, that these poor creatures have not been *allowed* to have the Word of God, preached fully among them."

In 1529, the Princes of Europe became disgusted with the insolent dealing of the Pope, and formed themselves into a league defensive ; and issued their famous *Protest* — hence they were called, " PROTEST-ANTS " — in which they declared their determination, to protect their people by the civil power, in the right, to embrace and enjoy, unmolested, the Reformed Religion.

In 1534, Henry VIII., of England ; imitated the example of the Continental Princes, by absolving the English from all allegiance to the Pope ; and declaring himself, as the head of the national church. Archbishop Cranmer was "the power behind the throne," in the formative stage of Henry's church. In the time of Edward VI. the liturgy was defined and established by law.

Among the ceremonials were many copied from Rome ; and which were so manifestly popish, that numbers of the bishops conscientiously protested against their adoption ; and in this noble stand, for complete *Separation*, they shared the ardent sympathy of multitudes of the People.

SECTION 2. — THE SEPARATISTS.

This conscientious opposition to the ceremonials, was intensified by the access of the People to the *First* PRINTED version of the Scriptures in the English Language ; translated by Tyndale ; and published by Coverdale, in 1535. This invaluable treasure they perused with the greatest eagerness, not as a Book of Ceremonials, but as a Divine Revelation ; an indispensable authority, in politics, morals, and religion. So strong and rapid was the growth of this sentiment, that multitudes were of one mind ; that all existing institutions, of Church and State — the social relations, and habits or every-day life, should all be made Conformable to this DIVINE MODEL.

The multitudes of this conscientious way of thinking, embraced persons of all ranks ; the humbler classes — yeomen — traders — mechanics — merchants — landholders — the nolility — and the clergy. Of these it is written — " The symmetry of their lives ; the Scriptural character of their Doctrines ; their faith in Christ ; their assurance of regeneration, and adoption, as the children of God by faith ; and the bold plans they entertained for social, civil, moral, and religious improvement ; brought them into sympathy with all that was right, and heroic in the Nation. They denounced the ecclesiastical ceremonials ; and presently the hierarchy ; and yet they entertained a profound reverence for the true Church, itself ; and a superstitious terror of Schism." The People holding these sentiments, were for distinction ; and reproach ; called PURITANS.

But, as revolutions never go backward — and as Henry VIII. had set the example, in repudiating the pretensions of Pope Paul III., in 1534 ; for the purpose of organizing a separate form of Worship ; and now that multitudes were full in the faith, that they would lose nothing by separating from the King's Church ; some of the more conscientious, ardent, and bolder ones, among the Puritans ; took counsel of the Lord, and went forward. Traditional " reverence for the Church," *per se*, and terror of Schism, formed a Rubicon, across which some of them dare not pass ; but with others, the power of superstitious reverence, to charm; and the terror of schism to frighten; had passed away. Ere long they conscientiously dared to follow their convictions by renouncing the King's church, and setting up another, upon what they conceived to be the BIBLE model.

These "Separatists" of England, were greatly encouraged by the example of the Reformers, on the Continent; especially in Germany, where under the reformation of Martin Luther, they succeeded in compelling Charles V., in behalf of the Pope; to sign the "Peace of Religion," in Sept. 25, 1555. This gave such of the countries of Europe as chose, the right to refuse the Church of Rome, and accept the Protestant faith. Thus "Separation" grew.

Quickly following this event, was the attempt to force upon the Netherlands; the yoke of the papal church. The policy of this attempt was "to exterminate heresy, by exterminating heretics." In opposition to this horrible plot, arose the immortal "WILLIAM; PRINCE of ORANGE;" who knowing the inwardness of this measure, was first moved with compassion, for those who knew not their fate. It was during his herculean efforts, to roll back the flood that was to carry, the Inquisition into the Netherlands; that the bloody "Massacre of St. Bartholomew," occurred. This noble endeavor he prosecuted to a glorious success, even to the end of his life — by assassination. When the Prince of Orange, *fell;* the "Inquisition" fell, in the Netherlands; and then began its demolition throughout the civilized world. Thus Holland, thro' this renowned Prince, was the first Country of Europe, to throw off the Papal yoke, and in place of it, proclaim *Religious Liberty;* and it soon became the refuge of the oppressed for conscience' sake, from England ; and other Countries.

All these bold movements on the Continent, encouraged the English "Separatists," to "obey God rather than men ;" and to take the stand, Luther did at the Diet of Worms, in 1521 ; "Here I stand : I cannot do otherwise, God help me. Amen." This growing Spirit of Freedom in Worship, caused a division between the bold, and timid, Puritans ; the latter conscientiously remained *in*, the establishment ; while the others conscientiously left it, for a purer model, in 1582. The Conformist, "Puritans," signalized their religious zeal, by calling loudly for severe penal statutes ; against the Catholics, whom they denounced as idolaters. The infamous "Court of High Commission ;" was established ; as a check upon Catholics ; and ".Separatists" too ; in the reign of Elizabeth. Its vocation was the same, as that of the Spanish Inquisition.

Upon the accession of James I., in 1603, Prelacy was greatly strengthened, and the bishops set up pompous claims to the Apostolic succession ; they also maintained a supernatural efficacy for the ordinances of the Church, as administered by themselves : and all this conscientiously for the purpose of bringing into contempt, the religious observances of the "Separatist" assemblies. By these measures, and the persecutions of the Court; most of their meetings were broken up, and all "Separatists" from the Church, were compelled to worship in secret — as, "from fear of the Jews."

Two of these Congregations, existed in the counties of Nottingham, Lincoln, and York; in the North of England. Mr. JOHN SMYTH; and Mr. RICHARD CLIFTON; were their first Pastors. Mr. JOHN ROBINSON; who succeeded Mr. Clifton as pastor, was among his converts. Mr. William Brewster, was chosen Elder and Teacher. After being harassed, fined, and imprisoned by the bishops, beyond endurance; they resolved upon Flight to Holland; where Religious Liberty could be enjoyed.

But even this was rendered extremely difficult, by a law passed in Elizabeth's time, which made such migrations an offence against the crown. All ports and harbors were carefully watched to prevent any "Separatists," getting away. Upon its being known that these congregations in the North of England, were preparing to flee, strict orders were given, that they should not be suffered to depart. On one occasion a company of them had secured passage, and their effects were on ship-board; when the treacherous captain set sail, and after proceeding a short distance, returned, and delivered these terror-stricken "Separatists," to the resentment of their enemies.

### SECTION 3.— THE EXILES.

But, gaining wisdom by this failure, and fearless of the law, made to crush them at home; in less than a year, a second attempt was made to escape their ecclesiastical tormentors; but, while a part of the men had gotten on board the ship, the barge that was to take their wives and children, to the vessel, was detained by low water; when a body of armed men from the King's

Church, came upon them. The captain of the ship, fearing for his own safety, hoisted sail and made off for Holland; leaving those helpless families, in the hands of their captors. The ship that bore the men away, encountered a heavy storm on the coast of Norway, and barely escaping shipwreck; all reached shore in safety. They, who had those families on their hands, could make no ready disposition of them, and yet were obliged to provide for their support; were glad to let them go; and the next year, these families were re-united in Holland. A church of English exiles, who had preceded them, under the care of their pastor, Mr. Ainsworth, at Amsterdam, extended their hospitalities; in the free land of William Prince of Orange; to these their fellow-sufferers for conscience' sake.

This first company of exiles from Scrooby, England, were soon followed by others of their number. While now enjoying repose from the persecutions of the Prelates; Pastor John Smyth, betook himself anew, to the study of the Scriptures. He soon found that conscience, consistency, and Scripture; required of them not only to separate from the Church of England; but also to renounce their Episcopal ordination, and baptism. In these views he was conscientiously opposed by Pastors Robinson, Clifton, and Ainsworth. Mr. Robinson, sought advice of Bishop Hall, in the matter. The bishop replied, — "Mr. Smyth tells you true . . . either you must go forward to him, or come back, to the Church, of England. All your Rabbins cannot answer the charge he makes against you."

As the result of this discussion, Mr. Smyth was conscientiously disfellowshipped by the other pastors, and the Amsterdam church ; as the easiest way to evade his logic. But this did not end the matter; for his influence soon became so formidable, that many were conscientiously drawn to his views, and he received the appellation, of — the "GRANDEE, of the Separation." Mr. Smyth and his followers became Baptists ; and returned to England ; where they united with their brethren, in conscientiously "CHALLENGING KING AND PARLIAMENT, TO THEIR FACES ; DETERMINED NOT TO GIVE WAY, NO NOT A FOOT ; UNTIL THEY HAD OBTAINED RELIGIOUS LIBERTY FOR ALL PEOPLE." This was achieved, at the accession of William III, and Mary, in 1688. He was grandson of William Prince of Orange, of Holland.

The boldness and success of Mr. Smyth, "threatened to swallow up all the separation besides " — of which there were many in Amsterdam ; and hence to avoid discussion with them, they ; with their pastor, Mr. John Robinson, removed to Leyden. Here they remained in peace for 10 or 12 years, but finding it difficult to obtain a livelihood ; and that their children were leaving them as fast as they grew up ; they were satisfied that their little band would ultimately become extinct.

Colonization in America, being much agitated at this time, these "Separatists," resolved to emigrate to the New World ; where they might be away from the temptations and vices of the Old World, for their children's sakes ; and where they might enjoy uncontaminated, and undisturbed, by the State Church ; "Freedom to Worship God." At first they proposed to go to Guiana, where the Dutch had trading-posts ; but upon afterthought, concluded to settle in North Virginia ; "provided they might establish a separate plantation, and be *allowed to arrange religious matters, according to their own ideas.*"

Forthwith two of their number; Robert Cushman, and John Carver, were sent to England as their agents, to procure a Grant of land from the Va. Co. This was readily promised; and a promise from the King, that they should not be molested, on the subject of Religion. But a bare promise, even from his majesty, was not satisfactory, to a people who had resolved to enjoy "LIBERTY OF CONSCIENCE WHATEVER IT MIGHT COST."

Another attempt was made to obtain a grant of the Dutch, which also failed; when Mr. Cushman, and Mr. Brewster, proceeded to England and made a second attempt, to obtain a grant of the Virginia Company; and were successful. Mr. Thomas Weston, and a few other London merchants, out of sympathy with their religious views, agreed to advance the necessary means, to plant the Colony; not however on very favorable terms to the Colonists: as every $50 paid in, was to represent the same interest in the Corporation, as an able-bodied man, who should join the Company. The whole property, was to remain a joint-stock for seven years; at the end of which, a division of the proceeds, was to be made, and the co-partnership dissolved. The banks of the noble Hudson River, near its mouth, were designated as the future home of these "Separatists."

Preparations for their departure, were immediately commenced. It was arranged that Mr. Robinson should remain with those who did not go in the first company, and that Mr. Brewster should accompany the pioneers. It was also agreed that each part should be considered a distinct; separate; independent church; neither one of them under any ecclesiastical jurisdiction to the other; nor to any Synod; Convocation; or Council; whatsoever. Those who remained, were expected to follow in due time.

The formalities of departure, were as follows: —

First. — A fast Sermon, by Pastor Robinson. His text was, in Ezra 8:21. "Then I proclaimed a fast there, at the river of Ahava, that we might afflict ourselves before our God, to seek of him a right way for us, and for our little ones, and for all our substance."

In the course of his Sermon he said — "Brethren we are quickly to part from one another, and whether, I may ever live to see your faces on earth any more, the God of Heaven only knows. . . . I charge you before God and His blessed angels, that you follow me no farther than you have seen me follow the Lord Jesus Christ. If God reveal anything to you by any other instrument of His, be as ready to receive it, as ever you were to receive any truth by my ministry; for I am very confident that the Lord has yet more truth to break forth out of his Holy Word. . . . The Lutherans cannot be drawn to go beyond what Luther saw . . . and the Calvinists, you see, stick fast where they were left by Calvin, that great man of God, who yet saw not all things."

And yet, Mr. Robinson himself, was not conscientiously willing to be drawn forward to the views of that "instrument of God," Mr. John Smyth; not even with Bishop Hall to urge him on.

Second. — The embarkation. About July 22, 1620, a company of devout men and women, with their children, went on board a frail vessel, at Delft Haven, Holland; some standing in little groups in earnest conversation; others, gazing upon familiar objects for the last time; many were hurrying to and fro, solicitous that all things be made ready for the important adventure. When the hour of their departure arrived, the Pastor and the little company kneeled together upon the deck of the ship, and in a most fervent prayer, he commended them to the Kind protection of their Heavenly Father.

Third. — The parting farewell. After the religious services were over — "with mutual embraces," they took leave of those who had come from a distance, to give them the parting hand, and pronounce upon them their farewell blessing. Governor Bradford writes — " Truly doleful was the sight, of that sad and mournful parting; to see what sighs, and sobs, and prayers, did sound among them; what tears did gush from every eye, and pithy speeches pierced each other's hearts; that sundry of the Dutch strangers that stood on the quay as Spectators, could not refrain from tears."

Fourth. — The final adieu. Governor Winslow writes — "When they separated, we gave them a volley of small shot, and three pieces of Ordnance; and so lifting up our hands to each other, and our hearts for each other, to the Lord God, we departed and found His presence with us."

From Leyden, the Pilgrims sailed to Southampton, Eng., in the vessel Speedwell; where they found Mr. Cushman and the rest of their company, preparing to sail in the larger vessel, Mayflower; under Captain Jones. While tarrying there, they received a comforting letter from Pastor Robinson; which they came together and heard read with great pleasure. The whole company was divided into two parties for the voyage, each party with the consent of their ship captains, chose a Governor, and two or three Assistants, who were to have a general supervision over them.

On the 5th of August, the two vessels went to sea on their adventurous voyage; but they had not proceeded far, before the Speedwell was found to be in a leaking condition, and both vessels put back to Dartmouth. About Aug. 21 they went to sea the second time, and after sailing nearly 100 leagues the Speedwell was found to be leaking again; and both vessels returned to Plymouth. It was now determined to sail in only one vessel; and among those who could not go, was the energetic Mr. Cushman. Captain Jones took on board the Mayflower, 101 persons, and their stores, and on Sept. 6th, started the third time.

### SECTION 4. — THE PILGRIMS.

How thrilling the moment! This expedition surpassed in importance, that of the famed "Argonauts"— or that of "Dido"— or of "Æneas"— or even that of "Columbus"— just in proportion as one event in God's providence surpasses another. This was the first band of Christian adventurers; driven from home and country for *conscience*' sake, to go forth and seek a place to worship God. No aid from the Government of their country, not even of transportation; which felons, would have had. But glory, was to rest upon their memory in history; and execration, upon that of their persecutors. Like the modern Missionary, they could say — "Native land, Farewell"— but unlike the Missionary, who goes to a nation sitting in darkness — a nation in darkness was to follow the light of the Pilgrims; they carried the "torch of Liberty" — that light which followed them was Christ.

The Mayflower had not been long on her way, before she encountered a fearful storm; and it was only with the utmost exertion that girding irons and other helps, were applied to certain parts of the ship, that the brave souls on board strengthened her for the voyage. So, as those, who first fled to Holland met a fearful storm on the coast of Norway, were preserved on their way safely; these also, were kept, amid the perils of the Sea. One is reported to have died on the way; and one was born; before they landed, so keeping their number good. On Nov. 9th, the cheering cry of "Land, Land," was heard. Although their destination was the Hudson River, they had become weary with their long voyage, and finding the coast both difficult and dangerous to navigate, they resolved to land inside of Cape Cod Bay. Nov. 21st, religious services were held on board the Mayflower, to offer thanksgiving for their preservation at sea, and to supplicate Divine favor in future.

Before landing however, they concluded, that, as the place was outside the grant of the Va. Co. whose Patent they held; and, as "some of the party were not well affected to unity and concord, but gave some appearance of faction;" it was necessary to institute, a "COMPACT:" or form of Government. Accordingly the following document was considered and adopted: —

"Having undertaken for the Glory of God; and the advancement of the Christian faith; and honor of our

King and Country; A voyage, to plant the First Colony, in the northern parts of Virginia: We do by these presents solemnly and mutually, in the presence of God, and one another; Covenant, and combine ourselves together into a civil body politic, for our better ordering and preservation, and furtherance of the ends aforesaid: — and by virtue hereof to enact, constitute, and frame such just and equal laws, ordinances, acts, constitutions, and offices, from time to time, as shall be tho't most meet and convenient for the general good of the colony: — Unto which we promise all due submission, and obedience."

This important document was signed by all the Men, on Nov. 21, 1620, in the cabin of the Mayflower. Their names, were as follows: — John Carver: William Bradford: Edward Winslow: William Brewster: Izaac Allerton: Miles Standish: John Alden: John Turner: Francis Eaton: James Chilton: John Craxton: John Billington: Moses Fletcher: John Goodman: Samuel Fuller: Christopher Martin: William Mullins: William White: Richard Warren: John Howland: Stephen Hopkins: Degory Priest: Thomas Williams: Gilbert Winslow: Edmund Morgeson: Peter Brown: Richard Bitteridge: George Soule: Edward Tilley: John Tilley: Francis Cooke: Thomas Rogers: Thomas Tinker: John Ridgdale: Edward Fuller: Richard Clark: Richard Gardiner: John Allerton: Thomas English: Edward Dotey: Edward Leister.

The choice of Governor, in this compact, based upon the consent of the governed, fell upon Mr. John Carver, unanimously; thus conferring upon him the distinguished honor of being the first Governor in New

England, chosen by the people. He was reported, as "A pious and well-approved gentleman." Mr. Miles Standish, was chosen as Military commander; he having seen service and acquired some distinction, in the Spanish army. Thus the civil government of the Pilgrims, was organized, and officers chosen before they left the deck of the Mayflower. "Exiles," sometimes become rivals.

We need not look to the founding of ancient Republics, for a better example than this, of a clear and just conception of what constitutes the germ of self-government. Indeed the prophecy, that — "The Kingdoms of this world shall be given to the Saints of the Most High" — is to be fulfilled thro' the compacting together of Christian men, "for the glory of God; the advancement of the Christian faith; and the honor of our country;" choosing "pious and well-approved gentlemen," to the highest offices in the gift of the people. It is the following out of this thought, so far, and so nearly as we may have done it; that has given to the United States of America, the enviable, and unsurpassed distinction, accorded to this Nation, among all the Nations of the earth.

In this compact, of the Pilgrims, we see no vestige of the Union of Church and State. They were a church in Yorkshire, they were a church in Leyden, and a church when they went aboard the Mayflower; but had reached Cape Cod Bay, before their civil compacting, took place: and in the compact nothing is said, concerning the church: each was separate and distinct from the other; the one, "Rendering unto Cæsar the things that are Cæsar's" — the other "Rendering unto God the things that are God's." Such is the safe "path, which shineth brighter and brighter," in which the Church ; and State, of America ; are advancing, from Glory to Glory.

### SECTION 5. — THE LANDING OF THE PILGRIMS.

Behold these, Pilgrims from Scrooby, safe at anchor within Cape Cod Bay — out of the way of England's cruel Prelates — safe from the perils of the deep — Thanksgiving and prayer duly observed — the Compact accepted in the presence of God, and of each other — the next step was to enter the land of promise, and of perpetual inheritance.

The First, party of 16, under Capt. Standish, was sent on shore to search for a place to inhabit; with orders to return in two days. In this tour they saw a few Indians, and some wild game. Upon finding some excellent springs of water, they state — "We sat us down and drank our first New England water, with as much delight as ever we drank drink in all our lives."

They found a large copper kettle, and a small quantity of corn ; of this they took the kettle full, and also filled their pockets ; intending to compensate the owners, if they could be found. This corn served as seed for planting, the next spring.

The Second, party. After returning to the ship, and relating their adventures ; another company was sent out in a Shallop, to search along the shore for a landing-place, but returned without success. While this party was absent, a young son was born to Mr. White and wife, on board the Mayflower ; this was the first English child born in New England. He was named,

"Peregrine White;" and lived to be 83 years, 8 months old; he died in Marshfield, Mass., July 1704.

The Third, party. On December, 16, a company of 18 men, was selected to look for a place of landing; consisting of — "Ten of our Men"— Miles Standish: John Carver: William Bradford: Edward Winslow: John Tilley: Edward Tilley: John Howland: Richard Warren: Stephen Hopkins: and Edward Dotey. "Two of our seamen " — John Allerton: and Thomas English: "with six of the ship's company " — two names only are given: Masters Copin; and Clarke.

Those 18, in an open shallop, who, after spending a large part of two days, "in getting clear of a sandy point, which lay within less than a furlong of the ship — the weather being very cold and hard, two of their number were very sick; one of them almost swooning with cold — and the gunner for a day and night, seemingly sick unto death; they found smoother water and better sailing on the 17th, but so cold that the water froze on their clothes and made them many times, like coats of iron." Obtaining at last a night's rest the next morning after prayers were over; they were attacked by Indians. A combat ensued, the savages rushed upon them with hideous yells and showers of arrows; but with the superior weapons of the white men, they were soon put to flight. This is called, "The First Encounter."

After offering thanks for their victory, they returned to their shallop. While on their search for a landing a violent storm arose, and after being driven helplessly about for several hours, "they found themselves, when the darkness of midnight had almost overtaken them, under the lee of a small island, where they remained all that night in safety; there mast split in three pieces, keeping their watch in the rain." In their record we find — "Here we made our rendezvous all that day, being Saturday.

"20 of December, on the Sabboth day wee rested."

Here is the first instance of the observance of the Christian Sabbath in New England  This Island, was called "Clark's Island," in honor of the Master Clark, of the Mayflower; who was with them at this time. Near the centre of the island is a large bowlder on which it is reported they held divine service, on that Sabbath; now called "Pulpit Rock." Upon the suggestion, of the Hon. R. C. Winthrop, LL.D. in his Oration at the 250th anniversary of the Landing of the Pilgrims, the above sentence; — "On the Sabboth day wee rested "— has been engraved upon "Pulpit Rock," on Clark's Island.

Farther inland they discovered in their search, a beautiful river emptying into the Bay, which they named Jones River; in honor of Capt. Jones, of the Mayflower.

Mr. Winthrop in his Oration says: — "It does not require one to sympathize with the extreme Sabbatarian strictness of Pilgrim, or Puritan, in order to be touched by the beauty of such a record, and of such an example." The record of the next day after — "We rested " — runs as follows : — " On Monday we sounded the harbour and found it a very good harbour for our shipping : we marched also into the land, and found divers cornfields and little running brooks, a place very good for situation ; so we returned to our ship again with good news to the rest of our people, which did much comfort their hearts."

This, was the Famous "LANDING OF THE PILGRIM FATHERS." Not the going ashore of the whole company from the Mayflower; but, the landing of the 18, from the Shallop, who were sent to "spy out the land" — and "to seek of God a right way for us, and for our little ones, and for all our substance:" December 21, 1620. The shortest day in the year — in mid-winter.

Dr. Winthrop, says — "They have landed at last, after 66 days of weary and perilous navigation. . . . And when the sun of that day went down, after the briefest circuit of the year — New England had a place and a name — a permanent place, a never to be obliterated name — in the history, as well as the geography, of civilized Christian man."

During this searching and landing, the Mayflower was still in the harbor of Cape Cod, with the rest of the men, women, and children, awaiting the return of the successful expedition. Returning, Mr. William Bradford, met the sad news; that, the next day after the shallop set out, Mrs. Bradford, fell overboard — very mysteriously, and was drowned.

On Friday Dec. 25; Christmas Day, they weighed anchor, and on Saturday the next day, the Mayflower, "came safely into a safe harbor." Another, "Sabbath they rested;" and on Monday the 28th, the famous "Plymouth Rock" — not another bowlder like it, all along that shore of sand, was known — was pressed by the feet of the Pilgrims, as they Landed. Little did they think of the fame to which this stepping-stone to Freedom, would attain — but with the chief corner-stone in Zion, they were familiar.

"On Christ the solid Rock I stand,
All other ground is sinking sand."

Gradually, safely all were Landed.

By these Pilgrims, a church was planted in the New England wilderness. Says Winthrop — ". . . That event was in its inception and completion, eminently and exclusively a religious movement.

The Pilgrims left Scrooby as a church. They settled in Amsterdam and in Leyden as a church. They embarked in the Mayflower as a church. They came to New England as a church. Without any Patent to a foot of the land, where they settled — without indulgence, from the Pope — without permit from King: or Primate — without license from Council; or Synod — Independent of Men; but under Law to Christ."

In remembrance of the kindness shown them in their distress, by their friends in Plymouth, England, from which they finally set sail, they called the place now chosen as their future home — NEW PLYMOUTH. These, were the "PILGRIM FATHERS."

## CHAPTER II.

### SETTLEMENT OF THE PILGRIMS AT PLYMOUTH.

> " What gave them strength 'mid all their toil.
> In every hour of need
> To plant within this sterile soil,
> A glorious Nation's seed ? "
> HEMANS.

SECTION I. — PEACE WITH THE INDIANS. — SICKNESS AND WANT.

SOON after, "the Landing;" the whole Company of the Pilgrims was divided into 19 Families ; each single man, being required to join himself, to some one of these families. They were soon very busy in felling trees, and erecting their cabins. One main building was first provided 20 feet square, as a "common rendezvous;" until they got their houses built, and their families, and goods removed from the Mayflower. While Gov. Carver, and William Bradford, lay sick in this main building, it took fire, and tho' no one was injured, the building was consumed. Their houses when finished — "stood on rising ground, in two rows, with a storehouse in the midst."

As a measure of precaution, suggested by the suspicious movements of the Indians, the Pilgrims extemporized a Military Organization ; at the head of which, they appointed Capt. Miles Standish, as Commander-in-chief — Jan. 1621. A few small cannon, were soon landed.

But to their great surprise and joy, on Friday morning March 16, an Indian walked boldly into the place, and began to cry out — "WELCOME ENGLISHMEN; WELCOME ENGLISHMEN." His name was Samoset; and thro' him, and another friendly Indian, named Squanto; a league of friendship was formed between Gov. Carver; and Massasoit; Chief of the Wampanoags, on Narragansett Bay.

This was a remarkable interposition of Divine Providence, in behalf of his cause, now in the hands of the Pilgrims; for altho' they held a Charter from the Virginia Co., to settle on the banks of the Hudson River; that instrument was of no use to them, now that they were settled at Plymouth. Hence this "Welcome Englishmen," gave the Pilgrims a Home, "on a wild and savage shore." By this happy turn, they were neither intruders, nor usurpers; and no longer, "Pilgrims and Strangers." The strong and lasting friendship between the Pilgrims and the Wampanoags, gave them a better title to their lands, than they could have obtained even from the King of England; out of all the lands he had usurped from the Red Men of America. All, white Men's titles, were not thus good, in those days.

During their first winter in Plymouth, the Pilgrims were visited with a severe sickness, which swept off nearly half of their number by death; among them Gov. Carver; who died, April 5. On the same day the Mayflower left, for her return to England. Mr. William Bradford was next chosen Governor.

On the 10th Nov. the Colonists were made extremely

happy over the arrival of the Ship Fortune, with 35 new-comers; including among them, those left behind with the Speedwell, and also Mr. Robert Cushman, an ardent friend of the Colony. He soon found some "discontents already apparent," arising out of the "joint-stock" system, which was the financial basis of the Colony; not altogether favorable to the Colonists.

Mr. Cushman, altho' a Layman, preached a Sermon on; "the Sin and Danger of Self-love." This he did in hope of allaying those discontents. He took for his Text 1 Cor. 10: 24. "He said the parts of the text, are two —

I. A dehortation — 'Let no man seek his own' —

II. An exhortation — 'But every man another's wealth.' In handling of which I will —

1. Open the words.
2. Gather the Doctrine.
3. Illustrate the Doctrine. By the Scriptures — by Experience — and by Reason —
4. Apply the same, to every one his portion." Following, is an extract from his Sermon —

"The difference between a temperate good man, and a belly-god, is this — A good man will not eat his morsel alone, especially if he have better than others; but if by God's Providence he have gotten some meat which is better than ordinary, and is better than his other Brethren have; he can have no rest in himself, except he make others partake with him. But a belly-god, will slop all in his own throat; yea, tho' his neighbor come in and behold him eat; yet this gripple-gut shameth not to swallow all."

This *first*, New England Sermon, was published in

London in 1622, and has passed thro' several editions in America. Mr. Cushman returned to England with the Ship Fortune, in Dec., as agent of the Colony; carrying with him a cargo, worth about £500; as the first remittance to the Company from New Plymouth.

Early in 1622, chief Canonicus sent to the Colonists a bundle of arrows, tied up with the skin of a rattlesnake; when Gov. Bradford sent back the skin filled with powder and balls — but the Indians were so terrified with its contents, that after keeping it a while among them on exhibition; returned it to the white faces. This non-acceptance of the "challenge," did not remove from the minds of the Colonists, all suspicion, and they at once took the precaution, to surround their little village with a palisade. News reaching them of an Indian massacre in Virginia, they also proceeded to erect a fort of logs, on the crest of the hill within their palisade, and mounted it with two small cannon This structure was erected at a great cost of labor; but when finished, it served the purposes of Fort; Town-house; and Meeting House.

The Pilgrims, tho' men of peace, deemed it prudent to use means of defence. They went to meeting, with their weapons in hand; prefaced their battles with prayer. They took special pains to keep the Sabbath, as it deserved keeping; walked softly before God; and cautiously amid perils. In a letter from Mr. Robinson, in Holland; after a victory over the Indians, he expressed his regret — "Oh how happy a thing it would have been, that you had converted some, before you had killed any." When at peace, they took great pains to instruct the Natives in the truths of the Bible. The custom of the

Pilgrims in asking a blessing before meals, impressed them favorably, with the "White Man's Worship." They were much interested in the "Ten Commandments;" but objected to the 7th, or to "tying a man to one woman;" as they termed the institution of Marriage.

When reduced to straits for food, and obliged to depend upon fish, clams, and oysters; the Pilgrims gave thanks to God, that they could "suck of the abundance of the seas, and of the treasures hid in the sand." On the occasion of a severe drouth, a day of public humiliation, fasting, and prayer, was appointed, and kept with marked solemnity and earnestness; "the religious exercises continuing for 8 hours." In the morning the sky was cloudless, and unpromising for rain; but before the close of the meeting, "the weather was overcast, and the clouds gathered together on all sides; and on the next morning, distilled such soft, sweet, and moderate showers of rain, continuing some 14 days, and mixed with such seasonable weather; as it was hard to say, whether our withered corn, or drooping affections, were most quickened and revived — such was the bounty and goodness of our God."

This circumstance, also deeply impressed the Indians in favor of the white man's God. Such was the strait to which the Pilgrims were reduced in 1623, that, had their supply of corn been equally divided among them, they would only have had "5 Kernels apiece." This strait is commemorated, at Pilgrim dinners in Plymouth, by placing "5 Kernels," of parched corn upon each plate on the table.

## SECTION 2. — THE LYFORD CASE.

Mr. Winslow, who had been to England in the interests of the Colony, returned, in March 1624. On board the same vessel were Mr. John Lyford; and two others; Oldham, and Conant, associates with him. This Lyford, had been recommended, covertly, by some of the London Partners, as a suitable minister for the Colony. But Mr. Cushman, agent of the Colony in England, wrote to the Plymouth people in Jan. 24, 1624, that — "We send you a preacher, to whom Mr. Winslow and I gave way, to give content to some in London." Upon these recommendations, and Lyford's pretended friendship for the Pilgrims; "bowing and cringing" to them in a very obsequious manner; he so far gained the confidence of Gov. Bradford; as to be invited to his councils with Elder Brewster, and others. He was anxious to be admitted to membership in their church, and after giving evidence of reformation of life, and professing his belief in their doctrines, he was received into their fellowship.

His intimacy however, with Oldham, and Conant, awakened suspicions, that all was not right. As the vessel in which he came over, was preparing to return, Lyford was observed to be very busy in writing letters, to send to England. He even had the imprudence, as well as insolence, to boast of the overturn which his letters would bring about in the affairs of the Colony.

Gov. Bradford, took the precaution from those hints, to follow the ship out of the Harbor, and with the permission of the Captain, opened the letters of both, Lyford and Oldham ; he took copies of some, and kept some, of which he sent copies to England.

The unfaithful twain, not aware of what had been done, soon began to conduct themselves according to the times they hoped were coming. Oldham refused to do military duty, "and rose against the Captain with a deadly weapon." He was tried and sentenced to prison ; but upon confession and promise of amendment, he was released. Lyford showed his insubordination, by attempting to set up Church of England service, by virtue of his Episcopal Ordination. This he did in face of the fact, that he had united with the Pilgrims in Church fellowship.

A meeting of the people was called to consider these matters. Lyford demanded proof of the charges made against him, and his party. Governor Bradford was called upon, to respond in behalf of the Colonists. He took occasion to open up the whole case, by referring to the persecutions the Pilgrims had suffered for their religious opinions in England ; and that they had come here to enjoy those opinions free from molestation ; and enlarged upon the labors and painful sufferings this undertaking had involved. He also reminded Lyford, that altho' he had not shared in these early trials of the Colony, yet when he and his family came here, they were received by the Colonists, with marked kindness, and freely supported, at no small expense ; and that for him, now to plot their ruin, was an act of great "perfidy and ingratitude."

In reply to these charges Lyford expressed his astonishment, and made denial of the same ; and declared that he did not understand the language addressed to him. Upon this show of hypocrisy and effrontery, the Gov. "put in," the copies, and original letters, which he had taken on board the Ship Fortune in Lyford's own handwriting. In one of these he had written to those who sent him out, as a spy, that — "The Leyden Company, Mr. Robinson, and the rest, must be kept back; or all will be spoiled." Lyford was confounded at this evidence against him; Oldham was enraged, and urged his accomplices, to open and violent resistance; but no one dared venture on his bad advice. This conduct of Oldham was specially odious in him, so soon after his release from jail, on promise of good behavior.

Governor Bradford reminded Lyford of his treachery, in breaking open private letters of the Pilgrims; on his voyage from England; of his humble confession when received into their church; and of his promise not to perform the functions of a minister among them, until he had another call to the sacred office; but in violation of this promise, he had assumed the clerical profession, drawn a few followers after him, and had attempted to officiate at the "Lord's Table."

In defence of his ministerial officiousness, Lyford replied, that many persons had complained to him of various abuses which were practised in the Colony; and gave the names of his informants. These persons being called upon to testify, flatly denied the truth of his assertions. In the light of his own conduct, the evidence of his letters, and his own witnesses against him, he saw there was no hope of his acquittal; when he shed some tears. He then confessed that, his "letters against them were false and malicious; and that in his charges against the church; and the Government; he was influenced by unholy pride, and selfishness; he feared his sins were too great to be forgiven; and that if God should send him forth as a vagabond, and fugitive in the earth, it would be no more than he deserved." Altho' both these derelicts were notified to leave the colony, yet the time for Lyford's departure was postponed for six months ; and had his repentance proved sincere in that time, it was the intention of the Governor to pardon him.

His apparent hearty confession, gained for him many sympathies; but before the six months had half expired he actually wrote another libellous letter to his accomplices in England; but the bearer of it, delivered it to Gov. Bradford. Lyford left for Cape Ann ; where he had been called as a minister. He died in Virginia.

SECTION 3. — THE PILGRIMS INDEPENDENTS.

Captain Miles Standish went to England in 1625, in the interests of the Colony. Upon his return, he brought the sad intelligence of the deaths of Pastor John Robinson, of Leyden ; and of Mr. Robert Cushman.

Mr. Robinson did not come with the first Colony of Pilgrims in 1620, for the reason given ; that — when they concluded to colonize in America, one arrangement among them was, that Mr. Robinson should cast in his lot with the major part of the church, and go, or stay, as they might determine. Hence as only the minority concluded to remove, he remained, and Mr. Brewster came with the Pilgrims, in the Mayflower. After Mr. Robinson's death the Church in Leyden disbanded; Mrs. Robinson and family, and the greater part of the church finally came to New Plymouth.

Altho' Elder Brewster came with the Pilgrims as teacher, he steadily refused ordination, tho' often urged to accept it. In those days, the Pastor was the practical, and experimental; and the Teacher, the doctrinal, Preacher; while it was the exclusive privilege of the Pastor, to administer ordinances. The Elders assisted the Pastors, in the work of discipline and were usually ordained. It was the business of the Deacons to pass the elements, at the Lord's Supper, and care for the poor. On Sabbath afternoon a question was propounded, upon which all were at liberty to speak. Collections were taken by, "each one going down to the deacon's seat, and depositing his Contribution."

The Pilgrims, came out from the church of England, and formed themselves into a distinct church; without asking the right so to do, from any one, and hence were Independent.

A mutual agreement was made between those who remained in Leyden, and those who came to Plymouth, that each company should be a distinct, and complete church; thus consistently indorsing their separation from all Establishments — Synods — or Councils — and re-indorsing the doctrine, of separate; individual, Church Independence.

In this direct and simple form of Church Government, we see the germ of the Ecclesiastical Law, that has attained usage in the United States, and is fast becoming general. That is; every church after voluntarily forming themselves into a body, according to the Scriptures, has the exclusive right to choose their own Pastor; or call those to Ordination whom they approve, to exercise ministerial watch care for souls among them, to choose Deacons ; to admit such persons to membership among them, as they approve ; exercise discipline in the body; and to do all things which of right Churches ought to do ; being under Law to Christ, as Head of the Church, according to the Scriptures ; as no other authority for these purposes is named in the Word of God. Hence no other can rightfully be recognized to these ends, either inside or outside, of each Individual, Independent Church. Nor have civil Magistrates any dictation whatever over Churches.

Thus had the Pilgrims set their faces in the right direction, ecclesiastically — and were told by Pastor Robinson ; "to expect that God had yet more light to break forth from His Holy Word." In 1629, some of the men of Plymouth being at Nantasket found there a man, named Ralph Smith ; who had been inhibited at Salem, by Gov. Endicott; and who had officiated as a "Separatist" Minister, while in England. He having the appearance of an upright, pious, man, and wishing to go to Plymouth, they consented. After being there a while, and exercising his gift among them, he was invited to become their Pastor. This invitation he gladly accepted, and thus became nearly, if not actually, the First Pastor of New England. During his pastorate, was the time when Roger Williams, labored in Plymouth. The two offices of Pastor and Teacher, were soon united in that of Pastor. It was not many years, before it became a saying, that — "No Minister stayed long at New Plymouth."

From the foregoing facts, we gather the grand purpose sought by the Pilgrim Fathers — that, of Liberty of worship and Independence in church Order. Being

"Separatists," from the church of England; not willing to be imposed upon by others, thro' Lyford; calling and dismissing their own Pastors; all show their decided conscientious preference, for the Independent form of the Church of Christ. Their sincerity is manifest, in the patient sufferings they endured, for the principles they held, and for the privileges they ultimately secured and enjoyed. To the Pilgrim Fathers, belongs much of the associated honor; of establishing LIBERTY of CONSCIENCE, and CHURCH INDEPENDENCE, in America.

## CHAPTER III.

*THE SALEM PURITANS.*

SECTION I. — THEY LEAVE ENGLAND.

THE Puritans and Pilgrims tho' at first, both members in and of the church of England, are now known in History as two different classes of Reformers.

The Puritans, were the Evangelical part of the church. In composing the Liturgy of the church, of England, after the "Separation;" from the papacy a strong relish existed among the Clergy for popish ceremonials. To their retention in the English service, the Evangelicals conscientiously remonstrated; and for this opposition were called "Puritans."

And yet upon these same questions, in which they agreed in the main, the Puritans, were divided into three classes —

1. Those who quietly remained in the King's Church, and yielded a general conformity, to its ritual, notwithstanding its errors.

2. Those who were conscientiously opposed to the errors of the church; and evaded Conformity to its popish ceremonials as far as possible, and yet clung to membership in its bosom. To this class belonged the Salem Puritans.

3. The radical Puritans, who both conscientiously denounced, and renounced the English establishment:

these were known as "Separatists"—and "Independents." Of this class were the "Pilgrim Fathers."

Mr. John White, of Dorchester, England, Puritan Clergyman, tho' not a Separatist, like the Pilgrims; persuaded several merchants of Dorchester, to attempt a settlement in New England, in 1624; as a station for supplies to be kept, for ships in distress; and also for the encouragement of the cod-fishing business. Cape Ann, was the point selected, for the beginning of the new Settlement. Lyford, and Conant, who were unsuccessful in Plymouth; were engaged in the enterprise.

The project was not successful at first, and given up by many, but Conant, encouraged by promises from Mr. White, of a patent; friends; goods; provisions; etc., if he would remain; "betook himself to Naumkeag, (Salem), as a fitter place for a settlement; in 1626, Mr. White, betook himself, to finding new adventurers in his enterprise; by holding correspondence with persons in London; Lincolnshire; and elsewhere.

The Puritans, were becoming conscientiously weary, with trying to stay in the English Church; and yet not conform to its ceremonials; and still unwilling to try open "Separation," from it—yet with the example of the Plymouth Colony to encourage them; the desirableness of a Puritan refuge across the Atlantic, was suggested, and favorably received. With this end in view, John Humphrey, John Endicott, and four others of Dorchester, at Mr. White's suggestion, obtained, of the "Council for New England;" under Charles I, Mar. 4, 1628; a Patent, for, "The Governor and Company of Massachusetts Bay." It was bounded by two lines; one beginning three miles North of the mouth of the Merrimac River, and following it 3 miles North of every and any part of it, to a certain point West — and the other ; 3 miles South of the mouth of the Charles River, and following that, in the same way to a certain point ; and then both lines to run parallel to each other, straight to the Pacific Ocean.

This belt of land across the Continent of America, the width of Massachusetts, would pass thro' what is now known as New York, Lake Erie, Canada, Michigan, Illinois, Wisconsin, Iowa, Nebraska, Dakota, Idaho, and Oregon. It was truly magnanimous in His Majesty, to be so liberal to the Puritan Colonists — but when we consider that this grant covered territory owned by the Six Nations, in Central New York — and ran thro' lands of other tribes, he knew not who — it savors more of monopoly.

Mr. John Winthrop, Sir Richard Saltonstall, and other wealthy Puritans, became interested in this Colony; and to prepare the way for a larger immigration — "The same year we sent Mr. John Endicott, a fit instrument to begin this wilderness work, and 60, or 70 others with him ; to start a Plantation there ; and to strengthen such as he should find there ; whom we sent thither from Dorchester and places adjoining."

Endicott was welcomed by Conant Sept. 14, 1628. Soon after his arrival a small party was sent by land to explore Massachusetts Bay, where, it had been already decided to plant the Capital of the Colony. In this movement the friends of the enterprise were encouraged, — " From whom the same year, receiving hopeful news, the next year, we sent divers ships over, with about 500 persons more."

Among those who came at this time were four ministers: Messrs. Skelton; Higginson; Bright; and Smith. The last, Mr. Ralph Smith, had secured his passage, and placed his goods on board the ship, before it was known that he was conscientiously a "Separatist." This fact, when found out, excited no little uneasiness among the Puritans; but thro' conscientious fear of making their movement unpopular, should they refuse Mr. Smith, a passage; he was allowed to come; but he was privately and conscientiously required, to promise conscientiously — " Not to exercise his functions (as a minister), within the patent, unless by Endicott's leave." This conscientious precaution of the Puritans, towards the "*Separatists,*" was the "ill-egg," in the Massachusetts Bay Colony.

On May 1, 1629, six ships left England, with many hopeful souls on board. When they passed "Land's End," Mr. Higginson called his family, and the passengers, upon the deck of the ship, and among other things; conscientiously said — " We will not say as the Separatists are wont to say " — (perhaps, an eye askance at Smith) — " Farewell Babylon! Farewell Rome! but we will say Farewell dear England, Farewell dear Church of God in England, and all Christian friends there. We do not go to New England as ' Separatists,' from the church of England." . . . And so he concluded with a fervent prayer for the " King; church; and state; of England."

Note the difference — The Pilgrims; were "Separatists;" and so was John Smyth, of Holland; who resolved to Challenge the King, the church, and the parliament; of England, for religious liberty. Not so, the Puritan;

"not Separatists;" says Higginson. This is the *one* — difference between Pilgrims and Puritans.

Before this fleet of Puritan emigrants set sail, they conscientiously took the precaution, to ferret out all persons from their number, whose companionship they could share; and relieved them; of "encountering the perils of the deep, and of the American Wilderness." Ralph Smith describes them, as "An absolute crew holding all, but such as themselves, as reprobate." During the voyage the seamen were surprised, and edified, at their conscientious observance of prayers, and the exposition of the Scriptures, two or three times a day. The Sabbath was spent entirely, in preaching and catechising; and repeated solemn fasts were held for the success of the voyage.

In these same ships came also the bulk of the Leyden congregation, including Pastor Robinson's Family. On the 24th of June, they arrived in Salem. In strict accordance with the conscientious pledge, taken of Mr. Smith; and the conscientious secret instructions sent to Gov. Endicott; Smith retired to Nantasket; outside "the Patent;" where he was found by the Plymouth men, as already stated. Thus "Separatists," were not "Welcome Englishmen," among the Puritans; but were; among the Pilgrims. A difference, to be noted.

Yet previous to the arrival of this Company, Gov. Endicott had become interested in the mode of Church Government, adopted at Plymouth; and the same was now concurred in by Messrs. Skelton, and Higginson. Not long after their coming to Salem, a day of solemn prayer and fasting was appointed, preliminary to uniting in Church Fellowship.

## SECTION 2. — FIRST CHURCH FORMED.

The day set apart for the organization of the First Church of the Puritans, in Mass. Bay, Colony was Aug. 6, 1629. Those who proposed to unite in church relation, (tho' "still members in and of the Church of England ") — and not " Separatists," as Higginson said, — and without announcing either the authority of the King's church or their membership in it — conscientiously publicly gave their consent to a Confession of Faith ; in part as follows — " We Covenant with Our Lord, and with one another ; and we do bind ourselves, in the presence of God, to walk together in all His ways according as He is pleased to reveal Himself unto us in His blessed Word of Truth." . . .

A most interesting part of the Organizing ceremonies, was the conscientious receiving of the right hand of Fellowship, by this new unseparated Puritan Church ; from delegates of the " Separatist " Pilgrim Church ; at Plymouth ; who had been invited by Gov. Endicott, to be present *for that special purpose.* In performing that service, the Delegates, told their Salem brethren, distinctly, that — " This act was simply one of brotherly recognition, as fellow-laborers in a common cause ; that neither Church has any ascendency over the other ; but *both alike ; distinct, free and Independent of each other ;* and responsible alike, and only to *Christ,* Our *One Lord and Master."* Mr. Skelton for Pastor ; Mr. Higginson Teacher.

This was the ground taken by the Separatists ; or Independents in England. When the Pilgrims left Holland ; and those who stayed there ; both recognized each other, as distinct, separate, Independent, churches. So in Plymouth, and now to the Salem Church; the Pilgrims maintain the same sentiment.

It is not a little, strange; that Gov. Endicott conscientiously would not allow the "Separatist," Smith; to stay in Salem; and yet he conscientiously sends for the "Separatist" delegates, to give the "not Separatist" Church in Salem; the right hand of fellowship!" After this act of "Organization," of which Church; were the Salem people members; their own; or of the church of England — or of both? The fraternal bond, thus formed; between the churches in Salem; and Plymouth; had its marked influence for many years after.

The total neglect of the English church ceremonials, in the formation of this First Church of Salem; was regarded by John, and Samuel Browne; as a glaring heresy and an insult to the mother church. These gentlemen, were ardent Episcopalians; one a lawyer; one a merchant; and both, members of Endicott's Council; and such was their chagrin, at this new departure in church ways, that they conscientiously and immediately instituted "Separate" worship; according to the church of England. The Brownes regarded the above act of Endicott and the rest, as "Separating" from the church of England.

SECTION 3. — THE BROWNES SHIPPED HOME.

Gov. Endicott, immediately upon the Separation of the Brownes; conscientiously availed himself of the clause in his instructions — "To send Home the incorrigible" — and shipped them to England, as "factious and evil-conditioned." As might be expected, the

Brownes made bitter complaint to the Company, of the Mass. Bay Colony; and Endicott was written to, as follows — "Let it therefore seem good to you, to be very sparing in introducing any laws or commands, which may render yourself, or us; distasteful to the State here, to which as we ought, we must and will have an obsequious eye." That conscientious eye, had not only "a beam" in it —but proved to be an "*ill-egg*" for the future peace of the Colony.

Sympathy was naturally enough with the Brownes in England; and prejudice, as naturally sprung up, against the Massachusetts Bay Colony; upon this first instalment, (after the ejection of Smith), of COERCION for "Conscience's sake." It has ever been, by perverted views, obtained thro' an "obsequious eye;" instead of an "eye single to the glory of God;" — that has misled the friends of the Puritans, into writing labored, and lame apologies, for them, on the pages of New England History.

The Pilgrims; and Smyth and his Friends, when in Holland, all had a conscientious purpose, far above all time-serving, in refusing to conform to the rights of the establishment; and in refusing to remain in her communion — in fleeing to Holland to escape her persecutions — and thence "going to America, to seek a place to worship God;" cost what it would. They conscientiously renounced the trammels of church and state, "plucked out the obsequious eye;" and were the true friends of *Religious Liberty*.

But the Puritans conscientiously "followed them afar off." They neither renounced the church of England; nor would they conform to its ceremonials; remained, members in the establishment; and voluntarily covenanted together in a church of their own, in Salem. Yet they accepted ministers, whose Episcopal ordination, they considered valid; but rejected Smith; because he was a "Separatist;" and accepted the right hand of fellowship, from the very "Separatist" church, Smith went, to serve as Pastor; and shipped their own Episcopal brethren, the Brownes; for objecting to their fellowship, with Separatists, and turning the cold shoulder, to the *dear* mother church! Not so, did the Pilgrim Fathers. Posterity need not question the "Conscientiousness"—of either Puritans; or Pilgrims; even tho' we may not be able to reconcile the difference between their Policies.

### SECTION 4.—UNABATED ZEAL.

Those interested in the Massachusetts Bay Colony, were encouraged at the turn of affairs, as, favorable to their aspirations. The reception and welcome given to Endicott, was far more cheering, than that extended to the Pilgrims by the Indian, who bade them — "Welcome Englishmen."

Besides a still more imposing and efficient movement was preparing in England, to follow up the fancied good beginning made by the first pioneers. Its agents and members, however, were not the victims of the wrath of the "Court of High Commission," as the Pilgrims were; who were forbidden to meet for worship in the country — and were forbidden to flee from the country; yet did flee to Holland, the land of William Prince of Orange; where *Liberty* of *Conscience*, was allowed. Not so with the Puritans; they were afforded the fullest sanction of the English Civil Court, and were furnished with ample powers for founding a colony, and performing all the functions of Civil Government.

This new movement was inaugurated with the utmost care and deliberation. In one of Mr. John Winthrop's letters about July 1629, he states — "1. It is granted that the worke is lawfull and hopefull of success, for the great good of the churche." The Pilgrim movement was not regarded by their enemies, as either; lawful, or for the good of the church. In article 7, He says — " . . . The members of that churche may be of more use to their mother churche heere, than many of those whom she shall keepe in her owne bosome." . . .

How far this conscientious sympathy for the established church; was participated in, may be a question; but the enterprise was legal, and churchly. Hence the Puritans had naught to fear, from either the King's church, or State.

But the puzzle for Posterity is this; — how to explain this ardent indorsement of the church of England; and its early abandonment, by the Puritans? Why they held to their new church way with such conscientiousness, and practised such rigidness, towards all of different views? And in conclusion, whether the care they took to plant themselves in Massachusetts Bay, does, or does not; debar the Puritans hopelessly, and forever, from all claim, to the honor; of being the Founders of Religious Liberty in America? On these points Posterity — will have their opinion.

## CHAPTER IV.

### *THE BOSTON PURITANS.*

THE coming of Endicott to Salem, was but the putting him forth as a "fit instrument to begin this wilderness work." Back of this, was the larger and more comprehensive scheme for the founding of a Puritan Colony; equipped with all the appointments for building up a civil State, religiously.

SECTION I. — THEIR CHARTER.

The parties conscientiously interested in this important undertaking did not propose to follow the example of the Pilgrims — in "Separating" openly and boldly from the king's church — or, escaping as best they could, like exiles and culprits to Holland — with no sympathy or recognition from king and bishops; only that, "they consented to wink, at their departure for America." Under no such uncertainties did the Puritans, of Massachusetts Bay, propose to launch their ship of State.

Accordingly a petition in due form was presented to the King, and on March 4, 1628 a charter was obtained of Charles I[st], Entitled — "The Governor and Company of the Massachusetts Bay in New England." The main provisions of this charter, conferred upon the Co., powers : —

1. Of self-government — "so far, as their laws should not be repugnant to the laws of England."

2. It gave them power to admit new associates.

3. To administer oaths.

4. It conferred military power — "for their speciall defence and safety, to incounter, expulse, repell, and resist by force of armes, as well by sea as lande, and by all fitting waies and meanes whatsoever, all such, person and persons as shall at any tyme hereafter attempt or enterprise the destruccion, invasion, detriment or annoyance to said plantation or inhabitants."

Brief, and limited in its range, as this instrument seems to have been, yet it was all-sufficient for their civil ordering. Comparing it with the "Compact" of the Pilgrims; and clothed with the sanction of the king of England; the "Charter," was an instrument of Royalty; while the "Compact," was an instrument of Loyalty.

It is important, in view of the grave proceedings, in the history of the Massachusetts Bay Colony, to note here, the entire absence of any provision whatever, in this *charter*, concerning the subject of *religion*. So remarkable was this omission considered at the time, that Gov. John Winthrop, takes special pains to set down the reason, therefor in his, Journal — which was; "The assurance that came to them, from the Privy Council — that his majesty did not intend to impose the ceremonies of the church of England upon us: *for that it was considered, that it was freedom from such things that made people come over to us.*"

No better evidence is desired; than this omission of any mention of the ordering of religion, in the Charter;

and Mr. Winthrop's explanation of it — to settle the question beyond the shadow of a doubt; that it was fully understood in England, and expected, from the conscientious opposition of the Puritans to coercion in matters of religion and conscience; and therefore demanded by public opinion; that in the Puritan Colony of Massachusetts Bay, there should be no legislation; much less any coercion whatever, in the establishment of religion, or the free exercise thereof: but, that undefined, unrestricted Religious Liberty, was to be the sacred heritage of all, who should go there to inhabit. Verily, verily, no more effectual door could have been opened, than was here flung wide open, thro' which the Puritans might have entered; and bearing aloft the unfurled Banner of Freedom of Conscience; they would have forever merited from all generations, the enviable and glorious distinction, of being the Fathers of Religious Liberty. But, with Charter in hand, to that end designed; they did not conscientiously so elect; and theirs; and there; and then; was the irreparable mistake.

Because it was not conscientiously in their hearts, to cherish liberty in religion; they procured a promise from Mr. Ralph Smith, — before he left England, in the same ship with Higginson and others, who were not "Separatists from the church of England" — that he "would not exercise his functions (as a minister) within the Patent, without Endicott's leave." And this exclusiveness they conscientiously formulated, before they had obtained their Charter from King Charles; which was silent; for Liberty in Religion. Another evidence of their foreordained conscientiousness, against too much liberty of conscience; is seen in an article of agreement between the Stockholders of the company — that, "The Stock, shall be chargeable with one-half the military; and ecclesiastical expenses of the Colony." This simply meant, the support of religion by Law. Thus confounding the things of Christ; and Cæsar.

But with their charter, such as it was, in full possession, with other arrangements completed; 15 ships were ready to convey to Massachusetts Bay 1,000 persons; some of them people of wealth and station at home, and among them four conscientious ministers of the gospel; Messrs. Wilson, Phillips, Maveric, and Wareham. Gov. John Winthrop, Dudley, and several of the newly appointed Assistants, having the Charter in custody, embarked on board the flagship Arbella. Being detained at anchor, by contrary winds, off the Isle of Wight, on Apr. 7, 1630, the day before sailing, they conscientiously issued an address — "To the rest of their Brethren, in and of the church of England, a sort of defence against the misreport of their intention to separate from the English church, which was spoken of in terms of warm affection, declaring that such hope and part as they had obtained in the common salvation, they freely acknowledged they had received it in her bosom and sucked it in her breast."

This plain statement conscientiously clears the Puritans of being "Separatists" in England, and of intending to be, in New England.

SECTION 2. — THEIR THEOCRATIC BASIS.

After a stormy and tedious passage the flagship of this fleet of conscientious, law-abiding, church-going

Puritans, with Gov. Winthrop on board; arrived at a point not far below Gloucester Harbor, about June 21, 1630. Thus the Arbella arrived, the longest day in the year — and the Mayflower the shortest day in the year: Dec. 21, 1620. The other vessels arriving by the end of July.

The first session of the Court of Assistants was held on board the Arbella, previous to landing; and while they lay at anchor in Charlestown harbor. At this session was conscientiously passed an Order; that — "Houses be built for the Elders, with convenient speed, and their salaries provided for at the public expense." Taking this magisterial order; with the provision in the Co's article, for "one-half the Ecclesiastical expenses, to be paid out of the Colonial treasury;" and the conscientious predilections of the Puritans for a restrictive Church system; it is easy to foresee, the fatal rocks, towards which their ship of Church-and-State was being piloted. How widely, different, this conscientious action on board the *Arbella;* from that of the Pilgrims, in forming the "Compact," on board the *Mayflower*.

The Capital of the Colony, was in as brief a time as convenient, located on its present site, and called, after its English namesake; BOSTON: in Sept. 17, 1630. The 2d and 3d Courts of Assistants, were held in Charlestown.

The Puritans, without any formalities of renunciation of the Church of England; or, declaration of any *intention;* conscientiously fell into the line of things inaugurated by Endicott; and soon organized at Charlestown; Dorchester; Watertown; and elsewhere; partly after the examples of Plymouth; and

Salem; distinct churches, which admitted their own members, and chose their own officers; yet not without regard to neighboring churches.

At once they were conscientiously charged, as by the Brownes at Salem; with "equivocation, and open Separation." To this they conscientiously replied, that — "The simple ceremonies employed in the induction of their ministers into office, were not a new ordination; repudiating, or superseding that which they had received from their bishops in England; but as mere marks, of their election and installation." Who can tell, whether the Puritans were "Separatists;" or Churchmen? They neither imitated the Pilgrims; nor the Brownes. What inference could "their brethren in and of the church of England," draw, from their "farewell address;" and this jilt of the prayer-book; and departing into the ways derelict, of Separatists; and Schismatics?

Unexpected discomforts, and privations, attended upon this coming to New England; so that about 100 persons returned in the same ships; (one of them was the Mayflower,) in which they came out. Among these were Mr. William Vassal, one of the Assistants, and Mr. Bright a Minister, both of them conscientiously disliking the fusion policy, of civil-and-ecclesiastical matters; the leaders of the Colony were conscientiously minded to pursue. Mr. Vassal, soon after returned, and found a congenial abiding-place at Plymouth: among a people who had conscientiously renounced Church and State — and set up an Independent Church — and a State, based on the consent of the governed.

A vigorous course was conscientiously marked out by the Puritans, in matters Ecclesiastical — and also Governmental. At the first session of the court Sept. 2d, ten weeks after they landed, a process was issued against Thomas Morton, of Mount Wollaston ; "for his many injuries offered to the Indians." At the 2d Session Sept. 17, the Court ordered Morton "to be set in the bilbowes — and to be shipped back to England — and payment to be made out of his goods, for a cannoe hee uniustly tooke from them — and his house burnt in the sight of the Indians, for their Satisfaccon, for many wrongs hee hath done them." So it seems the Puritans conscientiously classed the robbing of Indians — and setting up church of England service, in Salem by the Brownes ; as both alike, punishable with " shipping to England."

The winter of 1630–31, was one of intense severity, the colonists suffering greatly from the cold, and for want of supplies. A vessel had been despatched to England for help, but they were so reduced before relief came, that famine stared them in the face. In this peril they appointed Feb. 16, as a day of Public Fasting and Prayer ; to seek help of God. On the 15th however, the anxiously hoped for ship, Lyon ; arrived, — laden with provision ; and their appointed *Fast*, was quickly changed into a hearty Thanksgiving.

In this Ship were a few emigrants ; but as unexpectedly as the ship's coming ; among them was a young man named ROGER WILLIAMS — and MARY his wife. Gov. Winthrop reported his arrival — as a "Godly Minister."

When the Lyon returned, Sir Richard Saltonstall, and

a portion of his family embarked in her: he never came back.

At the 2d Session of the General Court, May 18, 1631; was conscientiously adopted the Theocratic Basis; "No man shall hereafter be admitted a freeman, that is, a citizen and a voter; unless he be a member of some of the Colony Churches." Not a fourth part, it is said, of the adult population of the Colony, were members of any of the churches.

A Puritan Church, as defined by them, was — "A Body of believers, associated together for mutual watchfulness, and edification." "Candidates for church-membership, were required; besides an orthodox confession of faith, and lives conformable thereto; to add a satisfactory religious experience, to be recited in the face of the congregation, of which the substantial part, was, an internal assurance of a change of heart, and a lively sentiment of justification, as being of God's Elect."

At first, a Minister, and Teacher, officiated in each church; but in a short time the Pastor filled both offices. They had also ruling Elders; "ancient, experienced, godly Christians, of lion-like courage, when the sound and wholesome doctrines delivered by pastor or teacher, were spoken against by any." Their Deacons; "were plain-dealing men, endued with wisdom from above, to manage the church Treasury."

These churches, were each complete in its organization, as were the Independents; "but no single church, could venture upon any novelties of doctrine, or discipline; nor appoint officers, nor retain them, without the approval of the other churches." The Magistrates, and General Court, aided by the advice of the Elders ; claimed and exercised, a supreme control in spiritual and temporal matters ; and even in causes wholly temporal, (if not carnal), the Elders were consulted, on all important questions. At Boston and other places, the system of defraying church expenses, out of the public funds, was preferred: while at Plymouth, the system of voluntary contributions, every sabbath, was adopted: the taxing system, was forced into practice, and finally was established by law.

Besides the Sunday services, which were protracted to a great length ; there were frequent lectures on week days. An annual Fast in Spring in place of "Lent ;" and a day of Thanksgiving in Autumn, instead of "Christmas ;" took the places of the various holidays of the Papal, and English churches. Baptism, instead of being dispensed to all, as in the churches of Rome, and England, was limited in its use, as a special privilege to church members, and their "infant seed." None but church members, were admitted to the Lord's Supper. Marriage was declared no Sacrament, in dissent from Papal, and English churches ; but a civil contract, and to be sanctioned by either ministers or magistrates.

An English Historian writes : — "Their Ministers were men of great sobriety, and virtue, plain, serious, affectionate preachers; exactly conformable to the doctrines of the church of England: and took a great deal of pains to promote a reformation of manners, in their several parishes. Many others godly and well-disposed Christians, and many with their entire families, to avoid the burthens and snares which were laid upon their consciences here, departed thither."

When Posterity shall search the records of the past, to find ; Who were the *Fathers* of RELIGIOUS LIBERTY, they will be particular, that, such "honor be given to whom it is due."

# CHAPTER V.

*CHARTER OF GOVERNOR AND COMPANY OF MASSA-
CHUSETTS BAY ANNULLED.*

At the mock-hearing given the Puritans, before the Hampton Court, Eng.; where the Prelates of the church had a private interview with the King; showing him their case as against the Puritans; and the next day the Puritans were permitted a hearing, in the presence of King and Prelates — James I, rendered his infamous decision upon their cause, as follows :—" If this is all your party have to say, I will make them conform themselves, or else I will harrie, (dog) them, out of the land, or else do worse — only hang them that's all." And yet it was from Charles I, his son, that they received their charter, for the Massachusetts Bay Colony, in New England, Mar. 4, 1628.

SECTION I.— THE RIGHT TO ANNUL THE CHARTER, RESERVED.

The difference between the threat of James, and the permit of Charles; to let the Puritans go out of the land, clothed with royal authority to found a civil state; is one of the many strange things in history. It is hardly possible to suppose that Charles had any sympathy with them, as a sect of Nonconformists, or Reformers. As Charles was about to begin the experiment of ruling without the trouble, of troublesome Parliaments; he might have fancied the new colony, an outlet for a class of his subjects, who would not be any help to him, in crushing out the spirit of liberty. Again, he possibly foresaw in it, the nucleus of a future empire, which might add to England's consequence, and advantage. But whatever the one, or many motives, for giving the Charter; King Charles did not let slip from his grasp, the power to control, or annul, the Puritan Charter.

This royal grip, was in the clause, giving — "The Company the function of self-government, so far, as their laws were not repugnant to the laws of England." The single word "repugnant," covered all the ground; for if the laws of the colony, were not contradictory to English Laws; yet, if they should be distasteful to the merest caprice of his majesty; the whole code of the colony could be declared "repugnant," and be annulled at a nod. However much the King, and prelates; might despise Puritanism, or might desire to trample it under foot; yet for the time being they were inclined to wink at it, with an "obsequious eye;" still, holding it firmly within the range of the royal power.

But the slyest trap of all; and the bait which would be most certain to lure the Puritans into repugnance, in case they should at all venture to be coercive; was that of silence, on the subject of religion in their Charter. Under the cover of silence, was hidden, the swivel, in the text of the Charter, about conformity, or nonconformity; in the church of England; or any other form of worship. That was left out, so that it might be left alone, by the Puritans; but if not, let alone, as the "forbidden fruit;" the touch of this unmentioned coil, could easily be made a pretext of "repugnance."

Had the Puritans conscientiously taken the King's Silence, on this point, as the "still voice of God," and come to New England determined; "To make no laws whatsoever concerning the establishment of religion, or the free exercise thereof;"—a halo of unshadowed, untarnished, and unfading glory, would have encircled their names; in the grateful remembrance of all Nations. Thrice happy, and honored; would the Puritans have been, had they conscientiously continued to cherish the fondness for the Mother church, set forth in their parting address — and worshipped with, or without the prayer-book; and left others to do the same; without prejudice or molestation, from Court; or Elders; yea thrice happy!

Prosperously would the Puritan Ship-of-State, have sailed over the waters of Massachusetts Bay! Yea Joyfully, Joyfully would they have built up the walls of their Puritan Zion; had their Magistrates simply protected all persons conscientiously from *civil* disturbance, whether at work; or at worship; and winked at the ways of others; as the King proposed to wink at their ways; in the same thing; then would it have remained a perpetual saying — "That it was *freedom* from *such things* that made people come over to us." Thus it was; that the silence of the Charter; on the subject of Religion; and the proviso in it, about "repugnance to the laws of England;" laid the two "trap-doors;" through which the Colonists were liable at any time, to be precipitately dropped into a sea of troubles; unless conscientiously guarded against; with a caution, watchfulness, and wisdom, well nigh *superhuman!* "Of these thou shalt not eat!!"

SECTION 2.—THE PURITANS CARELESS ABOUT LOSING THEIR CHARTER.

It was a matter notorious and surprising, that the Puritans; who dared not "separate" from the church of England, at the same time they obsequiously conformed to her distasteful ceremonials; should in their untenable position, be the conscientious advocates of the persecuting edicts of the Court-of-High-Commission; against both, Catholics; and "Separatists." Such an attitude was not inspiring of confidence, from those among whom they were in reluctant conformity; nor very begetful of respect, from those against whom they conscientiously inspired discomfort — out of the dens, of the "Commission."

The conduct of those who came to Salem, in being conscientiously unwilling to let Mr. Ralph Smith take passage with them, because he was a "Separatist;" and only allowed him to do so, upon his making conscientious promise, to be *silent*, or "depart their lymitts;" was a semblance — more like providing for restriction, than for toleration in matters, of religious opinion.

In addition to this oath taken of Mr. Smith; secret instructions were conscientiously sent to Gov. Endicott concerning him — "That unless hee wilbe conformable to our Government, you suffer him not to remaine within the Lymitts of our graunt." That is; imprecatory silence in freedom of speech upon religious opinions, or mandatory exit from the Colony, by the Civil Magistrate. So marked and so impolitic a proceeding, could not fail to excite the "repugnance" of their enemies, and fill the minds of their well-wishers, with apprehension.

The conscientious speech of Mr. Higginson, on the deck of the vessel, off Land's End — that, "We do not go to New England as Separatists" — and then conscientiously in Aug., to organize themselves into a church, wholly separate, from the church of England without any formal act of separation; or any notice to the Mother Church, nor even apology, for so doing: is most notable!

To the Brownes, it was evident enough, that the tender feeling of the Puritans for "their brethren in and of the church, had somewhat coagulated as to the use, of the prayer-book. Adding to this the fact, that Gov. Endicott was clothed with the conscientious function to adopt "a more severe course, when faire meanes will not prevaile" — what must have been the chagrin of the Brownes; when they actually found themselves homeward bound; as "factious and evil-conditioned?!" What speech could they make, as they came in sight of "Land's End;" sent home for *not* separating from the church; by those who had declared themselves; "not Separatists"? This was Episcopalian, conscientiously against Episcopalian.

No more effective agents could have been sent to England, from Massachusetts Bay, to incite "repugnance" against its charter; than were the Brownes. Men of wealth, and standing, at home; members of Endicott's Council; and with special grievances, on the subject in which the Charter was silent; their coercive treatment filled them with a frenzy of disgust. The moment their feet touched English soil, their tongues would be loosed to tell a tale, to listening ears; which could not fail to arouse a prodigious influence in the church of England, against the Massachusetts Bay Colony. No greater conscientious mistake could Endicott and those concerned with him, have made just at that time, than the shipping of the Brownes.

At the Session of the General Court in Sept. 16, 1631, one Henry Lynn was sentenced to be whipped and banished; "for writinge into England falsely and mallitiously against the government and execution of justice here." Possibly Mr. Lynn might have been mistaken — but from his testimony, and that of the Brownes; that of Sir Richard Saltonstall; and others; enough was at hand, that was irrepressible, to force an unfavorable influence. Thus the Puritans continued to add with their own hands, fagot after fagot, to the fire of prejudice, they had already kindled against themselves.

Enough had been done to disappoint and grieve all the well-wishers of the colony at home; and to cool all the love of "the brethren in and of the Church of England," for their Puritan-Episcopal brethren in the Bay; and to set in a flame the ill-will of their enemies, on both sides of the Atlantic. It only remained therefore, for the Puritans to indulge in some further misuse of their chartered power, "repugnant to the laws of England;" to enlist the King, among their numerous and increasing enemies. Indeed the Puritans had been in too small a degree careful, to avoid offending his majesty, tho' he had given them so lenient a charter; for within one year, the General Court, had passed the sentence of banishment upon fourteen persons. However ill-deserving all these parties may have been; the question with the King, would be first; as to the lawfulness of the laws; by which these edicts were issued and enforced. Even the King of England had no authority to banish his subjects out of the lymitts of the realm, without a special Act of Parliament, authorizing him so to do. But in the Bay we find this Chartered Court, with no Act of Parliament, giving them the right to do so; in 14 months, banishing 14 persons; which would have required 14 Acts of Parliament, to have authorized the King to have done as much. Hence they had by their own, considerate, or inconsiderate, acts, jeopardized their charter.

Posterity; will incline to an adverse judgment against the Bay; especially as the Examples of Plymouth Colony; and the Rhode Island Plantations; near by; never found such conscientious urgencies necessary. Chas. I., was willing Massachusetts Bay Colony, should be a Refuge — but not an Inquisition; nor a Star Chamber.

### SECTION 3.—MATTERS GREW WORSE.

No little complaint is made, by Puritan Apologists of the 19th century, because Massachusetts Bay had so many hostile enemies. True they took occasion against the Colony, but who furnished the *occasion?* Their conscientious attitude, towards Mr. Smith; and the Brownes; was assumed, within a year after the Charter was given. If complaints against the Colony, were not made before the occasion, for the Complaint was given; apologists need not complain; if Complaints began very soon after, the occasion was given.

The Puritan Court, might conscientiously declare in their edicts of banishment, that such and such persons were — "unmeete to inhabit here" — but that did not debar others from holding the opinion, that the mode of justice in the Colony, was "unmeete," also.

The harvest of all this sowing, began to be gathered into bundles, as soon as it ripened; and it ripened early. By the ships Mary, and Jane, news came to the Bay, as early as May 1633 — that, a "Petition had been presented to the King and Council, of many sheets of paper; accusing us to intend rebellion; to have cut off our allegiance; and to be wholly separate from the church, and laws of England." Allowing 66 days, as was usual, then, for a passage across the Sea; the time of presenting the said petition, must have been as early, or earlier, than Feb., 1633. Allowing also sufficient time for their acts to leaven the public sentiment; time for considering the method of action, to be taken; and time to get the petition before the King and Council; and it would carry this movement against the charter, back into 1632. Besides the occasion given for all this stir, would reach back to a still earlier date. So that in less than 2 years, after the Gov. and Co. of Massachusetts Bay began operations here, their conscientious, and "repugnant" courses, had stirred up this threatening, and formidable opposition: for which; whose — was the blame?!

A bold, conscientious — and for the time being, successful defence was made, by Messrs. Saltonstall, Humphrey, and Cradock; against the charges in the petition; and in behalf of the Colony; in their plea before the King and Council; that the charges made were overdrawn, and that matters were more hopeful, (at least they hoped they would be); than the petition represented. A favorable impression was made by them, upon the King and Council, and the matter postponed.

Hardly a year had passed, however, before the complaints were renewed, as might be expected; for the grounds on which they rested ; had not been removed. Following this movement, an Order in Council was obtained, Feb. 1634, demanding the surrender to the Board by Mr. Cradock ; of the Charter of the Massachusetts company. After a short delay, and as early as May 8, 1634, "the King re-assumed the whole business into his owne Hands — and gave an order for a Generall Gouernour of the whole Territory to be sent over."

So that, from the landing of Gov. and Company in Massachusetts Bay, June 22, 1630, to the presenting of the petition to the King and Council, in Feb. 1633, for the surrender of their Charter ; was only 2 years and 8 months. No wonder it was so soon recalled, when we remember that the beginning of the discontent, was as early as the shipping of the Brownes, by Gov. Endicott ; which took place within a very few months, of the giving of the Charter. Thomas Morton, whom the Puritans had shipped home, was not slow to write of this matter to one Jeffrey, here, in an exultant tone, who showed the letter to the Governor. Whom could the Puritans blame — whom — when, as a disagreeable off-set to conscientiously "shipping Home the Brownes,". they were ordered by the King, to "ship Home" their Charter ?

In place of this annulled Charter, "A commission was appointed, constituting the two Archbishops, and ten others of the Privy Council, a board ; to regulate all plantations ; with power to call in all Patents ; to make laws ; to raise tithes and portions for ministers ; to remove and punish Governors ; to hear and determine all causes ; and inflict all punishments, even to death." Here it may be well to Note — that this Board, with the powers granted them, were the only, legal and supreme, civil authority in the Bay. The Puritan Governor, Assistants, and Charter, of the Company, were all abrogated, annulled, and abolished, so far as having any authority or jurisdiction, by grant or otherwise, from the King of England. And hence, as their Charter was not restored, for many years ; nor any substitute for it given ; and as the Puritans made no Declaration of Independence, of England ; and formed no new "Compact" of civil Government, for themselves ; and still held on to their annulled Charter — they were much afloat for want of any lawfully authorized ; civil Government.

Here let us notice distinctly, that in place of the silence, on the subject of religion, in the Charter of the Puritans ; special power is given this King's Board, "to raise tithes and portions for Ministers" — which demonstrates, that the Puritans had the opportunity freely given them, to have established perfect Religious Liberty, in Massachusetts Bay, had they elected so to do. And hence it is plain, that their conscientious, yet, "repugnant" course with Smith ; and the Brownes ; and other proceedings on the question of religion ; were among the chief causes ; of their losing their Charter.

That the Puritans themselves understood, that they were without charter authority, is seen from their acts. "When the General Court met in Sept., 1634 ; with the demand for the surrender of their Charter — and the Document establishing the King's High Commission; confronting them — they made no reply to either; but promptly took order for fortifying Castle Island; Charlestown; and Dorchester Hights; and for drilling and disciplining the trainbands, and for collecting arms and ammunition." At the Session of the Court in Mar. 1635, a Military Commission was organized, — "to do whatsoever may be further behoovefull for the good of this Plantation, in case of any warr that may befall us."

To this end the Gov. and Company, had previously called together all the ministers of the Colony, to consider the question; — " What ought wee to do, if a General Gouernour should be sent out of England?" Answer. " We ought not to accept him, but defend our lawful possessions, (if we are able); otherwise to avoid, or protract." " A beacon, to be fired to alarm the country in case of invasion, was set up on what was thereafter known as 'BEACON HILL,' in Boston." " As the Massachusetts men held originally by Patent from the Council for New England, which had surrendered its Charter to the King; this amounted to robbing them of their property, and redistributing it to others." " Process was bro't in Westminster Hall, England, in Sept. 1635; in which Matthew Cradock made default, and was convicted of the usurpation charged; and taken to the King to answer for the same. The remaining patentees stood outlawed." What was the political status, of the Gov. and Company of Mass. Bay, thereafter? Viewed at the distance of 250 years, they seem to have been dwellers in this wilderness, on somebody's (?) lands; holding a repudiated Charter; basking in the delights of untenable "Squatter Sovereignty." Mr. John Cotton, of the New England, Puritans; held, that — " By the Patent we have Power to erect such a Government of the Church, as is most agreeable to the Word, to the estate of the People, and to the gaining of the Natives (in God's time) first to Civility, and then to Christianity." If their Charter gave them such ecclesiastical " Power," it must have been in its silence, on the subject ; for there was none in its provisions.

## CHAPTER VI.

*ROGER WILLIAMS ARRIVES IN BOSTON.*

IN their anxiety and distress, the Puritans of Boston had been waiting for the arrival of the ship Lyon — to bring them bread; and on Feb. 15, 1631, they were joyfully relieved. But God had a greater blessing for Boston, and the United States, in the persons of Roger Williams, and Wife — who came to bring the Bread of Religious Liberty.

SECTION I. — ROGER WILLIAMS' EARLY HISTORY.

Of the early history of Roger Williams, too little is known. The place, of his birth, as given by some, is Conwyl Cayo, in Carmarthen, South Wales, England. The date, of his birth, is variously conjectured, as between the years 1598, and 1606. Enough is known, to indicate, that his young life was blessed with the inestimable advantage of pious parentage; which so often brings forth its hallowed fruit in the lives of great and good men.

It is a currently received statement that while a mere boy, he was one day observed, by Sir Edward Coke, taking notes of a sermon. Curiosity led Sir Edward to ask the lad to allow him to examine his notes. So pleased was he with the evidences of talent in the notes of young Williams, that he solicited of his parents, the privilege of superintending his education. As Gamaliel a Doctor of the Law, knew not the great work he was doing for the Church of Christ, while instructing young Saul of Tarsus;— so, neither did Sir Coke, England's great expounder of Civil Law, comprehend the boundless influence, his interest in the education of young Williams, was destined to exert, in the Christianization of the Nations of the earth; by casting down the unholy Babel of church and State, and exalting Christ as Lord of all.

Thro' this favorable attention, and influence of his illustrious Patron, young Williams was elected scholar of Sutton's Hospital, about July 4, 1621, and as is supposed, he was matriculated a pensioner in Pembroke College, Cambridge July 17, 1625; and took the Degree of Bachelor of Arts, January 1627. Tradition says— he commenced the study of Law, under Sir Coke; but of this, and the reasons for his change of profession, little is known; for not long after, he was admitted to Orders in the church of England; and was beneficed, at or near, Sempringham, in Lincolnshire. While there he made the acquaintance of John Cotton, and Thomas Hooker, before any of them came to Massachusetts Bay.

Roger Williams' position, as a clergyman in the Church of England, gave him a most Providential opportunity, to observe the leavening influence of Conformity, and Nonconformity; going on inside and outside the English church and State, Hierarchy. Especially Providential was it, that he was located in Lincolnshire; the region from which had gone forth the Pilgrim Fathers, in their search for "*Freedom to worship God, cost what it would."* Doubtless he also found, perhaps in his own immediate parish, those who had embraced the views of Mr. John Smyth, in Holland; from which; as a part of the Scrooby Pilgrims: they returned to England, and joined their "Separatist" Brethren, in — "CHALLENGING KING AND PARLIAMENT TO THEIR FACES, AND NOT TO GIVE WAY TO THEM NO NOT A FOOT, UNTIL LIBERTY TO WORSHIP GOD WAS SECURED:" which was achieved in 1688, as a concession to Dissenters.

Yet it is not to be supposed; even with a knowledge of the facts; that, the Pilgrims, had gone to New England; and that the Nonconformists of England; were both warring a good warfare, for Liberty of conscience: that Roger Williams, had any conception of the great work God was about to call the Rector of Sempringham, to do in the world, for the cause of Religious Liberty. Much less did he dream; "the day I rode with Cotton, and Hooker, [from Essex, where he lived], to, and from, Sempringham" — what awaited, the three, in Massachusetts Bay. But subsequent events assure us, that young Williams, was not in darkness, or in doubt, as to what position he should assume, toward the great Nonconformist agitation.

It is easy to imagine; that, a change from the Ministry in the church of England, to a place in the company of *"Separatists"* from being a member of a Prelatical Hierarchy, to that of a "challenger of King and Parliament to their faces, for liberty of conscience, cost what it would" — which naturally enough, cost him something.

At a later date, in a letter to Mrs. Sadleir, daughter

of Sir Edward Coke, Mr. Williams wrote — "Truly it was as bitter as death to me, when bishop Laud pursued me out of this land, and my conscience was persuaded against the National church, and ceremonies, and bishops; beyond the conscience of your dear father. . . . The never-dying honor and respect which I owe to that dear and Honorable root and its branches. . . . That man of honor and wisdom and piety . . . was often pleased to call me his Son. . . . I say it was as bitter as death to me, when I rode Windsor way, to take ship at Bristol, and saw Stoke House, Buckinghamshire, where the blessed man was; and then durst not acquaint him with my conscience and my flight."

We are not to understand here that Mr. Williams' change of sentiments, was "bitter as death to him" — but, that what he suffered for conscience' sake, from his brethren, (like Joseph) yea, from his bishop; was cruel as the grave. For we find in his letter to Mr. John Cotton Jr., in Mar. 1671; this testimony: — "He [God] knows what gains and preferments I have refused in Universities, City, Country, and Court, in Old England, and something in New England . . . to keep my soul undefiled in this point, and not to act with a doubting conscience." . . .

And now like Paul, having no more place in those parts, Roger Williams, and Mary, his wife, embarked at Bristol, England, in the ship Lyon, Capt. Pierce, master, on Dec. 11, 1630.

SECTION 2. — ROGER WILLIAMS CALLED TO THE FIRST CHURCH IN BOSTON. — GOES TO SALEM.

After a tedious and tempestuous voyage of sixty-six days, the vessel which brought that God-sent, fearless, defender of Soul Liberty, and his young wife, Mary, to New England; arrived, off Nantasket, Feb. 15, 1631. Mr. Williams, was then according to different, reckonings, from twenty-five, to thirty-one years of age; a NONCONFORMIST; a "SEPARATIST;" a FEARLESS ADVOCATE; of perfect Religious Liberty; and an exile from home and country; thro' the bitter persecutions of the church of England. Gov. Winthrop notes his arrival, as that of "a godly minister." A title, of which he ever continued worthy.

Upon the arrival of Mr. Williams, he was invited to occupy the pulpit, of the First church in Boston. But the reasons for declining this call, he gives as follows : —

"Being unanimously chosen teacher at Boston, I conscientiously refused, because I durst not officiate to an unseparated people, as, upon examination and conference I found them to be." As the Puritans left England, avowed Episcopalians; and had never declared themselves, separated, from them; and yet had organized themselves into a church, having no semblance in form or ceremonials, to that church; it required not a little, "examination and conference"—to find their Ecclesiastical Environment. Mr. Williams plainly, uttered no "condemnation of this church" but simply states that they were "unseparated, as he found them to be." The Puritans themselves declared; "we do not go to New England as Separatists — and declared themselves to be members in and of, the church of England." If they had been, "separated," they could have said so; and Roger Williams would have conscientiously preached for them. But because they were not "separated," he "conscientiously refused to officiate." This was not condemning them; but "keeping his own soul undefiled." If the logic; and the facts; Roger Williams used in self-defence before those "ablest and best men;" were more than they could appreciate; they must blame the logic; not that "Godly Minister."

Roger Williams, knew what "separation" meant, and what it had cost him; as great a cost too, as had any of the Puritans sustained. "Separation," in those days meant "Orthodoxy" — coming out, from Rome; and Prelacy. If he were to pain his soul, by officiating to the "unseparated," in *New* England — he might as well go back to *Old* England — yea, back to the church of England. The Puritans also knew what "Separation" meant, and they feared it, conscientiously.

The Church in Salem, who had received, at their organization; the right hand of fellowship from the Plymouth "Separatist" Church — and it would seem, a portion of their spirit, too — hearing of Mr. Williams' "conscientious," refusal to officiate for the Boston church, gladly embraced the opportunity to invite him, to officiate for them, as Teacher. This invitation he "conscientiously," and cheerfully accepted. Here we may note, that the first two churches, constituted in New England; one at Plymouth, and one at Salem, were — *one* — of the "Separatist" Order. While the first Church of Boston, was the third in New England — and of the "unseparated" Order.

On April 22, 1631, the Governor and Council conscientiously wrote Mr. Endicott, that — "They hoped the Salem people would act cautiously, and not proceed in this matter of calling Mr. Williams, without due advisement: inasmuch as he had refused to fellowship the Boston church, and had broached novel opinions; that — "The Magistrate might not punish the breach of the Sabbath, nor any other offence, as it was a breach of the first Table." Here take special note; that some of the Magistrates of Boston, took open issue with Roger Williams, on the questions of CHURCH AND STATE; AND LIBERTY OF CONSCIENCE. Also by exhorting with the *Church* at Salem in the matter of *calling* a *religious teacher;* they violated the Silence of their Charter; on the subject of freedom in religion — conscientiously, of course.

Verily, verily; it must have given Roger Williams unutterable surprise; having just escaped a persecution, "as bitter as death;" to be thus embarrassed, "when landed after a voyage of 3,000 miles; in the North American wilderness!"

SECTION 3. — ROGER WILLIAMS IS CALLED TO PLYMOUTH.

Finding his way hedged up in Salem, as the Church; — thro' hesitation, from the conscientious attitude of the Court — "for the present forebore proceeding with him" — and receiving a call from the Church in Plymouth, he departed thither; as is supposed, in Aug. 1631; within six months, after his arrival at Boston.

Thus, for liberty of conscience, Roger Williams was obliged to seek refuge where he could, from the resentment of English Prelates ; and the warning from the Massachusetts Magistrates ; neither of them, having yet fully understood Christ's Magna Charta — "Render therefore unto Cæsar the things, that are Cæsar's, and unto God the things that are God's."

Here again Mr. Williams found sympathizing friends, in the Pilgrims, who knew what liberty of conscience meant, and what its *sacred* value ; and where he became a co-worker with Mr. Ralph Smith, the "Separatist ;" and who had like himself, to go outside of "ye lymmitts," of the Bay. There was plainly more sympathy between the churches at Salem, and Plymouth, than between either of them, and the Boston Church.

Gov. Bradford, writes of him — "Mr. Roger Williams (a man godly and zealous, having many precious parts, but very unsettled in judgmentes) came over first to ye Massachusetts, but upon some discontente left yt place, and came hither, (where he was friendly entertained, according to their poore abilitie), and exercised his gift amongst them, and after some time was admitted a member of ye church ; and his teaching well approoved, for ye benefite whereof I still bless God, and am thankful to him, even for his sharpest admonitions and reproufs, so farr as they agreed with truth."

It will be remembered that the Pilgrims did not fall in with Mr. Smyth of Holland ; (of whom bishop Hall said, to Mr. Robinson), "All your Rabbins cannot answer the charge he makes against you." As Gov. Bradford was familiar with the agitation in Holland, he might have seen something in Mr. Williams' views of *truth*, that reminded him of Mr. Smyth. Yet the Gov.'s testimony that " Mr. Williams was godly, zealous, and his teaching well approved," are the main points, and very valuable.

In the month of Oct. 1632, the people of Plymouth were favored with a visit from Gov. Winthrop, and his pastor, Mr. John Wilson, from Massachusetts Bay. Their method of conducting public worship is seen in Gov. Winthrop's note of it, as follows : — " On the Lord's Day there was a Sacrament, which they did partake in ; and, in the afternoon, Mr. Roger Williams, (according to their custom) propounded a question ; to which Mr. Smith, the pastor, spake briefly ; then Mr. Williams prophesied ; and after the Gov. Bradford of Plymouth ; spake to the question ; after him the Elder Brewster ; then some two or three more of the Congregation. Then the Elder desired the Gov. of Massachusetts, and Mr. Wilson, to speak to it, which they did. When this was ended, the Deacon, Mr. Fuller, put the congregation in mind of their duty of contribution ; whereupon the Governor and all the rest, went down to the Deacon's seat, and put into the box ; and then returned."

Besides his duties as Teacher at Plymouth, Mr. Williams took great pains to reach and do the natives good ; it was his soul's desire, and to that end, to have their language. In his own words he says — " And as to these Barbarians, the Holy God knows some pains I took uprightly in the Main Land and Islands of New England, to dig into their Barbarous Rockie Speech, and to speak something of God unto their souls. God was pleased to give me a painful, patient spirit, to lodge with them in their filthy smoky holes (even while I lived at Plymouth, and Salem), to gain their tongue. . . . I was known by all the Wampanoags, and Narrohigansetts, to be a public Speaker, at Plymouth, and Salem ; and therefore, with them, held as a Sachem. Ousamaquin, (Massasoit), and I had been great friends at Plymouth." He also made the acquaintance of most of the leading, Chiefs; and won their confidence and friendship, by the unselfish interest he manifested in their welfare. These advantages, tho' dearly bo't, were of the greatest possible service to him, in after days — and to all the New England Colonies.

It is also well known that while in Plymouth ; " Mr. Williams' time was not spent altogether in spiritual labors, and publike exercise of the Word ; (though as much as any others whosoever) ; but, day and night, at home and abroad, on the land and water, at the How, (hoe), at the Oare, for bread." His oldest child, was born there — his whole number, was six ; named as follows : — Mary ; Freeborn ; Providence ; Mercy ; Daniel ; and Joseph.

Of Mr. Williams' literary labors while in Plymouth, in part, was his, "Key Into The Language of America ;" published in England in 1643. His other work is known as a " Treatise, on the King's Pattent ; " a work written, " at the request of Gov. Bradford, of Plymouth, for his private satisfaction." The question treated, had reference to the rights of the Colonists, to their lands, by Patent from the King.

SECTION 4. — ROGER WILLIAMS IS RECALLED TO SALEM.

After an absence of about two years, the people of Salem, who had somewhat recovered from their dismay, occasioned by the conscientious advice of the Boston Courte not to engage Mr. Williams as their religious Teacher — and who in the meantime, had suffered no abatement of their esteem and love for him, invited him to return to them, as Teacher; with Mr. Skelton, their pastor, then in declining health. For this purpose he asked a dismission from the Plymouth Church; to that of Salem. "Which though some were unwilling to, yet through the prudent counsel of Mr. Brewster, the ruling Elder there . . . foreseeing (what he professed he feared . . .) that Mr. Williams would run the same course of rigid Separation and Anabaptistry, which Mr. John Smyth, of Amsterdam had done; the Church at Plymouth consented to his dismission; and such as did adhere to him, were also dismissed, and removed with him, or not long after him, to Salem."

Note; when Mr. Williams removed from Salem to Plymouth, it required the conscientious counsel of the civil Court to induce the people to loosen their hold upon him! Now he is recalled there, it requires a "prudent, foreseeing Elder" — to soothe the apprehensions, of the people, to let him go back again. Whom the "rulers fear;" and the people do not fear; is not always a dangerous man. Nor did Mr. Brewster take the counsel of pastor Robinson, given the Pilgrims in Holland, as they were about leaving: that — "If God reveal anything to you by any other instrument of His, be as ready to receive it, as ever you were to receive any truth by my Ministry . . . for the Lord has yet more truth to break forth out of His Holy Word." But Elder Brewster conscientiously said, "let him go."

It may be well to note, here that, upon his return to Salem, Mr. Williams had been in New England about two years and six months; and not a little tossed upon the billows of public opinion. Our best authorities place the date of his removal from Salem to Plymouth in the month of Aug. 1631, and that of his return from Plymouth, to Salem, in early winter 1633.

In view of important considerations to follow, let it be specially noted here; (and see Chap. V. Sec. 3): that the report received in New England, that — "A Petition had been presented to the King and Council, against the Massachusetts Bay Charter" — was brought over, in the ships Mary, and Jane, which arrived here, in May, 1633; nearly six months, before the return of Roger Williams from Plymouth, to the Bay. These facts will enable us to see, presently, that the adverse influences, which tended to "undermine the civil foundations of the Colony," culminated in the abrogation of the Charter. Towards that "undermining of the foundations;" Mr. Williams had as yet, done nothing; and yet, the "undermining" of the Charter was going on apace; nor did its fall long delay.

The year of Roger Williams' return to Salem, 1633, is also noted for the arrival in the Bay of Messrs. John Cotton; and Thomas Hooker. The two latter became prominent leaders in the Puritan churches, and left no uncertain record of their conscientious attitude towards Mr. Williams; and Liberty of Conscience. During the ride of the three together "to and from Sempringham,"

England; they were of *one mind*, upon "Nonconformity;" but upon the question of "Liberty of Conscience," in New England, they were *not*, of one mind.

During Mr. Williams' absence in Plymouth, the Puritan State Church of the Bay, had conscientiously adopted still more urgent measures for the ample support of religion. It was provided that in every township, there should be set apart, land, to be known as, "The Minister's Lot." Whoever was first settled on these lots, became the permanent Minister of that parish, for life. Observation was on the watch, what kind of ministers settled on those lots. If "the powers that be," used their benign influence to give the minister a permanent home, it was presumable that he would not, for small considerations, be seduced into "Contempt of authority;" especially while faring well at the hands of a system, in which, "all who were church members were voters — and none could be voters who were *not* church members."

Measures were also adopted, subjecting to assessment, and payment, all who did not conscientiously and voluntarily contribute, according to their ability, to all town charges; "*as well for upholding the ordinances of the churches*, as otherwise." Those who slandered the Government, or the churches, or wrote home discouraging letters; were to be whipped, cropped of their ears, or banished! The Puritans doubtless, felt obliged, conscientiously, to adopt these prudent measures, to maintain their jeopardized authority, now that their Charter was to be removed. Into the "lymitts" of these "unseparated people," as Roger Williams "found them to be," at first; he is about to take up his abode, a second time.

Well aware as he must have been, from his first experience in the Bay; and that the attitude of the Magistrates towards men of his views, conscientiously remained unchanged; Mr. Williams must either, have been very conscientiously persuaded in his opinions; or, very persuaded, that his views would survive all opposition. Possibly; he was both, fearless, and confident in the Lord. At all events, he CAME; he MAINTAINED; he TRIUMPHED.

### SECTION 5. — ROGER WILLIAMS OPPOSED BY THE MAGISTRATES.

As the church in Salem, had lost none of their attachment, to Roger Williams, during his two years' absence in Plymouth; so, neither had the Magistrates lost any conscientious apprehension of him; ever, after he "durst not officiate for them as an unseparated people." For that refusal, he conscientiously — never made them any apology. In that "conscientious" utterance of his, was involved, the whole question of "Religious Liberty" — in all its height, depth, length, and breadth. And, as they feared, to what a Toleration might, develop; so, towards Roger Williams, they manifested their faith by their works.

That we may see the thorny path he was about to enter; a few sentences from the Journal, will aid us —
. . . "The Gov. and Council, called all the Elders together to consult where John Cotton should settle . . . divers of the ministers took part in the discussion which ended in fortifying Castle Island . . . all the

ministers were summoned to advise the Court what to do in case a Gov. General should be sent over." . . . In Palfrey's, Hist. of N. E. we read —. . . "The clergy, now thirteen or fourteen in number, constituted in some sort, a separate estate of special dignity. Though they were excluded from secular office, the relation of their functions to the spirit and aim of the community, which had been founded, as well as their personal weight of ability and character, gave great authority to their advice." . . . Could Mr. Williams expect to return to Massachusetts Bay; from which he had already been conscientiously intimated out; by this Minister and Magistrate Court; and not be again memorialized by them?

He did not so expect, nor was he happily disappointed. Indeed the old authoritative notification upon his first going to Salem, had not been annulled; nor the conscientious Spirit that prompted, it; changed; for careless license. John Cotton writes — "The magistrates . . . advised the church of Salem not to call him to office." Cotton Mather writes —. . . "The Government again renewed their Advice unto the People to forbear a thing of such ill consequence." Here then we find that the old unrest, founded upon his refusal to the "unseparated church of Boston;" still nestled in the bosom of some of the Magistrates; and was the conscientious fire, from which they drew their most ardent apprehension against his "opinions."

No sooner had Mr. Williams returned to Salem, than a conscientious query was raised about his "Treatise on the King's Pattent." As already stated, this was a manuscript work, he had written while in Plymouth;

"for the private satisfaction of Gov. Bradford." So far from having any unworthy motive about it, Mr. Williams writes, — "I should not have stirred any further in it, if the Governour had not required a copy," of him.

This document, wherein "treason, might lurk;" at a meeting of the Governor and Assistants, Jan. 7, 1634, was submitted for their examination. The Gov. reports upon it, as follows; — "Wherein, among other things, he disputes the right to the lands thy possessed here, and concluded that, claiming by the King's grant, they could have no title: nor otherwise except as they compounded with the Natives. . . . There were three passages chiefly whereat the Court were much offended: — 1. For that he chargeth King James to have told a solemn public lie; because in his pattent he blessed God that he was the first Christian Prince that had discovered this land. 2. For that he chargeth him and others with blasphemy for calling Europe, Christendom, or the Christian world. 3. For that he did personally apply to our present King, Charles, these three passages in Revelation: Chaps. 16:13, 14. 17:12, 13. 18:9. 4. For concluding us all heere to lye under a sinne of unjust usurpation upon others' possessions."

A modern publication claims, that the objectional bearing of this Treatise, was — . . . "in a way to undermine the foundations of their social order; by assaulting openly institutions at home in a way to bring the settlement into disfavor there, and so imperil its, as yet uncertain, life." The attentive reader will see, that this charge is without any truthful foundation. In chap. V. sec 3, we have given proof that — "the Charter in which all their legal rights as a plantation were bound up;" was already, under process of being annulled, before Mr. Williams' treatise, had been conscientiously criticised. Again, so indifferent was Mr. Williams about it, that he wrote privately to the Gov., and officially to him and the Court; "offering his manuscript, or any part of it to be burnt." Also at the next session of the Court in Feb. 3, 1634, it was again considered; and upon the advice of Elders Cotton, and Wilson, "they agreed to deal gently with the offender, and pass over the offence; as the influence of the Treatise, might not be so great as they had feared." *And so ended the offence concerning the Treatise:* no harm intended by it, no harm done by it. No "undermining the foundations of the Colony," by Roger Williams, as alleged.

The date of Mr. Skelton's death, is given as occurring on Aug. 12, 1634. After which Mr. Williams continued to exercise tho' not in any office, as the church was still under the conscientious dehortation of the leaders of the Court; "*not to ordain him.*"

The next conscientious misgiving about Roger Williams, by the Court, was in reference to his Preaching.

"As the Autumn drew on with its ill tidings from England, of the danger threatening the Charter, and all the interests of the plantation" — the Court appointed the "27th Sept. as a day of publique humiliacon," throughout the Colony. Let it be observed, here, that up to this date in 1634, *nothing whatever* that Mr. Williams had done, had any influence in any way, in making, "the dangers that threatened the Colony, from England." Yet by this proclamation of the Court, it is evident there *were* dangers of which they stood in great fear. And well they might, when they themselves, were said to have so far averted its provisions, that "an Order in Council," had been obtained in Feb. before, of this same year, for the *surrender* of *their Charter*. And in "May 8, 1634, the King reassumed the whole business into his owne Hands." The Charter of Mass. Bay was annulled, and gone. Who, "undermined the foundations of the Colony?" Not Roger Williams; surely!

As was the custom, then; Mr. Williams was called upon to improve the occasion by preaching. In his discourse, he "discovered eleven publique sinnes for which he conscientiously beleeved it pleased God to inflict, and further to threaten publique calamities."

Three weeks had scarcely passed, when the Court was conscientiously informed, that — "Mr. Williams of Salem had broken his promise to us in teaching publicly against the King's patent, and our great sinne in claiming right thereby to this country; and for usual terming the Churches of England, anti-Christian." Instead of the Court proceeding at once against him for this, Mr. John Cotton writes — "I presented (with the consent of my fellow-Elders and Brethren,) a serious Request to the over-ardent, Magistrates, that they would be pleased to forbeare all civill prosecution against him, till ourselves (with our Churches) had dealt with him in a Church way, to convince him of sinne: alledging, that myselfe and brethren hoped his violent course did rather spring from scruple of conscience (though carried with an inordinate zeal,) than from a seditious Principle."

We can't exactly see how Mr. Cotton was going to

"convince, Mr. Williams, of sinne," if his "zeale did spring from scruple of conscience." The latter was a conscientious contender for the faith. He "conscientiously refused" the call of the Boston church; even against his own temporal interest. It is suggestive that Mr. Cotton should interpose, to shield Mr. Williams from "civill prosecution," by the court, in matters of "scruple of conscience!" Did neither of them see, that such a course was protecting Mr. Williams, in his "special whimsey; that Magistrates should not punish men for matters of conscience?" But all this flourish of trumpets ended quietly; so that no charge can be made here, that Roger Williams, in this Fast day Sermon, did "undermine the foundations of the Colony;" especially, as the "foundations" were already gone; with their Charter.

The next conscientious call of the Courtiers upon Mr. Williams, was a summons to appear before them at their session on May 10, 1635, to be dealt with in regard to his teaching concerning the "Resident's Oath." The Magistrates, now anxious for their fate, upon the loss of their Charter, laid hold of every means, to sustain their revoked authority. The so called "Resident's Oath," was a kind of Oath of Allegiance conscientiously required of every person, to sustain the civil authority of the General Court. This Oath was, in part, as follows — " I ; A. B. being by God's Providence an inhabitant . . . do heere sweare, by the Greate and Dreadfull Name of the Everlyyveing God, that I wilbe . . . . Moreouer, I do solemnly bynde myself. . . . So, helpe me God, in the Lord Jesus Christ."

Mr. Williams' objection to this Oath, was not to it, as

a civil measure; or to perplex the Magistrates; now that their charter was gone; nor to excite the lawless to anarchy; as his enemies maintain — but he "queried" at it on conscientious, religious grounds. He claimed that it was Christ's Prerogative; to have this office; established by Oath. Hence his opinion, that, "Christian men conscientiously ought not to take Oath, which is part of God's Worship; to establish mortall men in their office." He also maintained that, "carnall men ought not to be required, to take a religious oath; or perform a religious act, to set up men in civil office." His scruple was, to keep civil; and religious things; in short, "Church and State;" separate. As we see above, the "Oath," was a compound, of religion and politics; precisely of the whole type, and trend, of the Theocracy.

Further than this, Mr. Williams foresaw, that this Oath; would bind the inhabitants to sustain the Court, in their measures in all things; even to taking the lands of the Indians; and also, bind him; to sustain them; in opposing his efforts, for "Liberty of conscience!"

Mr. Cotton, informs us that Mr. Williams' positions were so well taken and conscientiously maintained, that — "His course threatened the Authorities with serious embarrassment, the more, as his reputation for usual sanctity; especially among the weaker and more influential sex; drew not a few good people toward his conclusion . . . so as to force the Court to retrace its steps, and desist from that proceeding." The conscientious popular will, sustained Roger Williams.

Hence, the defamers of Roger Williams, in the nineteenth century, will find it very difficult to convince Posterity, that he seditiously labored to "undermine the foundations," of civil order; when we remember that those foundations were already "reassumed by the King"—and that the *people, then living*, sustained him in his course; ("especially, the more influential sex;") and "forced the Court to retrace its steps." Civilly and Ecclesiastically; Roger Williams was more of a "Peacemaker," than the Court.

It may be well here to recall the fact, that on, "May 8, 1635; the King reassumed the whole business of the Bay Charter, into his owne Hands." Two days after, May 10, 1635, the Court of the Bay, without any charter; conscientiously summoned Roger Williams before them, to answer concerning the "Resident's Oath." Who, "undermined the foundations of the Colony?"

For a wonder; during the graceful retirement of the Court, at the pose of the "more influential sex;" the church in Salem, and their teacher, enjoyed a brief repose, from Magisterial supervision. Yet, there still hung over their heads, the two, conscientious advices of the Court; "Not to call Mr. Williams to office; a thing of such ill consequence."

SECTION 6.—ROGER WILLIAMS ORDAINED PASTOR OF THE CHURCH IN SALEM.

The People of Salem, hoping that the composure of the Magistrates, would be prolonged, they conscientiously made no delay of inducting Roger Williams into the Pastoral office, according to the simple rites of the early churches of New England: the time of its occurrence was probably in June, 1635.

At this remarkable proceeding, the Court, no longer had the fear of the "influential sex" before their eyes; but at once sent forth their conscientious protest against church and pastor; characterizing their act in ordaining Mr. Williams over them; "as erroneous and very dangerous; and a great contempt of authority." They certainly, did not, show supreme deference, to the double suasive of the Court; but the question Posterity will ask, is; "By what Authority, did the Court conscientiously inhibit the church at Salem, ordaining any man they might please, as their Pastor?" Surely not by any authority in their charter; now gone!

The conscientious hope of the Church, that "they might have rest and be edified," was dispelled by the Summons from the Magistrates, for their Pastor to appear at the next Court, in July 18, 1635, to answer to complaints conscientiously made against him. The Court assembled. Earnest debate followed. The Elders were called in to give the aid of their conscientious judgment as follows: — "He who should obstinately maintain such opinions, (whereby a church might run into heresy, apostasy, or tyranny, and yet the civil Magistrates could not intermeddle), ought to be removed, and that the other churches ought to request the Magistrates so to do." All ended in notifying the Church, and their Pastor conscientiously " to consider the matter until the next General Court, and then to recant; or expect the Court to take some final action " — conscientiously of course.

In this most remarkable advice, for Christian Elders,

to conscientiously give a Civil Court, we see plainly; it involves the whole question of "church and state;" Conformity and Nonconformity; Religious Restriction; or Religious Liberty. No charge of "sedition" is made against Mr. Williams; only that — " *He*, who should conscientiously maintain such opinions." . . .

At this same Session of the Court, a petition, previously made to the Court ; for the papers, conveying the Title ; to a piece of land, belonging to the people of Salem; was renewed. Influenced no doubt by the advice of the Elders; and by the "contempt of Authority," of the Salem church, in ordaining a pastor of their own choice — The Great and Generall Court conscientiously responded to this petition — thus — " We will wait before giving answer to your request, until there shall be time to test more fully the quality of your own allegiance to the power which you desire should be interposed in your behalf." Yet that " Power " — had lost their charter!

According to the Theocratic Basis of the Puritans ; " no person could be a citizen, and voter, unless he were a church-member " — hence the members of the Court were all within the church ; and of course amenable to church Discipline. Mr. Williams who was accustomed conscientiously to distinguishing between, " the things that belong unto Cæsar, and those that belong unto God ;" quickly saw ; that the Court, while sitting in their civil office, had ; by conscientiously refusing the Salem petition, committed a moral injustice. Thereby laying themselves open, " to be dealt with, in a church way."

Being a man not much given to hesitation, in conscientiously doing his duty, when Providence gave him an opportunity — Mr. Williams, by, and with, the cooperation of the Salem church — "Wrote Letters of Admonition unto all the churches, whereof any of the Magistrates were Members; *that they might conscientiously admonish the Magistrates of scandalous injustice for denying the Salem petition.*"

The Elders, who were first to receive these "Letters," quickly saw the trap, they had set for themselves; in their Theocratic Basis; for if the Magistrates were put under Church Discipline, and proved contumacious and conscientiously refused, to "confess their fault, and repair the offence;" the inevitable result MUST BE EXCOMMUNICATION! This would carry with it, not only church-membership; but citizenship; and impeach, the General Courts! "And Great would be the Fall!" Besides they saw that; to discipline the Magistrates, would be, to sustain the charge, of the Salem Church; and their Pastor; in their Letters: in short, sustain Roger Williams; and condemn themselves: and that too according to the logic of their own Church Polity! So much the worse, for the Polity!

The Elders not caring to be seen running down that steep place, to be choked in the pool of stultification; quickly began a search for a way of escape from their dilemma. The first gap open to their relief, was to conscientiously intercept the offensive Letters. This was done, by the Elders, of the "unseparated," church in Boston. Their *excuse*, for so doing, which they gave; in a letter to the church in Salem, under date of Aug. 1st, 1635; was; for "not seeing their way clear to publish to the body the Salem document."

Observe; these Elders conscientiously assume, to withhold a letter to their church; not to them — and then assume; to reply; to that letter, without being authorized by their church to do so: as follows — "1. That the admonition of the Salem Church was a 'gift' which should not be offered until that church had reconciled itself to the Magistrates. — See Matt. v.: 23, 24. 2. That the act of the Magistrates was rather a private, than a public offence. 3. That it was not fitting to deal on the Lord's day in a worldly business; nor to bring a civil matter into the Church." Was it fitting to carry an Ecclesiastical matter into the Court; as they had Mr. Williams' Ordination?

The next gap, of escape, for the Elders, was, to retort in kind; and conscientiously commence church Discipline, with the church, and Pastor of Salem; by Letters from other churches, "presenting before them the offensive spirit and way of their officer, Mr. Williams; both in Judgment and Practice." This was the happy hit, which sustained the Magistrates, in refusing the Petition — shielded them from Church Discipline — and saved to them, their Church Membership, and their Citizenship.

So we are informed, that: — "The neighboring churches, both by Petitions, and Messengers, took such Happy Pains with the Church of Salem, that it pleased the Lord, to open their hearts to assist us in dealing with him." As Cotton Mather writes: — "That Holy Flock was presently recovered to a Sense of his Aberrations." They were not so *Holy*, however, when they "ordained him, in contempt of Authority."

It is not difficult to imagine; with what tact, and

conscientious zeal; those Messengers to the Salem Church; with the special motive of upholding the whole system of the Puritan Theocracy; backed by the concurrence of the General Court: would beseech; and urge; and promise, "the lande betwixte the Clifte and the Forest Ryver, neer Marble Head;" if but a *bare majority*, would conscientiously agree to repudiate Roger Williams. To gain this, was to "cut the Gordian Knot." This was the "vulnerable point, in the heel of Achilles."

Nor did they labor in vain, but, with the result, of speedily winning to the view they took, the small majority of the Salem Church; and persuading them conscientiously to unite with others in dealing with him. Like Endicott they "yielded to truth." Imagine who can, the bitter disappointment Mr. Williams must have felt, when those who had so lately; recalled him; and ordained him; in face of the inhibition of the court; should so soon conscientiously forsake him and flee; and so delivered him to "Admonition"—for writing Letters of Admonition. When writing of it, he says: —" In my troubles the greater part of that Church was swayed and bowed, (whether for feare of persecution or otherwise), to say and practise, what, to my knowledge; with sighs, and groans, many of them mourned under."

The last Sabbath Roger Williams occupied the pulpit of the Salem Church, was probably on Aug. 19, 1635; only about two months, after his ordination as pastor! He left Salem in Aug. 1631: and came back there from Plymouth late in 1633. Mr. Skelton died in Aug. 1634. From 1629, to 1634, the church met for worship in an unfinished building. In 1634, a framed house was erected, 20 feet by 17, with a gallery across the end over the door. What remains of this latter house, is still preserved in the rear of Plummer Hall, Salem Massachusetts — a sacred relic of the conscientious struggle for Religious Liberty. It was no doubt built, in anticipation by the church, of long enjoying the ministry of Mr. Williams. But in that, they were prematurely disappointed.

During the week following the 19th of Aug. he fully considered the emergency forced upon him, and conscientiously resolved upon the stand, he must; and was willing to, take. Like Martin Luther, he could exclaim — "Here I am, I can do no otherwise, God help me. Amen." In the meantime he prepared a letter to be read to the church the next Lord's day. So — "It behoved Christ to suffer!"

On Lord's Day morning, Aug. 26, 1635, those who usually assembled there to worship conscientiously wended their way to their "Separatist" Meeting House — they entered it — but to see Roger Williams in their Pulpit; no more thereafter.

Elder Samuel Sharpe, conducted the services; during which he read the aforesaid letter. In this letter Mr. Williams expressed himself in very strong terms; concerning the false and unchristian basis, of the Puritan churches of the Bay. His conscientious declaration was : — "He could hold christian communion with them no longer. They were unclean, by idolatrous pollutions. They were defiled with hypocrisy and worldliness. They needed cleansing from anti-christian filthiness, and communion with dead works, dead worships, dead persons in God's worship. They ought to loathe themselves for their abominations; for they were false worshippers of the true God; liable to God's sentence and plagues; guilty of spiritual drunkenness, and whoredom; of soul-sleep; and soul-sickness; in submitting to false churches; false ministry, and false worship. Their doctrines were corrupt. Their ministry was a hireling ministry."

Concerning himself he conscientiously wrote:— "The breath of the Lord Jesus is sounding forth in me (a poor despised ram's-horn), the blast, which in His own holy season shall cast down the strength and confidence of all these inventions of men; in the worshipping of the true and living God."

To his church, he declared; when he saw that a meagre majority of them had forsaken him, and were even ready to take sides with his opponents; that — "He should communicate with *them*, no more, so long as they remained in fellowship with the 'unseparated,' State-churches of the Bay."

Posterity; will not be so much interested in the manner of characterizing, adopted on either side, as in the cause, which each labored to establish: Toleration; on the one hand — and Inhibition on the other.

Many in the Salem church were much grieved, at the stand their Pastor had taken, but to him, it involved the whole question of Church and State; Religious Liberty; or Ecclesiastical Domination. If he remained with his church, even while a small majority of them were in collusion with the first church in Boston; and the other churches; then he could no longer conscientiously refuse, "to officiate to the 'unseparated' church in Boston. He must either stultify his own conscience; go back on his own history; renounce 'separation;' and sustain the Courts in punishing men for religious opinions; — or he must continue to be the divinely chosen 'ram's-horn,' to trumpet forth to all the world, Christ's fundamental Text — 'Render therefore unto Cæsar the things which are Cæsar's; and unto God the things that are God's.'"

True to his conscience, and true to the truth — he opened his own house for religious services on the Lord's Day; and on Lecture Days; and so withdrew himself from all the assemblies of the churches of the Bay. John Cotton says — "For a season he withdrew communion in spiritual duties with his WIFE; who still went to the Parish Assemblies; till at length he drew her to partake with him in his opinions." Those who conscientiously sympathized with his opinions; flocked to the Meetings in his own house; and to these such increasing numbers were added, as to furnish a new occasion for alarm to the conscientious vigilant, and ever-watchful Boston Magistrates; "Lest the infection of his opinions should spread!!"

SECTION 7. — ROGER WILLIAMS' TRIAL.

Voluminous and vehement ebullitions have flooded the ages from the abyss of authorship — agonizing, to show that it was for other offences, than advocating toleration; (that, being set down, as an offence); which formed the basis of Puritan conscientious opposition to Roger Williams. But a careful investigation of all the facts, will bear us out in the conclusion — that all other charges the Puritans raised against him, would not have made their case a sufficient ground for their final action; had that question of Liberty of conscience been left out — and, that question alone, would conscientiously have been a sufficient one, in their judgment. See the conscientious advice of the Elders; at the Court of July 18 — "He that would maintain such opinions; the churches ought to request the Magistrates, to remove, (banish) him."

Already there was hanging over Mr. Williams' head, the conscientious summons of July, for him, "to appear at the General Court in 8 weeks thereafter." Already the court had succeeded in conscientiously persuading a small major part, of his church, to join them against him. This carried the main point; by shielding the Magistrates from the Admonitory Letters; changing the case; and conscientiously putting him and his church under Admonition, for admonishing the churches, to admonish the Magistrates.

Messrs. Hooker and Cotton, were conscientiously very active now; besides Petitions, and Messengers from the churches; to induce the "minority" of the Salem Church, and Mr. Williams, to conscientiously retreat from their "untenable position," Mr. Cotton, "had spent most of the Summer, in seeking to satisfie his scruples." But Mr. Williams saw clearly that the way they sought to satisfy his scruples, was, to submit all to the preferences of the Court: and put liberty of conscience; under the consciences of the Magistrates.

We have already noted in Section 5, that the Meetings of the General Court in May 10, and July 18, 1635, were both; *after their Charter was annulled.* Under the Charter this Court was composed of the Gov.;

Deputy Gov.; and Eight Assistants. As the Colony grew, and Townships were organized, provisions were made, for these towns to be represented by Deputies of two or three persons from each town, chosen by the Freemen, to sit with the General Court. At this time, there were twenty-eight Deputies; eight Assistants; the Deputy Gov.; and Gov.; in all 38 persons composing the General Court. There were now ten churches in the colony, having among them, 12 able Ministers, or Elders: who were eligible from their office, to sit with the Court as Councillors, on important occasions. Some 50 persons; the first men of the Colony, composed the General Court of Massachusetts Bay.

Promptly on Wednesday Sept. 12th, the Court met at New Town, (Cambridge). On Thursday, the case of Roger Williams; tho' he was not present; was taken up.

The Magistrates made no attempt at concealing their conscientiousness about the action of the Salem Church, and Pastor, in sending out the "Admonitory Letters;" concerning their attitude on the Petition, about the Marble-Head land.

They took the conscientious view, that — "They were not accountable to the churches for anything they might do in their civil office." If so; why could they hold Roger Williams and his church accountable to them; for anything they might conscientiously do, in their Ecclesiastical Office?

Conscientious, upon having — contumacious Salem, more conscientious about "contempt of authority;" the Court sent home the three Deputies from Salem; Capt. William Traske, and Messrs. John Woodberry, and Jacob Barney; "to fetch satisfaccion for those offensive letters; or the names of such as indorsed them; or els the arguments of those that will defend the same." Evidently the Magistrates were not in a conscientious mood to be Admonished, by the church, and Pastors of Salem.

Upon this exhibition of the conscience of the Court, a scene of excitement followed, which furnished a demoralized example; of "brethen dwelling together in unity." Ex-Gov. Endicott was present, and being noted for dealing out his holy indignation, with unstinted measure, when occasion required; he availed himself of this opportunity. He poured forth his scathing invective upon the course matters had taken. Some of the Court, not being edified at hearing his Oration, "incensed beyond endurance retorted; and upon call, by generall ereceon of hands ordered that he be committed; (to jail) for contempt of Court." By some, it is stated, that "Endicott yielded to truth." The records state; that "the same day he came and acknowledged his fault, and was discharged." He took— "Admonition."

The Court passed this order — "If the major part of the ffreemen of Salem shall disclame the Letters sent lately from the church of Salem, to severall Churches, it shall then be lawfull to send Deputyes to the Generall Court." Evidently some of the Magistrates did not conscientiously relish being under censure, by the freemen of Salem.

It is plain with what conscientiousness the Court kept an eye on Roger Williams. Already they had gained a small "major part," of the church against him, by promising their land. At this Court, they "won to Truth," his ever helpful friend, Endicott ; by the Order of committal — and as a conscientious — persuasion — offered the three Deputies of Salem Seats to disown the Admonitory Letters.

Thus matters stood at the close of that day. Either for prudent — or some other reasons ; the Court adjourned, for five weeks — to Oct., 18.

During this interval for the gathering storm — intense excitement prevailed thro'out the Bay. The Court who were soon conscientiously to pass a Sentence, upon a conscientious, "godly minister" — were excited. The churches who had conscientiously evaded the exercise of admonition, upon the Magistrates — were excited. The Elders, who had conscientiously procured the major vote in the church at Salem against their pastor — were excited. Those members, who had just taken part in the ordination of Mr. Williams, contrary to the Order of Court ; and now had turned against him — were excited. Those who conscientiously attended his "separate service, marked by his popular ability," knowing that he was to be sentenced — were excited. And no doubt, Roger Williams himself, as "the poor despised Ram's-horn, of the Lord Jesus Christ" — was aware of the prevailing excitement. Endicott was a little cooled-off, and as many as felt the contagion of the popular excitement — were excited. Mr. Cotton said to one — "The Court are so incensed against his course, that it is not your voyce, nor the voyces of two, or three more ; that can suspend the Sentence." The Court "*Conscientiously*" incensed !

SECTION 8. — ROGER WILLIAMS BANISHED.

The rising Sun of Thursday Oct. 18, 1635, shone upon the paths along the fields and forests, which converged at New Town; in which, the Gov., Dept. Gov. Eight Assistants, and Twenty-Five Deputies — (the three from Salem being unseated) ; and whoever had occasion to be present ; were hastening to the Court. Mr. Williams, speaks of his "travells by day and night to goe and return to their Court." "All the ministers of the Bay," had been conscientiously invited, by the Court to attend for consultation with them, on this occasion. Very little consultation would be needed, as the Elders, had before conscientiously advised ; that "any one holding such opinions, ought to be removed by the Magistrates, at the request of the Churches."

The case of Mr. Williams, was finally reached ; and the charges, in their indictment ; made out at the Court of July 18, were reproduced, as follows : —

1. "That the Magistrate ought not to punish the breach of the First Table, except when the Civil Peace should be endangered.

2. That an Oath ought not to be tendered to an unregenerate man.

3. That a man ought not to pray with the unregenerate, even though it be with his wife or child.

4. That a man ought not to give thanks after Sacrament, nor after meat."

Behold, this conscientious Puritan indictment ! What is there of it, besides the all absorbing matter ; of taking the usurped power of persecuting men for religious opinions; *out* of the hands of Civil Magistrates? That; and that supremely, was the chief ground of the conscientious impatience of the Puritans, toward the conscientious contender for SOUL LIBERTY. From his decline of the call from the "unseparated Boston Church;" to this time; they had conscientiously disfellowshipped his opinions. The composition of this august body was as follows:—

John Haynes: GOVERNOR.
Richard Bellingham: DEPUTY GOVERNOR.

### ASSISTANTS.

John Winthrop; Atherton Hough; William Coddington; Simon Bradstreet; Thomas Dudley; Increase Nowell; John Humphrey; and Richard Dummer.

### DEPUTIES.

At this session, when the Salem People were much concerned in the action to be taken; the three Deputies from that town, Capt. William Trask; John Woodberry; and Jacob Barney, were absent from their seats. Twenty-five others from towns took seats: viz:— John Talcott; John Steel; Daniel Dennison; Richard Brown; Ensign Wm. Jennison; Edward Howe; Wm. Hutchinson; Wm. Colburn; Wm. Brenton; Dr. George Alcock; John Moody; Wm. Park; John Mansall; Thomas Beecher; Ezekiel Richardson; Nathaniel Duncan; Capt. John Mason; Wm. Gaylord; Joseph Metcalf; Humphrey Bradstreet; Wm. Bartholomew; Capt. Nathaniel Turner; Edward Tomlyns; Thomas Stanley; and John Spencer.

ELDERS.

"All the ministers of the Bay," had been invited by the Court, to be present on the occasion and assist by the way of consultation." The names of the Churches, in the order of their formation; with their respective ministers, were as follows : — *Salem;* Roger Williams : *Dorchester;* John Wareham ; and John Maverick : *Boston;* John Wilson; and John Cotton: *Watertown;* George Phillips : *Roxbury;* Thomas Welde ; and John Eliot : *Lynn;* Stephen Bachiler : *Charlestown;* Thomas James: *New Town* (Cambridge) Thomas Hooker ; and Samuel Stone: *Ipswich;* Nathaniel Ward : *Newbury;* Thomas Parker ; and James Noyes.

Such was the composition ; of the conscientious lords, commons, and clergy, of the Greate Court ; whose presumptive jurisdiction, exceeded that of the King of England — and of the present Legislature of Massachusetts ; convened to sit in judgment upon the conscientious opinions of the Great Apostle of Religious Liberty in America. Gladly would they have washed their hands like Pilate ; but they had conscientiously undertaken to solve the problem ; — "what shall we do with him, that is called, Williams?"

Posterity will never cease to be conscientiously interested about the manner in which, "a godly minister ; towards whom many were drawn thro' apprehensions of his godliness ;" was disposed of, by the conscientious Puritan Court of Massachusetts Bay Colony.

If the Court moved against Mr. Williams, because of his views on the "Patent ;" or the "Resident's

Oath;" or his "Ordination;" or the "Admonitory Letters;" then, their case wo'ld have had some show. But judging from the indictment; and "what is written, is written;" the only thing namable, is, his *opinion* of the limitation, of the power of Magistrates, to "civil things only." For; defending Religious Liberty—advocating, freedom of *conscience*—urging Separation of Church and State—and promoting "a Toleration;" the Puritans conscientiously dealt with Roger Williams.

When his case was fully reached, and when conscientiously enquired of, whether he were prepared to give satisfaction to the Court, in these matters; Mr. Williams, justified the ADMONITORY LETTERS; AND MAINTAINED ALL HIS OPINIONS. When asked whether he would take another month for reflection, and then come and argue the matter before them; he conscientiously and distinctly declined; choosing, "to dispute presently."

They then appointed Thomas Hooker;—minister of the church at New Town, (Cambridge) in whose rude structure, which served them as a Meeting House; where the Court was sitting, corner, Dunster and Mill Sts.—to argue with him on the spot,'for the endeavor to make him see his errors. With the day far spent, all ended where it began; in that neither the Court; nor Mr. Hooker; found it possible, "to reduce him from any of his errors." His positions, to his mind, had a "Rockie Strength." He was conscientiously ready, for them; "not only to be bound, and banished, but to die, also, in New England; as for most holy Truths of God in Christ Jesus."

Tho' all seemed to be ready for the Sentence; yet

conscientiously an adjournment of the Court was ordered, to the next morning. The question arises, why this adjournment? Mr. Williams, was ready, and why were not they ready also? It needs but half an eye to see, that they had come to a most unwelcome task. Their only hope of relief, lay in the possibility that the Brother at the Bar, would *recant.* By his so doing, they would be sustained in all they had done up to this point — and gain a concession for the Theocracy; over Roger Williams. Hence the forlorn hope in an adjournment — but He, held to his " Rockie Strength."

That night — such a night — ended with "cock-crowing ;" the dawn, stole between the eye-lids of the conscientious Magistrates — the rising Sun, proclaimed the morning of Friday, October 19, 1635. The hour of Court arrived; all were in painful waiting, for the *Deed*, that was to be *Done.*

Whereupon the Court, with "all the ministers approving it *save one*" — conscientiously passed the following Sentence —

"Whereas — Mr. Roger Williams, one of the Elders of the Church of Salem, hath broached and dyvulged dyvers new and dangerous opinions, against the authoritie of Magistrates, as also writt ltres of defamaccon, both of the Magistrates, and Churches here, and that before any conviccon, and yet mainctaineth the same without retraccon —

"It is therefore Ordered — that the said Mr. Williams, shall depete out of this jurisdiccon within sixe weekes nowe nexte ensuing ; wch if hee neglect to performe, it shal be lawfull for the Gour and two of the Magistrates to send him to some place out of this jurisdiccon ; not to returne any more without licence from the Court."

Should thinkers of Posterity ever be troubled to know, the reason ; why, this Company should assume to act as a " Court " — with their Charter, annulled ; and having never declared themselves Independent — of either the Church ; or Crown — of England ; and had never organized themselves — into a body Politic — or Ecclesiastic —

Why — should they assume — to pass a Sentence — so imperious — and stilted upon accusations, so beardless, and baseless ? ! ! — the answer is — upon their traditional conscientiousness.

## CHAPTER VII.

*SOUL LIBERTY IN PROVIDENCE, RHODE ISLAND.*

SECTION I. — ROGER WILLIAMS OSTRACIZED, LEAVES MASS. BAY.

WELL might Roger Williams now say, as he did when bishop Laud pursued him out of England; "it was as bitter as death unto me?" As he retired from the Puritan Meeting House; [corner Dunster and Mill Sts.] in New Town, (Cambridge) Oct.. 19, 1635; where Thomas Hooker was pastor; he went out ostracized, by the General Court of Massachusetts Bay; (tho' they had no legal authority from the Crown to sit as a Civil Court:) and by "all the ministers of the Bay, save one" — ostracized; for *no crime;* yet, ostracized by Conscientious Puritans; for defending Toleration in Religious Opinions; conscientiously.

It was no doubt, Mr. John Cotton, who was the, "save one," of the Elders, who did not approve, the Sentence of Banishment against Mr. Williams. So that with all their conscientious zeal in accusing, and sentencing him, their greatest minister, their principal Ecclesiastical magnate; sympathized, with the Distinguished Prisoner at the Bar.

In a letter of Mr. Cotton's, to Mr. Williams on the subject he Wrote : " Let not any prejudice against my person, (I beseech you,) forestall either your affection or judgment, as if I had hastened forward the Sentence, of your civill Banishment; for what was done by the Magistrates, in that kinde, was neither done by my counsell, nor consent; although I dare not deny the sentence passed to be righteous in the eyes of God."

To this Mr. Williams replied — "That Mr. Cotton consented not, what need he [consent] not being one of the civill Court? But that hee counselled it, (and so consented,) beside what other proofe I might produce, and what himself here under expresseth, I shall produce a double and unanswerable testimony. 1. Mr. Cotton teaches the doctrine of not permitting, but persecuting, all other consciences and ways of worship, but his own. 2. Divers worthy Gentlemen, told me they should not have consented to the Sentence but for Mr. Cotton's private advice and counsel. I desire to bee as charitable as charity would have me, and therefore would hope that either his memory failed him; or that else hee meant, that in the very time of the Sentence — passing, hee neither counselled nor consented, (as hee hath since said, that hee withdrew himselfe, and went out from the rest), . . . and yet if so, I cannot reconcile his owne expression."

To this Mr. Cotton rejoined; — "I have professed that I had no hand in procuring, or soliciting, the Sentence of his Banishment." Why not, if it were a "*righteous*" one?

How could Mr. Williams have any other than "*unsettled* judgments," — (as he is accused of) — upon the contradictory statements of Mr. Cotton; and the testimony of the "divers Worthy Gentlemen"?

Taking Mr. Cotton; and these "Gentlemen;" out of the Elders; and of the Court; and we know not how many others, of their opinion; and it is plain that they were far from unanimous in the Sentence.

Owing to excessive engagements, which had been long continued, a reaction set in, after the Court had ordered him Banished, which prostrated Mr. Williams, with a severe sickness; in consequence of which the time of his departure out of the Bay was extended, from "sixe weekes," until spring; on condition, that, "he should not go about to draw others to his opinions." Altho' he did not "go about to draw" people to him, yet so many were drawn to his house to hear him, that it was conscientiously reported, — that, "all Salem was filled with the infection of Anabaptism." And the fact that, "twenty persons had been gained to his opinions, provoked the Magistrates; rather than breed a winter's spiritual plague in the Countrey; to put upon him a winter's journey out of the Countrey."

Hence we find the Gov. and Assistants, met in Boston Jan. 1636, conscientiously ordered Mr. James Penn; Marshal of the Court; to serve a warrant upon Mr. Williams at Salem, "to come presently to Boston, to be shipped to England, by a vessel then lying at Nantasket, ready to depart." Had they so sent him; which would have been regarded as most repugnant to the laws of England: the prisoner sent; or the act of the Magistrates in sending him; specially after their Charter was gone?

> "But 'tis their mandate hither sent by me,
> That thou to Boston presently repair;
> A ship there waits, now ready for the sea,
> Homeward to bear thy HERESY — and thee."
> DURFEE.

As Mr. Williams was conscientiously indisposed; bodily; and mentally; to walk to Boston, for the sake of a felon's ride, to England; a committee from Salem waited upon the Boston Magnate, Penn; and informed him that their minister might not be expected to respond to this summons. Promptly, as they always acted, and "conscientiously;" towards that conscientious "Ram's-Horn" — Mr. John Underhill, one of the two chief officers of the Plantation, and who was that year chosen Captain for Boston; was ordered, with 14 men to go in a pinnace, by way of Marble Head to Salem, and conscientiously take Mr. Williams by authority, and kindly place him on board the ship aforesaid. In the mean time, Ex Gov. John Winthrop had kindly and *privately* given Mr. Williams, a "hint from God" — to "arise and flee into the Narrohiganset's country free from English Pattents."

But when this naval expedition, arrived at his house; Roger Williams; had been three Days Gone! "Conscientiously" — Gone!

This was Roger Williams' 2d Flight. When he fled from bishop Laud, towards Bristol to take ship, he could not stop at the Stoke House, to say good-by to his esteemed friend Sir Edward Coke. And now he flees from the General Court, by a kind hint from Gov. Winthrop towards the wilderness; nor could he stop at Boston; to be "shipped to England." Likewise Moses, fled to Midian — the Spies, from Jericho — David, before Absalom — Elijah, before Jezebel — Matthias, before Epiphanes — Jesus, before Herod — Paul, before Aretas — Cyprian, from Carthage — Luther, from Worms — Pilgrims, from England. So the woman in Rev. 12: fled to the wilderness, and the Dragon made war upon her seed, which kept the commandments of God, and the testimony of Jesus Christ. Fleeing to the dens and caves of the earth, is a badge of the saints of the Lord, as all History shows. But how glorious the returns from all these Flights — and how deep the stain that rests, upon all the persecutors of the saints of the Most High. "I would palliate not a particle of the persecution or cruelty which [Roger Williams] suffered; from whatever source it may have proceeded, or by whomever it may have been prompted."

HON. R. C. WINTHROP.

### SECTION 2. — ROGER WILLIAMS SETTLES IN PROVIDENCE RHODE ISLAND.

> "Williams," he said, "I come on message here,
> Of moment great to this blind age unknown,
> Thou must not dally, or the tempest fear,
> But fly at morn into the forest drear." — DURFEE.

It was a dire disappointment to the Puritans, when they found Mr. Williams had escaped landward; for having heard that he and his 20 followers in Salem, were intending to settle not far away, but outside Massachusetts Bay, and found a new colony; they were "conscientiously" exercised, to prevent it.

> ... "Think ye he would bow,
> Or yield to sufferings of corporeal pain,
> Whom God had summoned from the bigot's slough
> To plant Religious Freedom, and maintain
> Her standard firm in fair Mooshausick's plain!"
> DURFEE.

The fears of the Puritans were founded upon the fact, that, "the people being many of them taken with apprehensions of his godliness" — and the fear, that such a man, with such principles, planted near by them ; "the infection, would easily spread into their churches." Hence this early attempt to conscientiously discourage a new colony.

Leaving wife and all behind, tho' followed by many prayers for his welfare; Roger Williams went into a wintry howling wilderness, about the middle of January 1636, and spent, "14 weeks not knowing what bread or bed did mean." The hospitalities of the Red Men, whose acquaintance and friendship he had won, while in Plymouth ; were cordially extended to him. All of which, rude as they were, he preferred ; with the care of Providence ; to remaining where he was liable, to be conscientiously "shipped to merry England."

In this exile the weary Winter wore away ; and in the Spring Mr. Williams with his wife and family, reappear, at Seekonk, in his rude home, on a plantation, generously bestowed upon him by Massasoit ; Head Chief of the Wampanoags. But no sooner was this fact known to the ever vigilant, *charterless*, Court of the Bay ; than they "conscientiously" informed *Gov*. Winslow of Plymouth concerning the matter; in such a way, that he willingly, or otherwise, "conscientiously," sent a messenger, with his letter to Mr. Williams. In this letter the Gov. expressed his, and others', friendship for him, and lovingly advised him ; "since he had fallen into the edge of their bounds, and they were loath to displease the Bay ; to remove but to the other side of the water, and there he had the country before him, and might be as free as themselves ; and they should be loving neighbors together."

This event, bro't Mr. Williams to a third exile — a third scene, "as bitter as death to him." Not bitter, because of the difficulty of moving on, in either case; but bitter, because of the opinions of brethren behind him; "conscientiously" pushing him on.

> "In short, thou art on Plymouth's own domain;
> Nor hath our Winslow in his charge forgot —
> His former friendship — but right loath is he;
> To vex his neighbors, by obliging thee.
> . . . Hence therefore must thou speed —
> The Narragansetts; may protect thy creed."
>
> DURFEE.

Mr. Williams was well aware that not all, even of the General Court, were thus; conscientious towards him; especially Gov. John Winthrop; but that in the enthusiastic spirit of Dudley; lay the sharpness of the thorn that so often pierced his soul — in whose pocket were found after his death; of his own composing; the following lines —

> "Let men of God in Courts and Churches watch
> O'er such as do a Toleration hatch,
> Lest that ill-egg bring forth a cockatrice,
> To poison all with heresy and vice.
> If men be left and otherwise combine,
> My epitaph's; I dy'd no libertine."

In Mr. Williams' own words, he tells us — "I was sorely tossed for fourteen weeks — I left Salem in the winter snows — I found a great contest going on between the Chiefs — I travelled between them — I first pitched and began to build and plant at Seekonk — I received a message from Mr. Winslow — I crossed the Seekonk, and settled at Mooshausick."

Like the Pilgrims, denied a resting-place among

conscientious Christian Brethren — Roger Williams, with Five companions, pushed out from the white-man's — land, in their "Mayflower," canoe ; — silently, musingly, prayerfully, they paddled along their exile way — nearing the other shore, they saw a group of the natives. When they were come within hail, they were saluted by them in broken English — " Netop, "(friend) " wha-cheer! wha-cheer!!" Much like the salutation the Pilgrims received from Samoset ; "Welcome Englishmen Welcome Englishmen !" The place of their landing, is well known by the name of "What-cheer Cove." Why should not the sacred spot be more distinctly, and gratefully marked by an appropriate Monument?

"The first grant of land conscientiously made to Roger Williams, by Canonicus, and Miantonomo, was a verbal one ; of all the meadows and lands upon the two fresh Rivers, called the Mooshausick, and Wanaskatucket. But on March 24, 1637, they conscientiously confirmed this grant, by Deed ; and, "in consideration of the many kindnesses and services he was constantly rendering them." Evidently Mr. Williams regarded "kindnesses," better legal-tender, than ; "burning houses in sight of the Indians, for their satisfaccon." He also regarded this title of Indians' lands, from conscientious Indians themselves ; as more satisfactory, than that by " Pattent from the King."

> " As to our title then, we trace it thus : —
> God gave James Stuart this, James, gave us."
> DURFEE.

The "conscientious " jilting of Roger Williams, from England ; and from Salem ; and from Seekonk ; for conscience' sake ; only confirmed him in his desire, to promote the great cause of Religious Liberty. Behold Him! conscientiously disposing of the lands, the chiefs had given him; as his personal possession; among those who had followed him out of *Christendom*, into *Indiandom*. In a deed to these ends, he says:—"I having made covenant of peaceable neighborhood, with all the Sachems and Natives round about us—and having in a sense of God's merciful goodness to me in my distress, called this place, PROVIDENCE—*I desire it might be for a shelter to persons distressed for* CON-SCIENCE." . . . Thus, what he had "*freely* received, he freely gave;" to his friends in tribulation; "reserving no more to himself than an equal share with the rest; his WIFE; also; signing the deed."

In this noble act of generosity; philanthropy; and conscientious devotion to Liberty of opinion; we see nothing of the "conscientiousness," that witheld; the "Marble Head Land." No kind design in this, to ship men of a Toleration, to England, "lest the infection being too near might easily spread."

> "But when the welcome of 'what cheer! what cheer!!'
> Shall greet thine ears from Indian multitude,
> Cast thou thine Anchor, there, and Trust in God."
> DURFEE.

Indeed the Flight of Roger Williams from Seekonk, marks the *temporary* ascendency, of the queryful, conscientiousness in Mass.; and Plymouth Bay, Colonies. The Court had barely escaped, Church Discipline—the Church in Salem, or a "small major part" of them, had succumbed to the Magistrates — Endicott, had "yielded to truth"— Gov. Winslow, dared not, withstand "the truth"— and Roger Williams, was gone; conscientiously twice gone, outside "ye lymmitts!" Surely, the Bay could be at peace, and conscientiously have rest, now.

And yet Soul Liberty, had made greater progress, than Soul Trammel. Henry VIII., had demonstrated to the world, that; A Church of England; could be established, independent of the Pope; and still use some of the popish ceremonials:— the Puritans had conscientiously demonstrated, that, a church could be established, and omit the Anglo-popish ceremonials, altogether:— the Pilgrims had conscientiously demonstrated, that, a church could exist Independent, of establishment, and ceremonials, both:— and now, Roger Williams had gained a foot-hold in Providence; where he is about conscientiously to demonstrate to the world, that a church, can be established, without an "Establishment;"— be Independent, of "Independency;"— and rest securely on the "Rockie" basis, of Religious Liberty. For the prevalence of this truth, he conscientiously contended with all his powers; and for its Triumph, he "counted all things but loss." With what success he labored; Posterity; will judge!

Here we have then, Boston; at the Head of Massachusetts Bay; the home of John Cotton; and the seat of THEOCRACY—also, Plymouth; at the Head of Plymouth Bay; the home of William Brewster; and the seat of INDEPENDENCY—and, Providence; at the Head of Narragansett Bay; the home of Roger Williams; and the seat of RELIGIOUS LIBERTY. These three centres of influence; situated relatively, so as to form almost a perfect triangle. Whose sentiments shall most widely; potently; and permanently; prevail?

Mr. Cotton, maintained conscientiously, that, "democracy was not a fit government for either church; or State. "If the people are governors, who are the governed? "Monarchy and Aristocracy, are approved and directed in the Scripture; but only, as a Theocracy; is set up in both."

Mr. Brewster, "foreseeing that Mr. Williams might run into the same course of rigid Separation and Anabaptistry, as Mr. Smyth, at Amsterdam had done; conscientiously, and prudently counselled the church at Plymouth, to grant him a dismission, as he had requested, to return to Salem."

Mr. Williams conscientiously advocated perfect freedom of opinion, in religious concernments; and that in the State, submission, to Magistrates, should be limited, to "CIVIL THINGS ONLY."

Very soon after his settlement at Providence; Roger Williams was informed, that the Pequots, had sent messengers to persuade the Narrohigansetts, to join them in a massacre, of the Connecticut settlers. He conscientiously resolved at once, to do his utmost, to defeat this plot, and thereby to save the lives of some of those very men, who had conscientiously Banished him from Massachusetts. Setting out alone in a fearful storm he paddled many a weary mile to reach the Narrohigansett village. Altho' he nearly lost his life by interfering; yet after boldly pleading his cause for four days, he succeeded; in breaking up the league.

In a letter to Mr. Mason, Mr. Williams states that — "Gov. Winthrop, and some of the Council; of Massachusetts; were conscientiously disposed to recall him from Banishment; and confer upon him some mark of distinguished favor for his services." In these services we see Mr. Williams rendering good for evil. But thât kind of an "infection tho' so near," did not infect all the Magistrates of the Bay.

Nor has that act of justice in Revoking his Banishment — yet been performed; tho' conscientiously suggested so soon, after his Banishment; and by one who reluctantly participated in it. And yet 255 years have passed, and during which, the world has received 255 times more benefit, from his "distinguished services;" than the conscientious Winthrops, then dreamed of; and YET; IT IS NOT DONE! And still, those "services" *wait* — for their "Mark, of Distinguished favor." By whom — and when — will the Sentence of Banishment against Roger Williams — be "conscientiously" — REVOKED?

SECTION 3. — PROVIDENCE PLANTATIONS PROSPER.

The conscientious charges, made against Roger Williams; "of his hostility to all Civil Government, are utterly demolished; as we see him carefully building up the Civil Government, of his new Plantation, on the most substantial and enduring basis.

The conscientious Banishment of Roger Williams, for advocating Toleration; did not secure peace and quiet in the Bay. Among the many who came from England, having diverse sentiments and opinions, was one Mrs. Anne Hutchinson: "a woman of talent, ready eloquence, self-reliance, and an acute disputant. She presently and conscientiously assumed to hold meetings in Boston, and instructed the sisters of the church, in the most "recondite doctrines of Theology."

While Mrs. Hutchinson maintained with superior energy, the great doctrine of the Reformation — Justification by Faith — which the Puritans also accepted; yet she took issue with them, on their formal mode of Worship — the ascetic austerity of their lives — and their sanctimonious carriage; as giving no evidence whatever of their justification; change of heart; or acceptance with God. She conscientiously maintained that the only true evidences of having those graces, were; an internal revelation — an assurance — and an innate consciousness, on the part of the believer, that the Holy Ghost dwelt in him, and was personally united to him.

The issue in this case as usual, turned upon each party, conscientiously demanding of the other — "Show me thy faith without thy works, and I will show thee my faith by my works." The zeal manifested, and the subtleties used by the disputants; drew disciples to both views. On the side of Mrs. Hutchinson, were Gov. Vane, John Cotton; Mr. Wheelright, a minister much in favor with the Boston Church; and even a majority, of that Church. But, by Gov. Winthrop, Mr. Wilson, and most of the other Magistrates, and "Ministers, of the Bay;" the Theocratic worship and manners, were preferred. "But the whole Colony was rent with the controversy." Why so; now that Roger Williams, was Banished?

In view of the Pequot war, in Conn., and the dissensions of the times, a Fast Day was appointed; and Mr. Wheelright, was chosen to preach. In his Sermon, he was thought to lean towards Mrs. Hutchinson's views, inasmuch as he distinguished her adherents, as under, "a covenant of grace;" and her opponents, as under, "a covenant of works."

This was a conscientious alarm to the General Court; so at their Session in March 1637, Mr. Wheelwright was notified, and reminded: that — "The Court had appointed the Fast as a means for the reconciliation of differences, but that he had purposely set himself to kindle them." Notwithstanding petitions were presented in his behalf, by the principal inhabitants of Boston; he was conscientiously considered as faulty; of "Sedition, and Contempt of authority." Concerning this state of things, Cotton Mather in his "Magnalia," writes — "The Ministry of the country awakened by these noises about the Temple, had several Meetings, that they might set matters to rights; all which were ineffectual until the General Court called, the First New England Synod; of all the Churches, in the country to meet in Cambridge, in the year 1637." Anomalous indeed! The General Court, of "Cæsar," calling a General Synod of Christian Churches! Yet — Sanctioned by the most Sincere Puritan Conscientiousness.

"The Synod being assembled, there were produced, 82, false and heretical opinions; 9 unwholesome expressions; and diverse perversions of Scripture; which had been uttered in the country, by several men, at several times. Some of the Delegates from the Boston Church, objected to the Synod's entertaining such a catalogue of errors; thereby bringing the Colony into reproach. The names of the authors of these heresies were suppressed; hence some of the more hypocritical Sectaries began to grow at last pretty clamorous, in demanding the names of such as held the dogmas then opposed; for the true parents of the brats, began to discover themselves, when the Synod was going to employ the sword upon them. Some of the civil Magistrates then present, as members of the Assembly, were forced as Justices of the Peace, to preserve the peace of the Assembly, by commanding scilence to those litigious talkers; whereupon they left the Assembly." Likewise did the Protestants, at the Council of Trent.

The chief anxiety of the Synod, was, to get into harmony with the great " Elder, John Cotton ; who was not the least part of the country;" especially as he like Mr. Wheelwright sympathized with the Hutchinsons. How could they endure that *he* should be among the Sectaries? After a long and sharp contention they at length conscientiously agreed: — " We are not united and married unto the Lord Jesus Christ, without faith, giving an actual consent of soul unto it; — That God's effectual calling of the soul unto the Lord Jesus Christ, is, in order of nature ; before God's act of justification, upon the soul: — That in the testimony of the Holy Spirit, which is the evidence of our good estate before God, the qualifications, and the fruit thereof, proving the sincerity of our faith, must ever be co-existent, concurrent, and co-apparent, or else the conceived testimony of the Spirit, is either a delusion, or doubtful. A happy conclusion of the whole matter."

The Puritans were much pleased at gaining back to their field Mr. Cotton ; " not the least part of the country ;" but that achievement did not give the other part of the country; rest and peace. The Hutchinsons still maintained with conscientious persistence, the doctrine of "inward assurance;" while the Theocracy, contended with equal conscientiousness for the necessity of the "outward manifestation." So that Banishing Mr. Williams; *settled;* not everything.

But the Great and General Court, who aimed at settling everything, conscientiously took the matter in hand at their session in Nov. 1637. Upon learning that a majority of them were in favor of proceeding with summary measures; (their conscientious remedy for all ills of the body politic); no time was lost, in anathematizing the dissidents, who could not otherwise, be reduced from one of their errors.

Mr. Wheelwright was conscientiously disfranchised, and banished. Mrs. Hutchinson, was sentenced to banishment, but like Mr. Williams, two years before, was conscientiously permitted to remain until Spring. Capt. Underhill, who so readily and conscientiously went after Roger Williams, to ship him to England, was deprived of office, and disfranchised. Mr. Hutchinson, John Clarke, and others were instructed that unless they left the Colony of their own accord, they would be conscientiously assisted to do so. All other persons of Hutchinsonian proclivities were ordered to give up their arms. All this ended in a Law — passed; that — "All persons who dared defame this Court and its proceedings, should conscientiously be subjected to fine and imprisonment." Thus the First New England Synod, closed.

These banished ones, who were without where to lay their heads, were forced "to seek a place where to inhabit." A desirable spot was soon found in the Plymouth Patent; but the experience of Roger Williams at Seekonk, taught them that this would be within "ye lymmits;" and that to be safe from moving again, they must speed on.

"The Narrohigansetts may protect thy creed."

In this their time of need, to whom could they look under God, for a friend indeed? Seeking counsel of Mr. Williams; who had tasted the same cup, as had now been put to their lips; they immediately associated themselves together, and under the leadership of Mr. John Clarke, proceeded to purchase of the Heathen Narrohigansetts, the beautiful and fertile Island of Aquidnay; Mar. 24, 1637; just a year to a day, after the meadows of Mooshausick, were deeded to Roger Williams. They gave it the name of "Isle of Rhodes" — later, it is known by the renowned name of RHODE ISLAND. These exiles were soon joined by others from Boston; but those, "who savored of the rigid Separation, and of Anabaptism, removed to Providence; which now began to be well peopled."

Roger Williams, having obtained at the same time of the cession of Aquidnay, a formal grant, by special deed; of Providence: On Oct. 8, 1637, he admitted his Associates, and such others; "as the major part shall receive, into the same fellowship of vote," as joint owners. At the same time a voluntary Government was formally instituted, and by a solemn Covenant; all, conscientiously agreed — "To submit to the orders of the major part; in "CIVIL THINGS ONLY."

Behold the three Colonies; and Compacts; of the New England Fathers. Among the Pilgrims, they left England, as a church; entered into a civil Compact, on the Mayflower; no union of Church and State; received their lands from the Indians; conscientiously enjoyed; "Freedom to worship God, cost what it would."

The Boston Puritans, came over as a Colony; having their Patent of lands, and charter from the King of England; and conscientiously set up a Theocracy, on the Silence of their Charter.

The "Separatists"—went into the Narrohigansett Country; received their lands of the Indians; and conscientiously set up the Standard of Religious Liberty; and Separation of Church and State.

> "I sing the trials and sufferings, great,
> Which FATHER WILLIAMS in his exile bore,
> That he the conscience-bound might liberate,
> And to the soul, religious rights restore;
> How after flying persecution's hate,
> And roving long by Narragansetts' shore,
> In lone Mooshausick's vale at last he sate,
> And on RELIGIOUS FREEDOM based our State."
>
> DURFEE.

At a Fast in the Bay, Dec. 13, 1638, Mr. John Cotton conscientiously elucidated how he fell into the toils of the Mrs. Hutchinson controversy. It consisted in; "The errors she taught, being very artfully formed, so near the truth he had preached, that at first he did not perceive their enormity." To this he added a conscientious confession. He bewailed his own, and the church's security, and credulity. In Mr. Williams, this would have been called — "very unsettled in judgments."

The delighted ones of Mr. Cotton's day rejoiced, that — "By this reasonable concession, did that reverend and worthy minister of the Gospel, recover his former splendor throughout the country of New England." Of course, in the eyes of the Theocracy he was all right, notwithstanding his equivocal position upon the Sentence against Roger Williams. Besides, he conscientiously recovered himself, from the danger of being — "shipped to England;— or being whipped — or having his ears cropped; or of being Banished to Mooshausick!" Roger Williams; might have remained in the Bay, on the same recanting "conscientiousness."

### SECTION 4. — ROGER WILLIAMS FOUNDS THE FIRST BAPTIST CHURCH.

That portion of the Pilgrim Fathers, who conscientiously became Baptists in Holland, under the leadership of John Smyth, and returned to England; published in 1611, a Confession of Faith, having the true Gospel; and old Waldensian, *ring*, in it. This work set forth in a bold conscientious manner; that — "The Magistrate is not to meddle with religion, or matters of conscience; nor to compel men to this, or that, form of religion, because Christ; is the King and Lawgiver of the Church, and Conscience."

Amid the agitations these sentiments caused, during the youthful manhood of Mr. Williams, he was a conscientious and attentive observer; and when he encountered the New England conscientiousness, he did not hesitate to teach Magistrates, the same lesson here; and but for his conscientious advocacy of it; Soul Liberty; might have long slumbered under the "ADVICE of the Elders to the Boston Magistrates." For his zeal he has been rewarded as he deserves to be; with the glorious title of "Father of Religious Liberty, in America."

With these surroundings in his early life, we are prepared to understand what Mr. Brewster of Plymouth meant, when he conscientiously said; at the time of dismissing Mr. Williams, to return to Salem; "foreseeing that he would like John Smyth, run into Anabaptistry." So too we understand the charge; that — "he had in one year, filled all Salem with Anabaptist tendencies."

The same is seen in the Indictment of the Court, at his Banishment. No doubt the conscience of the Court, was whet to an edge, on Mr. Williams' opinions, upon the Patent — the Resident's Oath — Separation — and the Admonitory Letters; but none of these charges appear in the Indictment as crimes — these opinions were not of sufficient venality, even in the minds of the Puritan Court, to be named as such in the Indictment — and even fear, lest Posterity should have to blush for them, may have kept them from naming these opinions as crimes. But when that most dangerous, of all heretical postulates (?), was advocated, that — "The Magistrate is not to meddle with religion, or matters of Conscience:" — that offence, goes into the Indictment — for this they conscientiously Banished him. At the same time, this very Great Question, of Soul Freedom — was rocking the throne of England.

In 1639, Mr. Williams' "Anabaptist tendencies," conscientiously led him to embrace Baptist sentiments. "Many of that persuasion having fled to Providence." Being, as they were; exiles for *Conscience*' Sake from Old England; and from New England; they were without any visible Church Order.  Therefore in imitation of John, in Judea — "There being no Administrator, Roger Williams was first dipped by Ezekiel Holliman, one of the Brethren, in Benedict Pond — and then himself dipped the others; and so became Founder, and Teacher, of the First Baptist Church in America." The same being the First Baptist Church, Providence Rhode Island; which has since, and still remains to this day.

In 1641, one Samuel Gorton, calling himself — "Professor of the Mysteries of Christ," created a disturbance which Mr. Williams only, with great difficulty was able to quiet.  But soon after some of the inhabitants, led by one Benedict Arnold, so far opposed him in this matter as to invite the interference of Massachusetts Bay.

The Bay conscientiously responded, by a proposition; to interfere; that — "If this faction would submit themselves, by taking a non-'Resident's Oath' of allegiance to their jurisdiction; or, if they preferred; to that of Plymouth."

The Bay at this time were conscientious, but charterless.

Accordingly a few of the Arnolds; went to Boston, and "submitted."  Upon this, a warrant was presently sent to Gorton; citing him to appear and answer to their complaint.  He did not appear, but answered in a reply to — "The Great Idol General of Mass. Bay."

Alarmed at this conscientious interference of the Bay, and fearing that their Theocratic Solicitude might be extended over all their neighbors; Mr. Williams resolved to proceed at once to England, to solicit a

Charter, for a Government — a measure suggested, by the people of Aquidnay, a year before. "Not being allowed to go to Boston, without license from the Courte" — he went to Manhattan, (N. Y.), and obtained passage home by Holland.

Shortly after he left; an attempt was made by Massachusetts Bay, to get possession of Shawomet, near Providence; territory which Gorton had purchased of Miantonomo — on a pretence, that he had no title to the land. Under the conscientious advice of five, of the "most judicious Elders;" Miantonomo, was *tomahawked* — and thro' the treachery of Arnold; two petty chiefs; and Shawomet; submitted to the Bay. Thus, was Rhode Island edified by advising Elders.

In 1643, a Union was formed between the 4 colonies of Massachusetts Bay; Plymouth; Connecticut; and New Haven; for mutual defence against the Indians — known as the "United Colonies, of New England."

Remembering still, Roger Williams' decline "of the call of Boston Church " — his "contempt of authority," in being ordained at Salem — and the "Admonitory Letters" — but *forgetting*, that he had *protected the Bay* from an INDIAN MASSACRE — Rhode Island; "because they followed after his religious opinions;" was conscientiously *left out*, of this Union; notwithstanding they wished to join it. Similar to the "Marble Head Land" case.

During Mr. Williams' stay in England, he published his "Key to the Language of America" in 1644. Also his, "Bloody Tenet of Persecution;" in reply to Mr. Cotton's letter — "On the Power of the Magistrate, in matters of Religion." Cotton conscientiously replied in his — "Bloody Tenet, washed and made white in the Blood of the Lamb." Williams conscientiously rejoined — "The Bloody Tenet more bloody, by John Cotton's attempt to wash it white."

Mr. Williams, readily obtained a charter, from the commissioners appointed by Parliament, to superintend the affairs of the Colonies. It included the Shores, and Islands, of Narrohigansett Bay, west of Plymouth Bay and south of Massachusetts Bay; as far as the Pequot (Thames) River country; to be known as the "Providence Plantations." Liberty was given in it, for inhabitants — "to rule themselves as they shall find most suitable." A similar privilege was given in the Massachusetts Bay Charter, in its silence, . . . on the subject of liberty in religion. The Massachusetts Bay Men choosing to restrict all not of their way; because they conscientiously feared "Toleration" — while in Providence, "Toleration" was conscientiously Tolerated.

On his return, (not his flight, as he last left England :) Mr. Williams brought with him letters from several conscientious influential gentlemen, Members of Parliament; which made it *peremptorily* unnecessary, for him to have "license from the Courte" — or, to return, by way of Manhattan. He came to Boston; not however, that the Court might "ship him and his heresy," to England; but to go quietly, (not *hurriedly* as he went before), thro' the Bay; to Providence. At Seekonk he was met by 14 canoes, and escorted to "Wha-cheer Cove" in triumph; Sept. 1644. Note — a "safe-conduct," needed, to go through the land of the Puritans;. but conducted safely, in the land of "CANOES!"

Alluding to Holland; he wrote—"From Enchugsen, therefore; a den of persecuting lions, and mountain leopards; the persecuted fled to Amsterdam, a poor fishing town, yet harborous and favorable to the flying, though dissenting consciences. This confluence of the persecuted, by God's most gracious coming with them; drew boats—drew trade—drew shipping; and that so mightily, and in so short a time; that shipping, trade, wealth, greatness, honor, (almost to astonishment in the eyes of all Europe, and the world), have appeared to fall as out of Heaven, in a crown, or garland, upon the head of this poor Fishertown."

The glorious success of Mr. Williams, in the popularity he enjoyed in England; and in obtaining a Charter; gave great encouragement to the friends of Liberty of Conscience; and also carried consternation into the camp of his opposers. So alarmed were the Theocracy, that in Nov. 23, 1644, the General Court conscientiously passed the following Law—"For as much as experience hath plentifully and often pved yt since ye first arising of ye Anabaptists, about 100 years since, they have bene ye incendiaries of commonwealths, and ye infectors of persons in maine mattrs of religion, and ye troublers of churches in all places where they have bene;—and yt they who have held ye baptizing of infants unlawfull have usually held othr errors or heresies togethr therewith, though they have (as other hereticks use to do), concealed ye same, till they spied out a fit advantage and opportunity to vent ym by way of question or scruple;—and whereas divers of this kind have, since our comeg into New England, appeared amongst orselves, some whereof have (as others before ym), denied ye ordinance of magistracy, and ye lawfulness of making warr, and others ye lawfulness of matrats, and their inspection into any breach of ye first table: — wch opinions if they should be connived at by us, are like to be increased amongst us, and so must necessarily bring guilt upon us, infection and trouble to ye churches, and hazard to ye whole commonwealth —

"It is ordered and agreed yt if any pson or psons within ys jurisdiction shall either openly condemne or oppose ye baptizg of infants, or go about secretly to seduce others from ye appbation or use thereof, or shall purposely depart ye congregation at ye administration of ye ordinance, or shall deny ye ordinance of magistracy, or their lawfull right or authority to make warr, or to punish ye outward breaches of ye first table, and shall appear to ye Cort wilfully and obstinately to continue therein after due time and means of conviction, every such psonor psons shal be sentenced to banishment." All done in good "Conscience."

Any one living 250 years after the passage of such a law as this cannot fail, in view of such honest delusion, to feel that commiseration for the Puritans, as will prompt the prayer — "Father forgive them for they knew not what they did."

The famous Westminster Assembly of Divines, sat in 1644. Among other divine (?) and conscientious considerations; bro't before them, was this — "Our next work is, to give our advice what to do for the suppressing of the huge increase, of insolences intolerable, of — Anabaptists, Antinomians, and other sectaries." Whatever the Assembly did about it, some of the sectaries, survive even yet. Had the Assembly consulted "Gamaliel," he might have repeated his advice; "to let them alone."

Upon his return to Providence, Mr. Williams took measures promptly, to organize a liberal civil Government under his new charter. But unexpected difficulties were thrown in his way. Massachusetts Bay still claimed Shawomet. Tho' on no other ground, than that they gained, thro' Arnold.

Plymouth was also conscientiously solicited, by the Bay — (as when Gov. Winslow sent Mr. Williams, further on) — to set up a claim to Aquidnay; and also to Providence; itself; as within the dominion of Massasoit. But this coveting of Mr. Williams' homestead, by the Bay, after Gov. Winslow's promise to him, that — "they would ever be *loving neighbors;*" the Plymouth people, regretted, and *repudiated.* But, not content with their poor success in these claims, the Bay Court, conscientiously forbade, Roger Williams, "to exercise any of his pretended authority, in either of those places."

Did ever Roger Williams make so "dangerous, and seditious" an attempt at "undermining the foundations" of the Bay? Besides, the Court, at this time; had only the King's reassumed charter, as the basis, of their baseless — authority; while Mr. Williams had a charter from the British Parliament, for his, "pretended authority." Further; after they had lost their charter, they had never formed a *voluntary* Government among themselves, as the people at Plymouth; and Providence had. The Bay had their patent of land from the usurped right of the King; the others, had theirs from the Indians, themselves — the owners of the soil.

Nothing could be more unbenign than this interdict from the Bay; yet, it was conscientiously done, to intercept, if possible, the establishment of a colony so near, with the "infection, of Toleration," in it.

At the Session of the charterless General Court, in Oct. 1645, a petition was presented from divers Merchants, and others; conscientiously asking for some alteration in the Law against Anabaptists. A portion, (as always), of the Court, were inclined to favor this petition — but the ever-present, ELDERS, were conscientiously *present;* and diligently went, first to the Deputies; and then to the Magistrates; and represented what advantage the granting of that petition would be to that sect, whose notions were already fast spreading. As the result of this buttonholing by the Elders, the Court *conscientiously* — "Voted yt ye lawe mentioned should not be altered at all, nor explained." Blow after blow, conscientiously against Toleration.

In this same line of conscientious baffling, we find — "The Commissioners, For The United Colonies" — adding their support in an order, conscientiously advising — "The suppression of the influx of error, under the deceitful color of Liberty of Conscience." ·Thus the Aristocratical Government of the "4 Colonies;" conscientiously "obstructed Freedom of Conscience." And all this; done in the Ice, of a Charter, which was *silent* on the subject of Religious Liberty — and even that, was annulled.

· A petition was presented to the Court in 1646, praying for the enjoyment of the civil rights of English subjects; and complaining of the exclusive limitation of civil privileges, to Church Members — but it was conscientiously answered, with refusal.

A similar effort was made in behalf of Religious Liberty in Plymouth Colony, by Mr. Vassall and others. Even one of the Magistrates, made a proposal for "General Toleration" — and two others, had favored it. But Mr. Winslow in reporting it to the Bay, wrote — "You would have admired to see how sweet this carrion relished in the palates of *most* of the Deputies. But Gov. Bradford, sustained by a (small) majority of the Magistrates, refused to put it to vote; as being that indeed which would eat out the power of Godliness." To Posterity, it looks as tho' the "power of conscientious godliness" was well nigh "eat out," already — when "Toleration" was called "*carrion.*" Thus; sad spectacle; "Pilgrim" Plymouth Court; a small majority of them — had; after 16 years of "Puritan conscientiousness," been made, like the Salem church; and like Endicott — to "yield to Truth."

SECTION 5. — THE PURITANS RISE TO EXPLAIN.

Inasmuch as the Puritans had left England — "not as Separatists, but as still members with their brethren in and of the Church of England;" they found it difficult often, to make other people understand their Ecclesiastical whereabouts. Finally they saw their way clear to request, that — "Not the least part of the Country" — their Great Elder, Mr. John Cotton — prepare for them, a "Declaration of Faith, and a Form of Church Doctrine, and Discipline, from the Old and New Testaments." This he most diligently, and dutifully produced in his — "Keys to the Kingdom of Heaven."

In the "Keys," he very learnedly, Biblically; and conscientiously declares, — "That, as in the State, there is a dispersion of powers into several hands, which are to concur in all acts of common concernments; from whence ariseth the healthy constitution of a Commonwealth." In like sort he assigns the power in the Church into several subjects, wherein the united light of Scripture, and of Nature, have placed them; with very satisfactory distribution.

By following the light of Scripture and of Nature: conscientiously; he found, that — "A Presbyterated society of the Faithful, had in itself a complete power of self-reformation, or self-preservation; and may within itself manage its own choices of officers, and censurer of delinquents." This was just what the church in Salem conscientiously thought, when they chose Mr. Williams to office; and sent out the Admonitory Letters for the "censure of Delinquents."

He also conscientiously found, — "By a special statute of Our Lord, that women and children were excepted from enjoying any part of this power; and hence only Elders, and Brethren, were to be constituent members who may act in such a sacred Corporation. . . . The Elders only are to rule the church, and without them, there can be no Elections; Admissions; or Excommunications; and they have a negative upon the acts of the Fraternity; as well as 'tis they only who have the power of authoritative preaching; and administering the Sacraments. Yet the Brethren, have such a liberty, that without their consent, nothing of common concernment may be imposed upon them." And yet, the "more influential sex," conscientiously put the General Court at bay, in Salem.

"Nevertheless, because particular Churches of Elders,

and Brethren; may abuse their power with manifold miscarriages; there is necessity of Communion of Churches, in Synods; who have authority to determine, declare, and enjoin, such things as shall rectify the maladministrations, or any disorders, dissensions, and confusions of the Congregations, which may fall under their cognizance — but still so as to leave unto the particular Churches themselves; the formal acts, which are to be done pursuant unto the advice of the Council — upon the obstinate and scandalous refusal whereof, the Council may determine, to withdraw Communion from them, as from those who will not be Counselled, against notorious mismanagement of the jurisdiction which the Lord Jesus Christ, hath given them."

And yet, after the production of "Cotton's (*lucid*) Keyes," the Puritans conscientiously complained of the — "Injurious aspersions cast upon the Churches of New England, that the world knew not their principles; — whereas they took all occasions imaginable, to make all the world know, that — In the Doctrinal part of Religion, they had agreed entirely with the Reformed Churches, of Europe — and that they desire most particularly to maintain the Faith professed by the Church of England, the Country whereunto was their original."

Were the "injurious aspersions," they conscientiously complained of, any more injurious, than the Law, they passed against the Anabaptists; which they refused, either "to alter, or explain"? Any worse than the "aspersions" they conscientiously cast on Roger Williams? They claimed membership in and of the Church of England; and to maintain its Faith; and yet conscientiously would not permit the use of the

"Book of Prayer," in their form of Worship! They held conscientiously against Roger Williams for saying they were an "unseparated people" — and yet they *claimed to be, unseparated!* And then wondered that the world did not understand them!

Nor did their perplexity soon remove — as they were presently led to see that they did not clearly understand themselves.

" It was convenient, that the Churches of New England should have a system of their Discipline, extracted from the Word of God, and exhibited unto them, with a more effectual, acknowledged, and established recommendation ; and nothing but a Council, was proper to compose the system." Like the Council of Constantine, A.D., 325.

" Wherefore, a Bill was conscientiously preferred unto the General Court of Massachusetts Bay, in 1646 — at the suggestion of the 'Commissioners for the United Colonies' — calling the Second New England Synod, to meet in Cambridge ; whereby a Platform of Church Discipline ; according to the direction of our Lord Jesus Christ, in his blessed Word, might most advantageously be composed and published."

The Magistrates, in the Court conscientiously were ready to pass this bill at once: but the Deputies ; were conscientiously reluctant to take a step, by which, they feared a precedent might be established, for mingling Civil and Ecclesiastical matters improperly : (this would be called, a " Roger Williams whimsey ") but their scruples were disregarded. The Boston Church, conscientiously refused to send Delegates to the Synod, until Lectured ; to "*yield* to truth ;" by the great theocratic Norton. This great Synod, met, late in the Fall, and during this Session, conscientiously passed the following significant Edict —

"The Civil Magistrate, in matters of Religion, or of the First Table; hath power civilly to command, or forbid things, respecting the outward man, which are clearly commanded, or forbidden, in the Word; and to inflict suitable punishments, according to the nature of the transgression of the same."

As a preliminary measure to the great work before them, they also appointed John Cotton; Richard Mather; and Ralph Partridge; each, to conscientiously draw up a form; out of which to "extract" material for the "Platform." After a Session of 14 days, the Synod adjourned to June 1647, in order to secure if possible a representation by Delegates, from all the Churches.

In the above Edict, passed at this Session, we have the second instance of the conscientious yielding of the few iron wills; in the Court; to popular opinion. The first instance, was when the opposition arose as to the "Resident's Oath, which compelled the Court to retrace its steps and desist from that proceeding." This second instance, in the above edict — they plainly and conscientiously indorsed Roger Williams' views; and abandoned their own. It is very carefully worded; "in matters of religion, or of the first Table;" so as to seem to be the old position — whereas it is the same sentiment as stated in the Indictment of the Court against Mr. Williams — "That the Magistrate ought not to punish the breach of the First Table, except when the civil peace should be endangered." So the edict has it — "The Magistrate . . . hath power . . . respecting the outward man." . . . Had the General Court conscientiously passed such an edict as this in 1635, it would have saved them the trouble of Banishing Roger Williams — and saved them from the "quere" of it, in the estimation of Posterity.

"As a further demonstration to the world, of the Principles of the Churches of New England, the Synod at Cambridge in 1648, passed a unanimous vote, that 'Having perused and considered (with much gladness of heart and thankfulness to God), the Confession of Faith, published by the late Reverend Assembly of Divines, in Westminster, England; — We do judge it to be very Holy, Orthodox, and judicious in all matters of Faith; and do freely consent thereunto for the substance thereof. Only those things which have respect to Church Government, and Discipline, we refer ourselves to the Platform of Church Discipline, agreed upon by this present Assembly. . . . All of which we commend to the Church of Christ among us, and to the Honoured Court, as worthy of their consideration and acceptance.' Ah! Puritans! conscientiously turned from the 'breast of your Mother Church,' and taken to the Westminster Assembly! Not 'Separatists' — nor Independents — but Theocratic Presbyterians.

"And they hoped, that this proof of their being fellow-heirs of the same Common salvation, with the churches beyond the sea, would not only free them from the suspicion of heresie; but clear them from the character of schism also; inasmuch as their dissent from those churches was now evidently, but in some lesser matters of ecclesiastical Polity; and a dissent, not managed either with such arrogancy, or censoriousness, as are the essential properties of Schismatics."

It was at this session, of this Synod in 1648, that — "In the midst of the Sermon, there came a large snake into the seat where many of the Elders sat; when one of them more resolute than the others, immediately despatched him." Happy would it have been for the memory of the Puritan Fathers, if the Elders had conscientiously cast out the Dragon, of, "Persecution for Conscience' Sake"—from not only "the seat where the Elders sat," but from the Theocracy.

The work of this Second N. E. Synod, was not finished until 1649; when it was conscientiously and formally promulgated by the General Court; and has since been known as the "Cambridge Platform." It can be found entire in Cotton Mather's "Magnalia." Its provisions were arranged in Seventeen Chapters. How much of it was "*extracted* from the Word;" may be a question — but that some of it resembles more an "extract" of Cottonwood—or the bad egg of a "Partridge" there is no question.

We shall only note here, a few of its timbers, which seem so unsound as to render the whole Platform "erroneous and very dangerous."

"Chap. II. Sec. 5. The State of the Members of the visible Church . . . was, before the Law . . . in Families . . . under the Law, National; under Christ, Congregational: (The term Independent, we approve not"). A very Compound "Extract."

"Chap. III. Sec. 1. The Matter of the visible

Church are Saints by calling. Sec. 2. The children of such are holy." Very clear (?).

"Chap. X. Sec. 3. This Government of the church is a mixt Government, (and so has been acknowledged, long before the term Independency was heard of) : . . . In respect of Christ the Head and King of the Church, it is a *Monarchy:* in respect of the Brotherhood of the Church, it is a *Democracy:* in respect of the Presbytery, it is an *Aristocracy.*"

"Chap. XII. Sec. 2. The things which are requisite to be found in all Church Members, are repentance from sin, and faith in Jesus Christ. Sec. 7. The like is to be required of all such members of the church as were born in the same, or received their membership, or were baptized in their infancy, or minority, by virtue of the covenant of their parents, when being grown up into years of discretion, they shall desire to be made partakers of the Lord's Supper." Such a "mixt" mess as this, " extracted from the word," by Roger Williams, would be called by his enemies, " very unsettled judgments."

"Chap. XV. Sec. 2. When any church wanted light or peace among themselves, it is a way of communion of the churches, according to the Word, to meet together by their Elders, and other Messengers, in a Synod : Acts 15 : 22, 23.

"Tho' the Churches have no authority one over another, yet one church may admonish another, and if the admonition be not heeded, other Churches may join in the admonition, and if it be still unheeded, they are to proceed to make use of the help of a Synod, for their conviction." Sec. 5. " The Synod's directions, and determinations, so far as consonant with the word of God, are to be received with reverence, and submission."

"Chap. XVII. Sec. 9. If any church, one or more, shall grow schismatical, rending itself from the communion of other churches, or shall walk incorrigibly, and obstinately, in any corrupt way of their own, contrary to the rule of the Word; in such case the Magistrate, is to put forth his coercive power as the matter shall require." Cotton's "Keyes," were much "mixt," very. Thus the Puritans conscientiously, became; state-and-church — Congregational — Presbyterians.

Notwithstanding the conscientious injunction upon his "pretended authority;" Roger Williams and his associates, at length succeeded in uniting and organizing, Providence; Portsmouth; Newport; and Shawomet, under the Charter, he had obtained. The new Government was declared to be "Democratical" — which Mr. Cotton said was "unfit for either Church; or State: but which Mr. Williams has shown the world, is fit, for both — Church and State; "separate." *Freedom, of Faith and Worship, was conscientiously assured to all.* This, is the first instance in the History of the Kingdoms of Christ, and Cæsar, in which the legal establishment of Religious Liberty, was ever conscientiously promulgated in any Commonwealth, either in America or the Old World — "and this honor, under God, and His guidance of the skilful hand, and generous heart of ROGER WILLIAMS; is the rightful inheritance of RHODE ISLAND."

This instrument is the true basis of all Freedom: Civil — or Religious. *Every man of civil deportment,* was a voter ; " in civil things only ; " instead of — " none but church members, to be voters." In Rhode Island no one stood conscientiously in fear of Elders — Magistrates — or Synods — as to the the faith he held. Mark ye, the difference between the "CAMBRIDGE PLATFORM" — and the PROVIDENCE PLATFORM. On which, does Posterity prefer to stand ?

## CHAPTER VIII.

*RELIGIOUS TOLERANCE AND THEOCRATIC ARROGANCE.*

SECTION I. — TOLERANCE AND ARROGANCE MEET.

THE year of Our Lord 1649 — was one of marked events. Charles I., King of England, was beheaded Jan. 31. Quickly followed the English Commonwealth, under Oliver Cromwell. Gov. John Winthrop, died Mar. 26 1649. Thomas Dudley died, soon after. 'Twas he who did a "Toleration," *hate* — conscientiously.

In 1649, one Obadiah Holmes, a native of Preston Eng. ; and then of Salem ; now of Mr. Newman's church at Rehoboth ; with 8 others, conscientiously withdrew, and organized the first Anabaptist church in Plymouth Colony ; choosing Mr. Holmes as their Minister. Four petitions were soon filed in the General Court of Plymouth; conscientiously praying the Court not to grant them land, on which to build a Meeting House. The Court cited them to appear before them — when they were conscientiously enjoined, "to refrain from practices disagreeable to their brethren : " and Mr. Holmes and two others, were merely bound over, "in £10, one for another."

This "lenitic," did not please the Massachusetts Bay General Court, whereupon they conscientiously warned the Plymouth Court, as follows : —

"Wee have heard heretofore of divers Anabaptists, arisen up in your jurisdiccon, and connived at; the infeccon of such diseases, being so neere us, are likely to spread into our jurisdiccon; but being so few, wee well hoped that it might please God, by the endeavors of yourselves and the faithfull Elders with you, to have reduced such erring men againe into the right way. But now to our great griefe, we are credibly informed that your patient bearing with such men hath produced another effect, namely, the multiplying and encreasing of the same errors, and wee feare maybe of other errors also, if timely care be not taken to suppresse the same. Perticulerly wee understand that within this few weekes there have binn at Sea Cuncke" (Seekonk; original Indian name for Rehoboth), "thirteene, or fowerteene p'sons re-baptized (a swifte progresse in one toune;) yett wee heare not of any effectuall restriccon is entended." . . .

But land and protection were conscientiously granted them, as might not have been in Mass. Bay. Thus the Law against Anabaptists, conscientiously passed in Mass. Bay, five years before, failed of being enforced in Plymouth. These Anabaptists were not advised away from Seekonk, as Mr. Williams was, by Gov. Winslow. Mr. Holmes and a few others, afterward removed to Newport, and united with the church, formed there five years before; with Dr. John Clarke; who left Mass. Bay, among the exiles of the Hutchinson controversy; as their minister.

In 1649, also, a noble provision was made, based upon the felt importance of everyone being able to read the Scriptures in the English Language; and also to enable some to read them in their originals; the Hebrew, and Greek. The provision was; that — "Every Township be required to maintain a school for instruction in reading, and writing:--and every town of a hundred householders, to maintain a Grammar School; with a Teacher, qualified, to fit youths for the Harvard University;" (Cambridge). The Basis of the New England, School system, was thus laid.

In 1649, a further attempt was conscientiously made, to exalt the Theocracy, by the enactment of a Law; making death, the penalty for Blasphemy. Also, that any Christian, who shall go about maintaining certain damnable heresies, should be liable to banishment. Denial of the Scriptures, was made punishable with fine, whipping, banishment; or death. As the fruit of such conscientiousness two persons; one at Hartford, and one at Charlestown, were executed, for witchcraft; in 1651. The people of Warwick, R. I., declared as their conscientious opinion of such atrocities, that — "There are no other witches upon earth; nor devils; but the ministers of N. E. and such as they." Harsh language, indeed; but less harsh, than the hanging, of the victims.

Massachusetts Bay, still conscientiously claimed Warwick; by virtue of the "submission," of the two petty chiefs, with Arnold; and an alleged grant to them of the same from Plymouth. But the Plymouth authorities conscientiously denied, both the fact, and the legality of any such title from them. Fearing what their fate might be, the Gov. and Assistants, of Rhode Island; applied to the "Commissioners for the United Colonies" — demanding protection, and redress. But their appeal was conscientiously — disregarded.

Whereupon the Bay conscientiously applied to the "Commissioners," for aid; or at least, sanction, to subdue Warwick; by force of arms. Such was their conscientious; and unceasing determination to overthrow "Heresie" in the R. I. Colony. Plymouth thereupon conscientiously protested against so unjust a measure, by virtue of any cession of Warwick from them. A meeting of the "Commissioners," held at Plymouth the next year on the subject; ended abruptly — not to say, "in a Row." The General Court of the Bay, demanded satisfaccion, in a letter to the Gov. of Plymouth, on the subject, the next year — for "an affront given to one of their Commissioners, on the said occasion." For "contempt of authority," no doubt; the "unpardonable sin;" of *Salem!* Was there no "contempt of authority," in attempting to make war on Warwick? All this, because Plymouth was Tolerant, in religion.

This conscientious cloud of war from the Bay, put the people of Providence, Warwick, and Newport, into some fear of danger to their Independence; as a Colony; upon which they conscientiously resolved to appeal to England, for a confirmation of their charter, and protection under it. For this purpose a subscription was raised, and Roger Williams, and John Clarke, were deputed, in 1651, to go to England for that purpose. "Peace on Earth, and good will to" Rhode Island; came, tardily.

In all the charges against Roger Williams, for seeking to "undermine the foundations of the Massachusetts Bay Colony," he is nowhere charged with using intimidation; bribery; and threats of war; as the Puritans conscientiously did, for the overthrow of Rhode Island Colony.

How could Roger Williams "undermine the foundations"—after, the King resolved to reassume—the Charter into his own hands—*before* he was back to Salem—from Plymouth?!

SECTION 2. — THE LYNN EPISODE.

Before embarking for England, Mr. John Clarke, with two others, Mr. Obadiah Holmes, and John Crandall, were sent as delegates from the Baptist Church in Newport, to visit, one of the members of the Church, Mr. William Witter, a farmer residing at Swampscott, near Lynn—who was too aged to go to see his brethren in R. I. This gave the conscientious Massachusetts Men, a rare opportunity to impress on three special offenders how—"to do, as they would be done by."

Mr. Witter, had, it was said, conscientiously called "Infant Baptism," (a conscientious tenet, in the Bay) —"a badge of the whore." Also, "yt they who stayed whiles a child was baptized, doe worshipp ye Dyvell, and broake ye Saboath." Mr. Clarke, of Hutchinson notoriety, had been conscientiously notified to leave the Bay of his own accord, or be helped out. Mr. Holmes, had been excluded from Salem; had seceded at Rehoboth; and been protected by the Plymouth Court: and now this trio with a few others were about to congregate at Lynn.

Having reached the home of Mr. Witter, on Saturday July 29, 1651, they conscientiously concluded; rather than go to the Puritan meeting at Lynn, as their presence might disturb some; to hold religious service privately in Mr. Witter's house. After their meeting had begun; while Mr. Clarke was preaching two constables entered, and conscientiously removed them to the "ordinary" for safe keeping. Somebody was diligent, to find out, that these visitors had arrived; and at what time they were to hold service; warrants made out; constables ordered to the front; and the men put in "durance vile," by noon of Sunday — "conscientiously!!"

In the afternoon the officers took them to meeting — the prisoners having had no orders, to remove their hats, sat with them on — whereupon the constable conscientiously plucked them off;" Mr. Clarke in the time was conscientiously reading in a book. An opportunity was offered; when Mr. Clarke was allowed to speak, but he was soon hushed by authority. Possibly he might have said something akin to what Paul said, on a similar occasion — "God shall smite thee thou whited wall." The Puritan preacher on the occasion, was Mr. Thomas Cobbett; author of "a large, nervous, golden, conscientious Discourse, against the Baptists."

On Monday, the Magistrate, Robert Bridges, conscientiously assigned them for examination, and ordered them sent to Boston jail, until next Court. By some means they returned to the house of Mr. Witter where they celebrated the Lord's Supper. On Tuesday they were imprisoned in Boston.

On the next week Thursday, Aug. 10, 1651, they were brought before the Court for trial. In a conscientious sermon (possibly, "a golden Discourse"), by John Cotton, just before the trial, said; that — "To deny Infant Baptism, was to overthrow all; and was therefore soul-murder, and a capital offence." Mr. Clarke being charged with Anabaptism ("*re*-baptism"), conscientiously disowned the name; on the logical ground, that those who received infant baptism, were not Scripturally baptized at all; and therefore such, who were afterwards baptized on profession of faith, were not; "*Ana*," (re)-baptized. All the "prisoners," bore conscientious testimony before; and against the Court.

Ex-Gov. Endicott, in passing sentence, fell into a passion, and in some words with Clarke, charged him with success in teaching among weak-minded persons, opinions he could not maintain before the learned: and challenged him, to "try and dispute, with our Ministers." All ended as usual; whether in an Episcopal Star-Chamber; Popish Inquisition; or the conscientious Puritan Court; in return to prison; fine; and if fines were not paid; Whipping.

From his prison Clarke sent forth his acceptance of Gov. Endicott's challenge; "to dispute with our ministers." He proposed to maintain, that — "JESUS CHRIST; had the sole right of prescribing laws respecting worship; that baptism — that is, dipping in water — was an Ordinance to be administered only to those who gave evidence of repentance and faith; that only such visible believers, constituted the Church; that each member had a right to speak in the congregation; either to inquire for his own instruction, or, to prophesy for the edification of others; that, at all times, and in all places, they ought to reprove folly, and justify wisdom; and that no servant of JESUS CHRIST; has any authority to restrain any fellow-servant, in his worship; where no injury is offered to others."

But this acceptance of Endicott's challenge, by

Clarke, was "conscientiously" *not accepted*, by "our Ministers;" though the Magistrates were in favor of it. Whether it would be undignified, for "Our Ministers," to debate with a prisoner, who neglected to "take off his hat" in Mr. Cobbett's meeting; or, whether it would be "contempt of authority," to discuss questions; with this Anabaptist sectary; which had been settled (?) in the "Cambridge Platform;" by an Authoritative Synod; or, whether the Ministers, didn't quite like the job; or, whether they chose to blame Endicott for his rashness; so "passed the hat," among the "Elders," to pay Clarke's fine, and let him go. Mr. Crandall's fine was also paid, and they were released — conscientiously.

Mr. Holmes was easily fined £30; so obnoxious was his sectariness, to the calm, considerate, cool, conscientiousness of the pious Puritans. In a letter to friends in London, he writes — "As I went from the Bar, I expressed myself in these words; 'I bless God I am counted worthy to suffer for the name of Jesus.' Whereupon John Wilson, (pastor of the First Church of Boston, the 'unseparated people,' Rogers Williams declined to serve); struck me before the judgment seat, and cursed me (conscientiously,) saying — 'the curse of God, and of Jesus, go with thee.'"

Friends offered to pay his fine also, but he by faith "refused to accept deliverance." He felt willing to have Posterity know, that of the Puritans of Boston, the Scripture was fulfilled — "The Ploughers plowed upon my back; they made long their furrows." He was willing to suffer with Christ — "by whose stripes we are healed."

Whereupon he was "conscientiously" taken to the

Public Whipping-Post, on Boston Common. Of his sufferings he says — " I had such a spiritual manifestation, that I could well bear it, yea, in a manner felt it not; though it was grievous as the spectators said; the man "conscientiously" striking with all his strength; (yea spitting in his hand three times, as many affirmed,) with a three-corded whip, giving me therewith thirty strokes. When he had loosed me from the post, having joyfulness in my heart, and cheerfulness in my countenance, as the spectators observed; I told the Magistrates, you have struck me as with roses; although the Lord hath made it easy to me, I pray God it may not be laid to your charge."

" Of the Jews five times received I forty stripes, save one." Paul. " Father forgive them for they conscientiously know not what they do." Jesus.

John Hazel, and John Spur, came up and shook hands with Mr. Holmes, smiling and saying — " Blessed be God." They were arrested on the spot, and for "contempt of authority conscientiously fined 40 shillings, and cast into prison."

The severity of this punishment is seen in the fact that for several weeks Mr. Holmes was unable to lie upon his back, but got rest as best he could, upon his knees and elbows. In due time he returned to Newport where he lived to a good old age. In 1790, his descendants were reckoned at 5,000 persons. Such was the episode of Lynn. This is what it cost the Delegates, to pay a friendly visit to Bro. Witter, within "ye lymmitts," of ye Christian Puritans.

About this time, the town of Malden, having conscientiously presumed to settle a Minister, without consulting the neighboring churches, was imperiously and conscientiously fined. This means of grace by the Court, was perpetrated without any shadow of law for it; either local or by virtue of their charter; which was gone; but a law was soon passed, making it "essential to settling a minister, to obtain the conscientious consent both, of a Council of neighboring churches; and of some of the Magistrates." The civil power in Massachusetts Bay, was set for Religious RESTRICTION. The *civil power* of the Narragansetts Bay — was for Religious LIBERTY.

### SECTION 3. — ROGER WILLIAMS AND JOHN CLARKE GO TO ENGLAND.

This journey was undertaken in 1651, for the safety of the R. I. Colony, against the conscientious threatenings from the Bay. No permission would be given them to sail from Boston, the home of the Court. But at the Dutch settlement of Manhattan; a colony of Holland; the country of William Prince of Orange, who was contending for Religious Toleration, 100 years before; he could safely take ship there for England; without being "shipped to England, from Boston as factious and evil-conditioned," by order of the Court.

Messrs. Williams, and Clarke, were kindly received in England, by Sir Henry Vane, a leading member of the Council of State; and they very soon obtained a confirmation of the R. I. Charter; notwithstanding unexpected opposition. Thus in R. I. they retained their Charter, because they favored Liberty in Religion; while in the Bay "the King reassumed their Charter, because they restrained, Liberty in Religion."

Mr. Clarke published in London his book — "Ill news from New England;" conscientiously giving an account of the Lynn episode. Whereupon Sir Richard Saltonstall, wrote to Messrs. Wilson and Cotton, ministers of Boston: — "Reverend and Dear Sirs; Whom I unfeignedly love and respect, it doth not a little grieve my spirit, to hear what sad things are reported daily, of your tyranny and persecution in N. E. as that you fine, whip, and imprison men, for their consciences. First you compel such to come into your assemblies, as you know will not join you in your worship; and when they show their dislike thereof, or witness against it, then you stir up your Magistrates to punish them for such, as you conceive, their public affronts. Truly, friends, this your practice of compelling any, in matters of worship, to do that whereof they are not fully persuaded, is to make them sin. Ro. 14 : 23. These rigid ways have laid you very low in the hearts of the saints. Oh, that all those that are Brethren, though yet they cannot think and speak the same thing, might be of one accord in the Lord."

Note — we find no such rebukes, ever sent from England to Roger Williams, for his style of "Liberty of Conscience;" as this letter of Sir Saltonstall, contains, to Wilson and Cotton. When the Puritans left England they were popular — when Williams left England, he was unpopular — but in 1651, this was reversed; "in the hearts of the Saints."

To Sir Saltonstall's noble remonstrance, Messrs. Wilson and Cotton conscientiously wrote an elaborate reply. They say — "You know not, if you think we came into this wilderness to practise the courses we fled from in England. We believe there is a vast difference between men's inventions and God's institutions; we fled from men's inventions, to which we else sho'ld have been compelled; we compel none to men's inventions. ... We content ourselves with unity in the foundation of religion ; and Church Order." Ah Puritans ! there is no need of compelling men to *God's Institutions*, when men conscientiously believe them to be such ; and there is no good in compelling men when they do not believe. Many people in 1651, believed most "conscientiously" that the "Cambridge Platform," *was not* "God's Institution"—but Men's clumsy invention.

About this same time Mr. Williams, sent a warm conscientious remonstrance to his old friend Endicott, against these violent proceedings.

In 1654, another unlawful Law was conscientiously enacted by the Theocracy, tho' strongly opposed by many; Obliging every town to support a minister; "the burden to be laid upon the whole society jointly, whether in church order or not " Also, an order that — "No one should be allowed to sit as Deputy in the General Court, who did not hold to the Orthodox Creed." Were the above decrees; "God's Institutions"— or "men's inventions"?

In this same year, Mr. Henry Dunster, First President of Harvard College, was compelled to resign that position, for conscientiously declining to bring his child, to baptism. Probably Mr. Wilson would say ; that—"The Trustees were only conscientiously compelling him to 'God's Institution.'" Mr. Charles Chauncey, who was chosen his successor ; both men of acknowledged learning; "was also somewhat infected with the errors of Anabaptism," but he conscientiously promised to keep his opinions to himself. Had Roger Williams been thus pliant — conscientiously recognized the General Court, as "God's Institution"—and quietly "kept his opinions to himself"—on the subject of "Magistrates having no right to coerce men in matters of conscience"—he might, never, have been banished from the Bay! Possibly; if Dr. Dunster had venerated "Infant Baptism," and no less an Institution than Harvard College, in 1654; as both "God's Institutions;" he might not have been so soon succeeded by the accomplished Chauncey.

SECTION 4.—THE GOVERNMENT OF RHODE ISLAND STRENGTHENED.

Leaving Mr. Clarke to look after the interests of R. I. at the Court of Oliver Cromwell, the Protector, of Old England; Roger Williams returned, as conscientious Protector of New England. He brought back with him, a letter from Cromwell's Council; not permitting him simply, to land at Boston, as when he returned before; and hurry right on to Providence — but; to walk slow into Boston; with even more power than the General Court, who Banished him 20 years before; and *securing to him, free passage at all times, through all parts of the United Colonies."* Thus the General Court of the Bay; and the "Commissioners for the Colonies;" were invited to lower seats; while ROGER WILLIAMS, was *authorized*, to take a Higher Seat. "Tides Turn."

The fear of conscientious supervision over Rhode

Island by the Bay; which was the occasion of Messrs. Williams, and Clarke, going to England at this time; wrought some confusion, in their absence. Mr. Williams' reception on his return, was at first a little dubious; so much so, that he declared himself, "like a man in the fog." But after the reading of the letter he brought from Sir Henry Vane, containing, "his admonition and advice, respecting some disorders, and discontents, which had arisen among the people of R. I.," and Mr. Williams' own remonstrances concerning all — steps were soon taken, by the people, towards a reconciliation.

Mr. Williams was deputed to answer Sir Vane's most excellent and welcome letter. In doing this, he pointed out — "the complications of Coddington, and Dyer, with the interference, of the Bay; as the chief causes, of the discontents. But, (that we may not lay all the load on other men's backs,) possibly a sweet cup, hath rendered many of us wanton and too active; for we have long drank of the cup of as great liberties, as any people we can hear of under the whole heaven." No such report from the Bay.

Commissioners from the Four towns of Providence, Newport, Warwick, and Shawomet; Assembled; and it was conscientiously agreed: that — "The Government for the future, should be according to the Charter." (No such submission to, or its approval by, the people of the Bay, of the Charter of Chas. I., was ever made.) At a general election of the Four R. I. towns, Sept. 12. 1654, Roger Williams, was conscientiously chosen President. Letters of "humble thanksgiving," were ordered to be written to His Highness, the Lord

Protector; and to Sir Henry Vane. Nothing from R. I. "repugnant to the Laws of England."

No sooner was Mr. Williams settled in office, than a paper was sent him, indirectly implying that he held the doctrine, of "Non-resistance — and no-Government"—and covertly seeking his sanction to the same. To this he made a conscientious reply, which settled the question for that time — and for all future time; as to the clear and consistent basis, on which his opinions of Civil Government; and Religious Liberty — rested securely.

He said — "That ever I should speak or write, a tittle that tends to such an infinite liberty, is a mistake which I have ever disclaimed and abhorred. To prevent such mistakes, I at present shall only propose this case : —

"There goes many a ship to sea, with many hundred souls in one ship, whose weal and woe is common; and is a true picture of a commonwealth, or an human combination, or society. It hath fallen out sometimes that both Papists, Protestants, Jews and Turks, may be embarked into one ship. Upon this supposal, I affirm that all the liberty of conscience that ever I pleaded for turns upon these two hinges: That none of the Papists, Protestants, Jews or Turks, be forced to come to the ship's prayers or worship; nor compelled from their own particular prayers or worship, if they practise any. I further add, that I never denied, that notwithstanding this liberty, the commander of this ship ought to command the ship's course; yea, and also command that justice, peace, and sobriety, be kept and practised, both among the seamen and all the passengers. If any of the seamen refuse to perform their service, or passengers to pay their freight; in person or purse, towards the common charges or defence; if any refuse to obey the common laws and orders of *the ship, concerning their common peace or preservation;* if any *shall mutiny and rise up against the commanders and officers;* if any should preach or write, that there ought to be no commanders or officers, because all are equal in Christ, therefore no masters nor officers, no laws nor orders, no corrections nor punishments; I say: I never denied but in such cases; whatever is pretended, the commander, or commanders, may judge, resist, compel and punish such transgressors, according to their deserts and merits." They were conscientiously, not, the sentiments of the Bay at this time.

The Government of R. I. having been reorganized; at the general election May 22, 1655 Mr. Williams was rechosen, Governor. A letter from Oliver Cromwell was received, "confirming the Government as now established." Even the Magistrates of the Bay had forwarded a congratulatory address to Oliver Cromwell. In May 12, 1656, Mr. Williams was invited to Boston 21 years after his Banishment — "Where he presented a Memorial to the General Court, reiterating his former complaints concerning the title to Shawomet; as to which some redress was now granted." He was not conscientiously ordered to Boston, this time, "to be shipped to Eng." — OLIVER CROMWELL, was in England !

Rhode Island, was now, more than the peer of the Bay; as she had a recognized Charter — and Religious Liberty: while in the Bay they had forfeited their

Charter — and upheld Religious Intolerance; to the grief of their friends in England. The General Court was now humbled — with "all the ministers of the Bay — (the save one,") whoever he was, not excepted. The *sentence* of Banishment, against Roger Williams, which conscientiously forbid him, "to returne any more without license from the Courte" — was peremptorily overruled by Oliver Cromwell's "safe-conduct for him to go thro' all the colonies at all times." John Cotton died Dec. 23, 1656.

SECTION 5. — THE PUBLIC CONSCIENCE, AND COURT CONSCIENCE.

Altho' in the Bay, conscientious respect was shown for Roger Williams' "pretended authority," in R. I. out of respect for Oliver Cromwell; who sustained the R. I. Government; yet in the Bay, and other places where it could be done, respect for the Theocracy, was conscientiously enforced. In 1656, complaint was made to the "Commissioners for the United Colonies," that; "Plymouth, was conscientiously, wanting to themselves in a due acknowledgment of, and encouragement to Ministers of the Gospel." Accordingly a decree went forth the next year from the General Court of Plymouth, that — "All the towns should be taxed for the support of Ministers ; and Grammar Schools."

The same year is memorable for the trouble the Theocracy encountered with two Quaker Women, "witches,"(?), whose names "after the flesh," were Mary Fisher ; and Ann Austin. Signs of witchcraft were searched for, on these Quakeresses, but none were found ; not even, "devils' teats." Tho' the principal tenet of this sect, different from others, was that of the "inner light;" yet the Theocratic laws defined the Quakers, as "a cursed sect of heretics lately risen in the world."

In making the "law a terror to evil-doers," it provided that — "for the first conviction for Quakerism, one ear should be cut off ; for a second conviction, the other ear also ; for a third conviction, both males and females, were to have their tongues bored with a hot iron." And in far too short, a time, Plymouth ; Connecticut ; and New Haven ; adopted similar laws. Not so, in Rhode Island. Pity for the Quakers; if humanity was lost, in the Bay; that, in those other colonies, "respect for Oliver Cromwell, did not prevail."

In the year 1657 the Third General Synod of New England; was convened in Boston. The question to be settled at this time, was ; *conscientiously* "concerning the church-state of their Posterity?" Answer ; that — "Persons who had been baptized in infancy, and grown up unconverted, if they were not scandalous in their lives, and owned the covenant ; could have their infants baptized, if they desired it." This settlement, (?) of the question, was called by the Synod ; the "Half-way Covenant."

Whether it was "half-way," from error, to truth ; or half-way from truth, to error — Posterity must judge. At all events, this laid the sandy basis for the great "Separation," of the Puritan churches of N. E. into the two wings of Orthodox Congregationalists — and Unitarians. And yet the Puritans were amazed, at the stupidity, of the rest of mankind, who could not understand them !

But at last; yes at last; such was the conscientiousness of the Theocracy, that the "Commissioners for the United Colonies"—yes, even they; deemed, it expedient for the glory of God; to pass an Order, Sept. 23, 1658, to prevent annoyance from returning Quakers; that—"Such as returned a second time should suffer death." Mr. John Winthrop, Jr., Commissioner from Conn.; who would have been more tolerant, had his surroundings been more favorable—and who hesitated, (as did Edward VI. when he signed the death-warrant of Joan Bocher)—when he signed this death-sentence against the Quakers; said—"Looking at it as a quere; and not as an act, I subscribed." Yet alas, such a "conscientious quere" would strangle Quakers; nevertheless!

But it did not long remain a "quere," in the Bay; where a law was conscientiously enacted, by the General Court; in spite of a vigorous resistance, on the part of the Deputies—for exterminating returning Quakers, with Death. Under this law Marmaduke Stephenson; William Robinson; and Mary Dyer; were found guilty, of "returning to Boston." The two former were hanged; Nov. 6, 1659. Mary Dyer was reprieved on the gallows thro' the intercession of her Son, on condition of her leaving the Colony within 48 hours. She spent the winter away, but returned; and was conscientiously hanged, June 1, 1660! One William Leddra; who had been banished—"was under such necessity of *conscience*, that he could not forbear returning to Boston. He was offered life and freedom if he would go away; but he replied—"to make you a promise I cannot." He also, was conscientiously hanged. Another victim was in prison, but by this time, the popular "conscientiousness," had become so intense, that the General Court, retired, before the popular disapprobation. As in the case of the excitement in Salem, upon the "Resident's Oath," the Court desisted—conscientiously!!

The notorious apology offered as excuse for the Puritans; that, — "It is easier to find fault with our Fathers in this . . . than to put ourselves in their place, and declare, with confidence, how we should have improved upon their methods," — does not repair the conscientious "Blunders" of the Fathers. Twice; the General Court was rebuked; like Balaam; by a righteous public indignation at their methods; and often were they vehemently and justly rebuked; and shown a better way, by Roger Williams — why — could they not see?

They did not see themselves as seen in the withering reprimand of the people of Warwick — "There are no witches in the world, nor devils; but the New England Ministers, and such as they." Our Fathers! were they conscientious hangmen?

Finally; as if said for a sarcasm, or a jest;—"The General Court, willing to try all meanes with as much lenity as possible consistent with our safety"—conscientiously provided; that, "all returning Quakers sho'd be duly arrested, stripped naked from the middle upward, tied to a cart's tail, and whipped from Constable to Constable, to any the outermost town, and so to be whipped over the border."

Thanks to Heaven for so much improvement. Yea, the conscience of the Puritan Theocracy, reformed;

from hanging Quakers, to whipping them! " Inasmuch as ye have done unto one of the least of these My brethen, ye have done unto Me." Such — were the conscientious — " Blunders," of our New England Puritan Forefathers.

## CHAPTER IX.

*THEOCRACY OF MASSACHUSETTS BAY, UNDER CHARLES II., AND JAMES II.*

" They passed the turf, as they the cavern sought,
 Where fell the body of his earliest slain,
And Woban said, as paused he o'er the spot,
 ' The black Priest's comrade never wakes again :'
Then did he seize the body by the foot,
 And dragged the bleeding corpse along the plain,
And o'er the rocky steep the burden dashed ;
 It dropped in night — re-echoing thickets crashed."
DURFEE.

SECTION 1. — THEOCRACY REVOLUTIONIZED.

THE death of Cromwell in 1658 ; and restoration of Charles II., necessitated a great change in the American Colonies. Much of the work done under the charters of James Ist., and Chas. Ist., was undone, under Cromwell ; Chas. II., and James II. Among the earliest of the royal Orders, was the one requiring the suspension of corporeal punishment, inflicted upon Quakers. The General Court being in doubt as to what might next be the pleasure, or displeasure of his Majesty ; Bradstreet ; one of the Founders of the Mass. Colony, and a Magistrate from the beginning — and Norton ; the popular minister of Boston, were conscientiously sent as agents to Eng. They were courteously received, but they soon found things as unfavorable, there, for *them;* as matters were for "Separatists," in Boston.

These agents soon returned, with a royal LETTER; in which the Charter of Massachusetts Bay, which had been reassumed by Chas. Ist, in 1634, was now, after 26 years, reaffirmed. The document had all this time been in possession of the court, altho' it had no legal force. In this letter, touching the Theocracy, it ordered, that — "complete toleration be allowed the Church of England." This of course was the King's rebuke; for Endicott's "shipping home of the Brownes," from Salem; for using the Prayer Book. It also demanded the repeal of the Law; that — "None should be voters but Puritan church-members;" and requiring the admission of all persons of honest lives, to the "Sacraments of Baptism, and the Lord's Supper." Here was "CHURCH-AND-STATE;" mauling, "CHURCH-AND-STATE." It also, granted liberty, "to make a sharp law against Quakers;" which the Agents were conscientiously instructed to ask. These provisions were intended to curtail the repugnant courses of the Puritans, and bring them back within the charter of Chas. Ist; which was silent, on the subject of Religion.

This letter greatly encouraged the advocates of Toleration, to press their claims, under the King's demands. During the next 30 years the people of Massachusetts Bay were conscientiously divided into 3 parties.

*First* — Those who were conscientious ardent supporters of the Theocracy; a gradually diminishing majority. Thus, in 30 years, Theocracy had arisen; been dominant; and had received its death-blow.

*Second* — A party weak at first, but daily growing

stronger; drawing to their ranks, those who were conscientiously convinced that the Theocracy was no longer tenable, or desirable. Among the converts to this view, were Bradstreet, and Norton; the "agents;" who came back satisfied, that there must, and soon would be a change. So Roger Williams' opinions, went marching on, towards "God's Holy Time."

*Third*—Was the party that conscientiously advocated Religious Toleration, and equal rights, for all the people. The "Third Party," gradually absorbed all the rest, and Theocracy disappeared, as a conscientious blunder.

The way for this change had been preparing, from the adoption of the "Cambridge Platform"—and the "Half-way-Covenant." These instruments, defined the Church; "to consist of Saints, and their baptized offspring." Many of these offspring, grew up unconverted, but by virtue of their infant baptism, felt that they had a right thereby, to have their infants baptized; and a right to vote, (tho' not church members, and could not be tho' baptized; because they were not converted;) and yet according to the "Platform," the church consisted in part, of them. Here was a dissolving dilemma, for the Magistrates, and Elders. And yet the Puritans wondered that the "world couldn't understand them."

SECTION 2.— MORE SYNODICAL WORK.

The Fourth; New England Synod was called to meet in Boston, in 1662. The absurd "Half-way-Covenant," "created noises about the Temple," equal to those caused by the Hutchinsons, which made the First

Synod, necessary; and the Ministers of the country were obliged to give heed to them. "Yea it met with such opposition as could not be encountered with any thing less than a Synod of Elders; and Messengers; from all the churches of Massachusetts Bay." The trouble with the Covenant, was, that nobody knew, where; "half-way," was.

The First Great Question conscientiously before the Synod — was — "Who are the Subjects of Baptism?"

Answer 1. "They that according to Scripture, are members of the visible church, and are the subjects of Baptism." Very lucid (?).

Ans. 2. "The members of the visible Church, according to Scripture, are confederate visible believers, in particular churches, and their infant seed; i.e., children in minority, whose next parents, one or both, are in Covenant." This was pellucid.

Ans. 3. "The Infant seed . . . when grown up, are personally under the watch; discipline; and government of that church."

Ans. 4. "These adult persons, are not therefore to be admitted to communion, merely because they are, and continue members, without such further qualifications, as the word of God requireth thereunto. The children of these church-members, are to be baptized." With such light as this who could help seeing?!

The Second Question; conscientiously before the Synod, was — "Ought there to be a Consociation of churches; and the manner of it?"

After answering their own Question in the affirmative; they next put their veto conscientiously on Independency. "That it is the most to be abhorred maxim, that any religion hath made profession of, and therefore of all other the most contradictory, and dishonorable unto that of Christianity — that a single and particular society of men, professing the name of Christ, and pretending to be endowed with power from Christ, to judge them that are of the same body and society with themselves; should further arrogate unto themselves an exemption from giving account, or being censurable by any other, either Christian Magistrate, above them; or neighboring churches about them." Behold the Puritans, by advocating the coercive power of SYNOD; and COURT; in matters of religion, are far enough from being conscientiously friends of Religious Liberty; or church Independence. The iron band of Church-Members' vote, broke at last, and Theocracy fell in pieces: and "great was the fall;" and small the loss.

### SECTION 3.— RELIGIOUS LIBERTY THRIVES.

In Rhode Island, the people remained conscientiously firm, in their grasp upon the principle of Roger Williams; not of toleration; but of absolute, perfect, religious, Liberty; for any, and for all alike. They made declaration; that — "It is much in our hearts to hold forth a lively experiment, that a most flourishing *civil State*, may stand, and best be maintained; with a full liberty of religious concernments."

Their Charter — provided; that — "No person within the said Colony shall be molested, punished, disquieted, or called in question; for any differences of opinion in matters of religion; who does not actually disturb the civil peace: but that all and every person and persons may at all times freely and fully have and enjoy his and their own Judgments, and Consciences, in matters of religious concernments; they behaving themselves peaceably and quietly, and not using this liberty to licentiousness, and profaneness, nor to the civil injury, or outward disturbance of others."

The remarkable and lamentable difference, between the spirit of this instrument; and that which conscientiously prevailed in the Bay, is most palpable. This provision for perfect Religious Liberty, in the Charter was inserted both with the knowledge, and hearty approbation, of Roger Williams — how then can the charges of his enemies that — "he was a subverter of the civil foundations, of the Bay Colony," be true? He did oppose the civil intolerance, of the Bay; and the verdict of Posterity, sustains him in being "conscientiously contentious" — for soul Liberty.

No little uneasiness was felt by the Puritans, as to what the King might do in reference to the evasive reply, they had sent, to the royal letter. This uneasiness was rendered still more uneasy, in the reply to it, brought by Bradstreet and Norton; when it became known that "Commissioners were to be sent by the King, to look into matters generally, in the Colonies." If it were right, for the Bay, to employ the "Commissioners of the Four Colonies," to rectify — Rhode Island — was it wrong, for King Charles II., to rectify the Bay? True it was a little worse than his father did, in reassuming the Charter, and then appointing Commissioners to come over — for now, his son reaffirms the Charter of Chas. 1st; and then appoints "Commissioners," to overtop that.

Upon the arrival of the royal Commissioners in Boston in 1664; they met a very cool reception; but they gave the General Court, the time until their return from a tour through the Colonies, to prepare a reply to the King's letter. The Court presently met, and in the matter of the church-members' elective franchise, they conscientiously provided : that — "All Freeholders 24 years of age, rated ten shillings to a single rate; and certified by the minister of the town, to be orthodox in their principles, and not vicious in their lives, might be admitted Freemen; though not church-members." This was but little better, as all those whose orthodoxy, was not conscientiously theocratic, could only get the clerical "certificate," with difficulty. Yet even this measure, opened a door for freedom; not soon to be closed. Evidently the royal commissioners were not sent, to look after Roger Williams for "undermining the foundations" of Massachusetts Bay Colony. Nay verily, the Puritans themselves, conscientiously — yet unconsciously, dug their own politico-ecclesiastical pit ; and by their own inadvertence, "Theocracy;" fell headlong therein. Yet with its downfall perished ; the last attempt, at Union of Church — and — State; in New England — and it is devoutly to be hoped — the Last, throughout the World!

SECTION 4. — FIRST BAPTIST CHURCH OF BOSTON.

The heavy blows dealt by the royal hand against the unroyal Theocracy, gave great encouragement to all lovers of freedom, to push their claims to recognition. Some sympathy might be felt for the Puritans, under the crushing blows of Charles, if we were not obliged to recall their own conscientious assumptions, in obstructing others in religious concernments; under their Charter from Chas. Ist, which was silent on religion. Nor should we rejoice; even tho' the King had legal power to persecute; that he should use it to lay the Puritans low; and yet we can but concur, that in turn for conscientiously restricting others, they should be held at bay, until others could get upon their feet.

As early as 1656, one Thomas Gould, a member of the Charlestown Church, conscientiously declined to present his child for infant baptism. The church labored with him for his error, but to no purpose. In the spring of 1657, he was conscientiously dealt with by the County Court, for his error. The next year; "he was admonished . . . but continued conscientiously and contumaciously to justifie his weightie schisme."

Mr. Gould was joined by others, in holding meetings privately at his house, for over a year; when he with 8 others formally associated themselves together, and conscientiously organized, June 7, 1664, the First Baptist Church of the Colony.

In Aug. 9, the same year the Puritan Church conscientiously, "excommunicated them, for impertinency and schismatical withdrawing." The Court then took action; "when Gould and his companions were solemnly charged not to persist in such pernicious practices." All ended in their being disfranchised, fined, and for non-payment, were conscientiously imprisoned.

On their return from visiting the other Colonies, the royal Commissioners, took the liberty to cause the English church service, to be conscientiously celebrated, for the first time in Boston.  Obnoxious as this was to the Puritans, times had so changed, that the General Court dared not conscientiously ship the Commissioners to England; as Endicott did the Brownes; for using the English Prayer Book, in Massachusetts Bay. Besides, the Commissioners were not supposed to know, but that the Church-of-England Service would be acceptable to the Bostonians as they were "unseparated;" for their last conscientious declaration in 1630, off the Isle of Wight, was — "to their brethren in and of the Church of England . . . from whose breast they had sucked such hope as they had." But they had been so long weaned, they did not conscientiously relish being forced to the breast.  But this piece of arrogance by the royal Commissioners, might have served to open the eyes of the Puritans, to the conscientiousness they had just practised upon Mr. Gould and his Associates.  At all events it was "relished well in the palates" of those who looked on, to see "Greek meet Greek;" and behold persecutors, flog persecution out of each other; for the benefit of Religious Liberty.

SECTION 5. — UNHAPPY STRIFES.

It is said of the Bourbons of France, "They never learned anything; and never forgot anything."  The Puritans were slow to surrender their conscientious method; to learn to practise the Golden Rule; and remember; that — "One is your Master, even Christ, and all ye are *brethren.*"

Learning little from the conscientious insult they suffered from the royal Commissioners; in 1667, a letter was sent to Rhode Island, protesting against the "Toleration allowed to the Quakers" there — and this protest was coupled with a conscientious threat, of total non-intercourse; if they "refused to conform to the policy of the United Colonies." Posterity will see at once, that the policy, of the United Colonies; was that of persecution, as the threat; and protest; were against, "Toleration." So James Ist said to the reformers — "Conform or I'll harrie you, or hang you, that's all." "William the Silent;" heard in *silence;* the oath — "Extermination of Heresy, by Exterminating Heretics."

Nor was one letter, of protest, and warning, enough; but a second, was sent. To this the people of Rhode Island conscientiously replied, that — " To those places where the Quakers are most of all suffered to declare themselves freely, and are openly opposed by arguments in discourse, they least desire to come; so that they begin to loathe this place, for that they are not opposed by the civil authority, but with all patience and meekness, are suffered to say over their pretended revelations: nor are they like or able to gain many here to their way. Surely they delight to be persecuted, and are like to gain more adherents by the conceit of their patient sufferings, than by consent to their pernicious sayings."

Behold the conscientious difference of opinion, about Religious Liberty, in Boston; and Providence. They no more relished, "pernicious sayings," in Providence, than they did in Boston. But in the former, they repelled sayings, with sayings: in the latter, sayings, with scourgings.

This same year, Mr. Thomas Cobbett, (minister at Lynn when Clarke, Holmes, and Crandall, went there: and the "author of a golden discourse against Anabaptists") in consequence of having his salary reduced to £30; accepted a call to Ipswich; where the town voted to give him £100, and buy, or build him a house — "the expense of both to be levied on all the inhabitants"— conscientiously!!

Among those who conscientiously refused to pay the levy, was one George Giddings. Upon this refusal his pewter platters were conscientiously seized to answer the tax. Thereupon he brought suit for damages before Samuel Symonds; one of the Magistrates, and his case was conscientiously sustained. The opposition conscientiously appealed to the County Court; and the case was again sustained. Whereupon the taxationists conscientiously appealed to the Court of Assistants; where Giddings' case was likely to be again sustained — but before that was done, it passed into the hands of the General Court — the conscientious and ever faithful bulwark of Theocracy, which never flinched, (unless obliged to; before Roger Williams; and the "more influntial sex" — or Oliver Cromwell,) and when the Court arose; George Giddings, lost his "pewter platters."

In Feb. 1668, another set of Agents, returned to Massachusetts Bay, with still further demands; among them, were — "Toleration for all sects — except Papists. The surrender of the peculiar privilege of 'church-member's vote' — and the substitution of a property qualification, as the sole one, for admission to the freedom of the Colony."

This measure was insisted upon by the Third Party. This demand was a fatal blow, to the whole Ecclesiastical System of the Puritans. The King felt justified in these measures, from the fact that the Puritans had interpreted the silence on religion, in the Charter his father gave them; as a liberty, to conscientiously oversee others in religious concernments. This liberty he abolished.

SECTION 6. — EDICTS AND PUBLIC OPINION.

In wielding the Power of the General Court, conscientiously in their favor, the Theocracy were very successful; but they found it very difficult to keep thinkers, from thinking. Persecution, tireless, and long, they had conscientiously employed, to limit Toleration, and yet it spread; its votaries multiplied; and now the King, was helping the factious followers of Roger Williams.

It would seem as though the letter from R. I. about letting the Quakers alone, except with the weapons of speech, and logic — had furnished the Puritans with a hint, to try the same methods, with Baptists, in the Bay. Possibly they may have been reminded, that the challenge to discussion, "with our ministers;" given by Endicott; and accepted by John Clarke; had never been very manfully responded to, by the Puritan Elders.

Hence, we are prepared for a vast stroke of wisdom, in an order by the General Court; for a great debate in Boston, Apr. 24, 1668. Six of the most noted of the Puritan Elders, on one side — with Mr. Gould and seven others, 3 of them from Newport, R. I., on the other side. Two days were spent in close discussion "with a great concourse of people — the effect of which, was not as great in convincing their opponents, as the Court could have desired." So, what the Puritan Elders, lacked in wit, and wisdom, the Puritan Court supplied, with civil Power.

Gould, Turner, and Farnum, were conscientiously sentenced to banishment; but not being anxious to leave; they were again conscientiously imprisoned. A petition with 66 signers interceded for them. But Gould, was not set at liberty until 1670. The Church retired to Noddle's Island — a warrant was conscientiously issued against them there. We are not informed, whether the Court punished Gould, and his friends, for not convincing the Elders — or for not being convinced *by* them.

But as the Banishment of Roger Williams, did not give peace and harmony in puritan-land, but was followed with the distracting controversy with the Hutchinsons — so this *overwhelming* debate with Gould and Co.; did not prevent, a debate more perplexing, and an "effect," still *less* "desirable, to the Court."

The "Half-way (nobody knew, *where*, to,) Covenant," was still a subject of bitter controversy among the Puritans, themselves. Mr. John Davenport, the spiritual Father of New Haven, was conscientiously, and vehemently opposed to it. His views upon it, so well accorded with the views of the First Church in Boston, that upon the death of Mr. Wilson; they called Mr. Davenport as their pastor. So, that First Church, whom Roger Williams found to be an "unseparated people," began to incline conscientiously towards "separation," from Theocracy.

The New Haven Church were very ill-pleased, at losing their minister — and the minority of the First Church in Boston, were as ill-pleased, at securing him. Whereupon, the minority, of that "unseparated church," conscientiously separated — and in 1669 formed what was afterwards known, and is still known; as "Old South Church" — Boston. Posterity would like to know, what worse it was for Roger Williams and a "major part," of the church at Salem, conscientiously to "separate" from the other churches of the Bay; than it was for the minor part, of the First Church in Boston; conscientiously to separate, from the other churches of the Bay?

At the Session of the General Court, the next year, the opponents of the Half-way-Covenant, being in a majority, this Separation, of the minority of the First Church, was conscientiously declared to be "irregular, illegal, and disorderly." Shades of Dudley! Orthodox, Theocratic, Puritans; put under the ban of the Court; with Roger Williams, the "Arch-individualist!"

But another tilt was at hand. At the next election of members for the General Court, the friends of the Half-way-Covenant, had a majority — and the former decision of the Court was conscientiously reversed; and the Puritan "Separatists," were sustained. Court; against Court. Thus the Court sustained the Puritans, in committing the same Sedition; for which they Banished Roger Williams; and shipped the Brownes. All this paradoxicalness is the legitimate fruit, of violating Christ's rule — "Render unto Cæsar the things that are Cæsar's; and to God the things that are God's."

SECTION 7.—THE FIFTH NEW ENGLAND SYNOD.

Notwithstanding the unwearied and conscientious efforts of the General Court to sustain the Half-way-Covenant, and enforce the observance of its provisions upon the people, the opposition thereunto steadily and mightily increased. Whereupon the Court summoned the Fifth, New England Synod; to meet in Boston, Sept. 10, 1669. This was Called the Reforming Synod.

Upon assembling however, a serious question arose; Whether the Convocation were a regular Synod? This issue "was raised upon the occasion that some of the Churches; notwithstanding the desires of their Elders, to be accompanied with other messengers; refused to send any but their Elders." It is not a little amazing, that — altho' the Fourth Synod, in 1662, passed an Edict, that — " Independency is the most to be abhorred maxim " — yet now, the Puritan churches were some of them so Independent, as to conscientiously decline to respond to the call of the Court ; to send delegates to the Fifth Synod — and to persist in that refusal ; even after the solicitations of the Elders, who had to go alone. And yet the Puritans lamented, because "all the world didn't understand them." Did they understand themselves?

But in order that those who had come together might not lose their journey, they passed a vote — " Unanimously approving of the 'Cambridge Platform,' constructed in 1648." They also expressed their desire, that the churches might conscientiously continue steadfast in the observance thereof. Surely this did not better matters much, for out of the "Cambridge Platform," sprung up the "Half-way-Covenant," and now the fruit of this was so bad, as to be nigh unto cursing. Why with such a failure, go back and try it again?

They next proceeded to consider the Questions: I. "What are the evils that have provoked the Lord to bring His judgments upon New England?" This was conscientiously answered, by enumerating many vices, existing — coldness of professors — and above all, the sins of those who had set up their own modes of worship." Possibly in this latter class, the Lord may have included the Puritans themselves — who had not only "set up their own mode of worship," but with pains and penalties forced others, to their modes. If God were well-pleased with this; those who were forced, were not — as, the "Brownes" — and Roger Williams — etc.

Question II. "How are these evils to be reformed? A variety of expedients was suggested — till finally, the last, but not least measure, always relied upon by persecution — was an Edict by the Court: that — "all plantations are strictly forbidden to continue without the advantages of having the Word of God constantly preached unto them." The difficulty in this case would be, if the Court should conscientiously order the Word of God preached according to the "Half-way-Covenant;" and the "Plantation" conscientiously should not — then what?

SECTION 8. — FIRST BAPTIST MEETING HOUSE, BOSTON.

After the Great Debate between the Elders, and Baptists, in 1668, the church organized by Mr. Gould, and others, retreated to Noddle's Island, where they continued conscientiously to worship in secret, for fear (not "of the Jews,") but of the General Court. Encouraged by the decline of theocratic arrogance, and the increase of freedom of the franchise, through the royal orders, this church conscientiously ventured to erect a building in BOSTON proper, on Salem Street, for their use as a Meeting House. As they had been obliged so long to worship in secret, and to avoid attracting attention, lest their "heresie might spread"— they conscientiously gave no public notice of their intended use of this building.

But no sooner had their purpose "come to the Governor's ears," than the Court were conscientiously at their post, enacting laws, "like the Medes' and Persians';" for protection of the public weal, from the growth of those who "set up worship of their own." A law had been enacted forbidding churches being organized, without the consent of other churches; and the Court; but no guards had been set up against building Meeting Houses. So Mr. Gould, and others; had violated no law, in erecting their house, "without due advisement."

Alarmed at this sign of the growth, reaching over from Noddle's Island into Boston; the City Fathers awoke to their duty, and on May 1, 1678, conscientiously passed a Law — "Forbidding the erection of any Meeting House, except with the consent of the Freemen of the Town, and County Court; or by approbation, on appeal to the General Court." The penalty for the violation of this Act :— "Forfeiture of buildings, and land, on which they stood." Such, were the emotions, of Puritan Charity.

Taking encouragement from the royal Orders, the

owners of this building conscientiously ventured, to hold a service in their *own* house, March, 1680. As they expected, they were presently summoned before the Magistrates, "and straightly commanded" to refrain; but when they seemed inclined to go forward; "not having the fear of the Magistrates before their eyes" decided measures were deemed needful by the Authorities.

As they gathered for worship, they found their Meeting House Door conscientiously NAILED UP — and the following Order, appended — "All persons are to take notice, that by order of the Court, the doors of this house are shut up — and that they are inhibited holding any meeting therein, or to open the doors thereof — without license from Authority — till the General Court, take further order — as they will answer the contrary at their peril." This order; and the King's order; giving "freedom of worship to all, but papists" — were somewhat at variance — conscientiously — of COURSE!!

Measures were at once taken, by those owning this House; not violently to unnail the doors; but to erect a temporary shelter in the yard back of the Meeting House where to hold services, until the "further orders" of the Court, should be made known. These matters were brought to the attention of the Court, at its session in May. A plea was made that the house was built before any law was passed to prevent it, and was not therefore an unlawful act. This plea was so far conscientiously allowed; as that the past was to be overlooked — but they were not allowed to open their Meeting House Door. Thus matters rested, until the General Court discovered a need for their Nails, in the

Meeting House Door — and between two days ; those iron sentinels of the Court, conscientiously vacated their posts, and the Baptists found their Meeting House doors — Ajar. They were soon afterwards permitted to occupy their house, unmolested and regularly, for Public Worship.

Increase Mather, in his work on the "Divine Right of Infant Baptism ;" conscientiously charged the Baptists, with — "Setting up an Altar against the Lord's Altar ; — and of committing the sin of Jeroboam, who made priests of the lowest of the people." Mr. Mather did not inform the world, which — was the "Lord's Altar " — whether it were the General Court ; or the Cambridge Platform — or the Half-way-Covenant — or a New England Synod — or Roger Williams' — " pretended authority."

Be that as it may ; In March, 1682, the Messengers of the Mass. Bay Colony, were conscientiously instructed to inform Charles II. that — " As for the Anabaptists, they are now subject to no other penal statutes than those of the Congregational way." Thus in 52 years after the Puritans obtained their Charter of Chas. 1st, which was silent on the subject of religion — they had conscientiously set up their Theocratic system, contrary to the wishes of the King — for 'this and no other misuses of that instrument, it was conscientiously reassumed by the King — Cromwell had overruled (not Revoked) the sentence of Banishment against Roger Williams, by giving him FREE PASS, *in all the Colonies at all times."* Charles II. conscientiously restores the Charter of his father, still silent on the subject of religion — and by his royal decrees, dash — the whole Theocratic Juggernaut; consisting of "Cotton's Keyes;" the "Cambridge Platform;" "Half-way-Covenant;" "New England Synods;" "Law of 1644 against Baptists;" and "General Court;"—"in pieces, like a potter's vessel." Amen. Selah.

Chas. II. evidently considered it legitimate, for him to destroy the illegitimate system of persecution, the Puritans conscientiously fostered under the silence of his father's well-meant favor, to liberty in religion; and thus brought Mass. Bay Colony back, to the intention of his Father in giving the Charter. So perished Theocracy.

SECTION 9. — THE SIXTH AND LAST NEW ENGLAND SYNOD.

To all extemporized, and temporizing devices of men, there is an end. With delight we hail the record, that the Sixth and Last, New England Eccl. Synod, was summoned to meet in Boston, May 12, 1680. For 50 years the Puritans had maintained a conscientious unflinching, restraint upon the sentiment of freedom of conscience, and worship; as advocated by Roger Williams. By this policy they had caused mortifying griefs to their own countrymen, and brethren in Christ; inflicted needless, painful, grievous, inconvenience to their neighbors; conscientiously persisting in this way, not through blindness, or ignorance of a better way, as they were often warned. But to the praise of Divine Providence; some of the Puritans lived to see, and yield to a better course; and Roger Williams lived to see God's own "holy season," in which the inventions of men were cast down. Even Gov. John Winthrop, who died on March 26, 1649; when solicited on his death-bed, by the conscientious Dudley, to sign a decree of banishment, refused; saying — "*I have done too much of that already, in my lifetime.*" So also, with conscientious misgivings, the younger Winthrop signed the Law — "*As a quere not as an act, I sign.*". So in this last Synod, the usually conscientious — became more so!!

The purpose of this assembly being called, was to form, " A Confession of Faith." Evidently the times would no longer accept "Cotton's Keyes;" nor the decrees of previous Synods. If the Puritans themselves, had not outgrown their own "unseparated" conscientiousness; public opinion, had pushed them out into more light, and an open field; where their old, one-sided breastwork, would no longer cover them from the enemy's fire in the rear. Among the missiles most effective, and not to be withstood, were the annihilating *orders* of King Charles.

Of the Thirty-Two Chapters; into which the Contents of this Confession of Faith was divided, the most noticeable for our present purpose, is that, upon *Liberty* of *Conscience*.

Chapter XXIV. Section 3. "They who upon pretence of Christian Liberty, shall oppose any lawful power, or the lawful exercise of it, resist the ordinance of God; and for their publishing of such opinions, or maintaining of such practices, as are contrary to the light of nature, or to the known principles of Christianity; whether concerning faith, worship, or conversation, or the power of godliness, or such erroneous opinions or practices, as either in their own nature, or in the manner of publishing or maintaining them, are destructive to the external peace and order which Christ hath established in the Church; they may lawfully be called to account and proceeded against by the censures of the Church; and by the power of the Civil Magistrate. Yet in such differences about the doctrines of the Gospel, or ways of the worship of God, as may befal men, exercising a good conscience, manifesting it in their conversation, and holding the foundation, and duly observing the rules of peace and order: — there is no warrant for the Magistrate, to abridge them of their Liberty."

Many thanks to God, and his blessed Martyrs: Roger Williams, and others; that "ye Puritans;" have at last, come to acknowledge the truth. The above "section 3," embraces as near as words can, the whole question, and substance of all Roger Williams contended for; [see his declaration in Chap. VIII. sec. 4]. Had the Puritans been conscientious enough, to have avowed such sentiments at the time they Banished him, that obnoxious Sentence; would never have left its very bad blot, on the pages of N. E. Eccl. History. In passing this decree; the Synod cast a reflection upon the former "conscientiousness," of the General Court, against peaceable citizens; as Roger Williams; Clarke; Holmes; Gould; and others; and by such retroaction, the Puritans themselves passed upon the Ecclesiastical polity of the Puritan Forefathers, of Massachusetts Bay — in 1680; a condemnation more anathematizing, than they had issued, in the Sentence of Banishment against Roger Williams; or in the Law of 1644, against the Anabaptists. Truly the Puritan

Synod of 1680, "yielded to Truth"—much to be preferred, to that of the General Court of 1635—to which Endicott gave way.

SECTION 10.—DEATH OF ROGER WILLIAMS.

After an eventful, conspicuous, conscientious, godly, triumphant life, at the good old age of about fourscore years, ROGER WILLIAMS, was gathered to the Fathers, in March or April 1683. A life, coming into notice more and more every year; a life, the study of which, is becoming a necessity, as a key to a correct understanding of New England Eccl. History; a life; the study of which, must be commensurate with the glorious career, which Civil and Religious Liberty; are to win for themselves, among the Nations of the Earth; and in the Providence of God; during Ages to come.

His whole life was a series of triumphs. While a lad he won the admiration, affection, and aid of the fortune of "Sir Edward Coke, the greatest Master of English Law." He won golden laurels, at Cambridge, England's great University of Learning—he took an honored position, while only a youth,—among the Clergy of the Church of England. He fled precipitately from home, to save his life, and preserve his conscience; from the tyranny of bishop Laud—he came safely to Boston, in 1631, his arrival being reported by Gov. Winthrop, as that of "a godly minister:" an honor, even his enemies never denied him—he refused to compromise his conscience by preaching to a Church of Boston Puritans, while "unseparated," from the Civil State—he so influenced public opinion as to cause the General Court, for a time; "to desist from that proceeding" — he compelled the General Court, to name in their indictment, as a cause of his Banishment; his *denial* of the *right* of *Magistrates* to *persecute* for *conscience' sake* — he is honored as the Founder of Rhode Island, on the axiom, that — " The sovereign power of all civil authority is in the people — he limited in his Charter of Government, the coercive power of Magistrates, 'to civil things only' — he secured in the charter of the Rhode Island Government, the recognition of *perfect Religious Liberty, for all persons*, whatsoever."

Mr. Bancroft, in his History, writes of him — " It is wonderful, with what distinctness Roger Williams deduced his inferences, the readiness with which he accepted every fair inference from his doctrines, and the circumspection with which he repelled every unjust imputation. . . . If Copernicus is held in perpetual reverence, because on his death-bed he published to the world that the sun is the centre of our system — If the name of Kepler is preserved in the annals of human excellence for his sagacity in detecting the laws of Planetary motions — If the genius of Newton has been almost adored for dissecting a ray of light and weighing the heavenly bodies in a balance — Let there be for the name of ROGER WILLIAMS, at least some humble place among those who have advanced moral science, and made themselves the Benefactors of Mankind." And may each of the defamers of his irreproachable name; " first cast out the beam that is in thine own eye."

Besides the statue of Roger Williams; a gift from the State of Rhode Island, which has been placed in the National Capitol at Washington ; District of Columbia — " Providence ; " the city he founded, has added her appreciative testimonial to his ever-blessed memory, by accepting as a gift to the city ; from his Great-great-grand-daughter ; MISS BETSEY WILLIAMS; of 100 acres of land, once owned by Roger Williams, [a gift of love to him, from the Great Sachems Canonicus and Miantinomo] ; to be forever kept, and to be known as ROGER WILLIAMS; PARK. "The love she bore the city, her great ancestor founded, and her reverence for his memory prompted the bequest." She died Nov. 27, 1871.

On Oct. 16, 1877, amid ceremonies elaborate and appropriate, a Statue of Roger Williams, a gift of the city of Providence, was unveiled, upon this Park. In the Oration delivered on the Occasion, the speaker said — " We bring to a close in these services, a long purposed, work. . . . To the philanthropist whose abounding charity, recognized no distinction of race, or tongue, we erect this statue. . . . Here let it stand : . . . here let children as they turn from their play, gaze with reverence at him, who chose rather to taste persecution '*bitter as death to him ;*' than to act with a *doubting* CONSCIENCE."

Nor have God ; and Posterity ; yet done honoring him ; because he honored Christ's injunction — " Render therefore unto Cæsar the things that are Cæsar's ; and unto God the things that are God's." Nor is the measure of shame yet meted out to the book-writing defamers of Roger Williams. "He must increase, but they, must decrease."

SECTION II. — DOWNFALL OF THEOCRACY.

The year of 1685, brought James II. to the throne of England. He being a devotee of popery, N. E. Theocracy found in him a formidable adversary. In 1686, he sent out Sir Edmund Andros, as Gov. General of N. E.; who at once demanded the surrender of the Charters of the Colonies. The General Court could not delay this time; as they did when Chas. 1st, sent for their Charter to be returned in Feb. 1633. Plymouth Colony, was absorbed into royalty also. Andros demanded the Charter of R. I. but as the document did not arrive, with conscientious promptness; he proceeded thither, and by formal proclamation, dissolved the Existing Government. That however did not annul their Charter; nor prevent the people of R. I. electing officers under it as before. He did the same in Connecticut; where their Charter was "hid in the oak," until another day.

Thus James 1st. gave the Patent, of Massachusetts Bay Colony — Chas. 1st, gave the Charter, in 1629; and reassumed it in 1634. Under Cromwell, the Colony had no charter. Under Chas. II., after 26 years it was reissued. And now Under James II., after 26 years more, it is again, "reassumed" — and not again reissued. So that between the Kings of England and the General Court; the Massachusetts Bay Charter was pretty thoroughly abused; and more so by the Court, than by the Kings.

Upon his return to Boston, Andros caused the English Church Service to be celebrated, in the "Old South," Meeting House. In vain the building was claimed, as private property; in vain the sexton refused to ring the bell. No tenderness, akin to that of 20 years before, by King Chas.' Commissioners, was shown by Andros. The clergymen came forth, arrayed in the hated surplice, and the Puritan conscientiousness suffered an insufferable unpleasantness.

But why should they? When they left home, they declared themselves — "Brethren in and of the church of England." When Roger Williams found them they were still, "unseparated," from that church — and never did, formally, "separate" from it. Why be shocked at a visit from their "Mother"? Possibly they would have been less shocked; if Gov. Andros, had "nailed-up the doors, of their Meeting House"! Or, had he banished them, as they did Roger Williams, beyond "ye lymmitts." Or, hung them, as per Mary Dyer!

Oh Theocracy! Oh Prelacy!! Oh Popery!!!

King James', Declaration of Indulgence was proclaimed Jan. 1687; whereby Toleration, to Quakers; Baptists; and Episcopalians; was guaranteed in Massachusetts Bay — notwithstanding the conscientiousness of the General Court. Thus in about the same time, that Toleration was secured for Dissenters in Eng., (1688); after the return of John Smyth and his Church from Holland; the same boon was granted to New England a few years only, after the death of Roger Williams; in whom Elder Brewster tho't he saw a tendency, like Mr. Smyth. Both, tended towards Religious Liberty.

Soon after the King's Indulgence, the foundation of an Episcopal house of worship was laid, and the leaders of the conscientious Theocracy, were asked for contributions, to help build it. Thus the system of religious intolerance in the Bay, providentially received its death-blow, from a papal devotee ; who favored liberty for the church of England, to answer his own ends. Better for the Puritans, that they had listened to Roger Williams, in the first place, and saved themselves the trouble, of rearing their Platform — and the mortification of having it thrown down before their eyes.

But for the many other, "unsettled judgments," of the Puritans ; we should wonder that Messrs. Increase Mather ; Cooke ; and Oakes ; were sent from the Elders of the Bay ; conscientiously to present a letter of congratulation, to King James for his "Declaration of Indulgence." It must have been done with an "obsequious eye." For by this "Declaration," the King put under his heel, so much of the Puritan Ecclesiastical policy, as they had interpolated into their system, under the silence on religion, in the Charter of Chas. 1st. He undid, as far as possible, what the Puritans had no right, to do, in his opinion.

Mr. Mather and the others found themselves in a strange quandary ; for while they were abroad, James II. was obliged to abdicate, after the "Battle of the Boyne ;" in favor of William III., Prince of Orange [great-grandson of William the Silent, Prince of Orange ; of Holland] ; and Mary ; [daughter of James II. ;] who were called to the British throne. Mather was obliged to adapt himself to the new order of things.

Finding that the old Charter, reassumed by Chas. 1st. ; and was reissued by Chas. II. ; and again reassumed by James II. ; was to be supplemented, by a new one ; Mr. Mather conscientiously "bent to circumstances ;" and like Gov. Endicott, when likely to be jailed ; and "yielded to truth." For this respect for Authority (?), he was rewarded, by having left to him, the nomination of officers, to be appointed by the Crown ; under the new Charter. Thus complimented, he took wise care, conscientiously to name for the new Colonial Council ; "persons favorable to the interests of the Puritan churches."

Yet ; notwithstanding Mr. Mather's theocratic principles ; and tho' he bent to circumstances ; and tried conscientiously to make the best of all ; he was exposed ; as were so many agents before him ; to imputations from the sterner theocrats, from which he never was relieved ; — "of having sacrificed and betrayed the rights of his constituents." If among those *lost rights*, were those of "nailing-up Meeting-House doors " — of " boring Quakers' tongues with red-hot irons ;" etc., etc. ; Posterity will not pronounce a very harsh judgment, against Mr. Mather, if he did betray, *such rites*, of his constituents.

Early in 1692, Sir William Phipps arrived ; (nominated by Mather,) with the New Charter ; embracing both Massachusetts Bay, and Plymouth Colonies, in one, under the name of Massachusetts. Its main provisions on the subject of Religious Liberty, were — " Toleration to all religious sects, except papists." The church and State basis ; of church-membership, and ministers' certificates ; for citizenship and suffrage ; were swept away ; and those rightly conferred upon all inhabitants possessing a freehold of the annual value of 40 shillings ;

or personal property, to the amount of £40." Thus the assumptions of the Puritans, in favor of Theocracy, on which their old Charter from Chas. Ist, was silent; in the new one, are forestalled and prohibited, in favor of Toleration.

The last "Bartholomew Massacre," of the Puritan Theocracy, was engineered by that conscientious Inquisitor, Cotton Mather; the "Last of the Greeks;" during the Summer of 1692; and it is known as the episode of the "Salem Witchcraft."

The ceremonies opened by the conscientious "scourging of an Indian servant girl; by Elder Parris; until she confessed herself to be a witch." In June an old woman, poor and friendless, was tried and hanged forthwith. Five women, of "blameless lives," were convicted by the Court; and with five more victims afterwards condemned, were all hanged. Among those conscientiously hanged in August, was a Minister named Burroughs, who had denounced these barbarities. While on the scaffold, he made a speech, and repeated the Lord's Prayer so affectingly, as to draw tears from the eyes of the spectators. Mather, as Inquisitor General, rode among the crowd on horseback, and quieted them, by conscientiously quoting Scripture passages. An old man of 80 years, seeing that every trial ended in conviction, refused to plead his case, and was pressed to death. Twenty murders were thus committed before Mather was satisfied; and then he conscientiously wrote a work, for the purpose of persuading the General Court, to continue this Inquisition. But thanks to Divine Providence, it was abolished that same year. Yet Mather conscientiously justified himself, in his own eyes, to the last. Was the opinion of Warwick people far wrong? Williams "filled Salem with Anabaptism"— Mather didn't better it, much.

### SECTION 12.— THE NEW CHARTER.

The year 1692, is made very memorable, by the Union of Plymouth, and Mass. Bay, colonies, under a new Charter. The impulse given the Reformation under Cromwell; the Toleration of Dissenters in England, secured, upon the accession of Wm. III., and Mary, in 1688; raised a wave of Reform, that rolled over New England, and swept into the bottomless pit, the last remains of the "serpent that crawled into the Elders' seat."

At the first meeting of the General Court, after the Union of the two Colonies under the New Charter— the following sentiments on the subject of "Liberty of Conscience," are found in the sermon delivered on the occasion — in part, as follows : —

"Things will go well, when Magistrates are great promoters of the things that good is, and of what the Lord requireth of them. I do not mean that it would be well for the civil Magistrate, with a civil penalty, to compel men to this or that way of worship, which they are *conscientiously* indisposed unto. He is most properly the officer of humane society, and a Christian, by Non-conformity to this or that imposed way of worship, and does not break the terms on which he is to enjoy the benefits of humane society.

"A man has a right unto his life; his estate; his liberty; and his family; altho' he should not come up unto these and those blessed institutions of our Lord.

When a man sins in his political capacity, let political societies animadvert upon him ; but when he sins only in a religious capacity, societies more purely religious, are the fittest then to deal with him. . . . It may be feared that things will not go well, when heresies are not exterminated ; but I pray. . . when did fines or gaols ever signifie anything for the cure of hereticks?

" The primitive church for the first 300 years of Christianity . . . by sound preaching ; by discipline ; by catechising ; and by disputation ; turned to flight the armies of the aliens. Afterwards indeed, the Emperors were engaged unto severities upon the hereticks of those days ; but what got they by it? When a wicked Manichee, a sort of Quaker, was put to death, it was a most wretched example, and it made the heresie spread the more. Such persecutions do but give a principle, which would be most fatal to the Church of God ; yea, they do but afford a root for Cain's club to grow upon. These violences may bring the erroneous to be *hypocrites*, but they will never make them to be believers ; no, they naturally prejudice men's minds against the *cause*, which is therein pretended for, as being a weak, a wrong, an evil cause.

" Wherefore that things may go well, I would willingly put in a barr against the persecution of any, that may *conscientiously* dissent from our way. Possibly the zeal in some famous and worthy disciples of our Lord, among ourselves, have been reported and reckoned, as having once had a little too much fire on this account ; but the churches of God abroad, counted that things did not go well among us, until they judged us more fully come up unto the Apostolic rule, 'to leave the otherwise minded to God.' Nor would I desire myself to suffer persecution upon a clearer cause, than that of testifying against persecution of other christians, that are not of my opinion. I am sure that things will not go well, as long as we incur the fulfilment of that awful word; 'If ye bite and devour one another take heed lest ye be consumed one of another.'

"Moreover it belongs unto Magistrates, to punish all the vices which disturb the good order and repose of human society; and hence also liberty of *conscience* is not to be admitted as a cloak for liberty of profaneness.

"To live without any Worship of God, or to blaspheme and revile his blessed name, is to be chastized as abominably criminal; for there can be no pretense of *conscience* thereto. Things will go well, when we go thus, and when there is an accomplishment of that word, in Romans 13 : 3. 'For rulers are not a terror to good works, but to the evil.'"

Had the Puritans conscientiously embraced such sentiments as the above, in 1635, when they were urged upon their attention by Roger Williams; they would have left a fairer record, and secured a juster claim to grateful remembrance by Posterity. But if those who "live without any worship of God — and blaspheme and revile;" are to be chastised at the "Whipping-post," by Magistrates; will it not "make *them* hypocrites, and not believers?"

### SECTION 13. — THE LAST GUN.

Seeing the end, not afar off, the Puritans conscientiously did their best for their last. At the Second Session of the New General Court, Oct. 1693, they passed Acts, obliging every town, to support a minister of the "Standing Order." All the people of the town, even those belonging to other societies; were to be "taxed, for his support." The right of *calling* the minister, was with the particular church — but the *fitness* of such call, must be left to the decision of a Council of neighboring Churches; yet he could not be *settled*, so as to make the town liable for his support, without the *concurrence*, of a majority of the legal voters. So settled, the Minister held a life-tenure of office, from which he could not be removed except for cause.

Great advance had been made toward Roger Williams' views of Religious Liberty. These last Acts, for saddling posterity with a cast-iron-system, served well for "bones-of-contentions," for too many years. Thus were the sandy foundations of the New England Theocracy, gradually and surely undermined: "and it fell."

## CHAPTER X.

### TRIUMPH OF RELIGIOUS LIBERTY.

* " From Chief to Chief the Calumet they past;
    Sate in solemn silence, the Council, bound;
    Each thrice inhaled, thrice forth the vapors cast;
        First, to the Power, that bids the Thunder sound —
        Then to the gods, that ride the angry blast —
        Then to the fiends, that dwell beneath the ground:
        These made propitious, they the hatchet gave —
        The bloody hatchet — to a peaceful grave."
                                        DURFEE.

SECTION I. — THE PURITANS ADVOCATE TOLERATION.

IT required but a few years; after the adoption of the New Charter of Massachusetts; which was brought about by the leavening influence of Roger Williams' doctrines, of Liberty of Conscience; and the demolishing blows, of Kings, Chas. and James, against Theocracy — conscientiously to turn public opinion into new moulds of thought. It would seem, out of place, for the Kings of England to use the civil power, in overturning the Ecclesiastical System, of the Puritans; but as the Puritans took a liberty, which the Charter of Chas. 1st, did not give them, to set up a coercion; even against the King's Church; as well as others; his successors deemed it their prerogative, to disfellowship what was done in the King's name, without the King's consent. So while one Church and State, was demolishing; another Church and State; Toleration, went marching on to victory.

> "Then silence reigned again — but still they stared —
>   Some clasped their knives — some their arrows drew;
> Then from his seat, his form our Founder reared,
>   Beneath him rocking, rolled the frail canoe;
> His hand he raised, and manly forehead bared,
>   And straight their former Friend the Sachems knew;
> Netop, What cheer! broke on the listening air;
>   What cheer! What cheer! was echoed here and there."
>                                                    DURFEE.

The First Baptist Church of Boston, had in the days and persons of Thomas Gould, and others, suffered much from the obstructions of the General Court; but in the settlement of Mr. Elisha Callander, in 1718, as Pastor of this Church, *both the Mathers*, Increase; and Cotton; ASSISTED AT HIS ORDINATION. At the ordination of Roger Williams; in Salem; 83 years before, not one of the Elders of the Bay was there; yea more the General Court, had interdicted his ordination, and when it was done, the act was conscientiously held up as a "great contempt of Authority." But those dreadful years had taught the successors of the Old Puritans, a lesson of wisdom — the same lesson, taught their fathers.

Even the Sermon, at Mr. Callander's ordination, was preached by Cotton Mather: the Chaplain at the Salem witch-hanging. The title of this sermon was — "Good Men United." Text Gen. 49: 7. "Cursed be the anger, for it is fierce; and the wrath, for it is cruel;" . . . Good for nothing, but only to make divisions in Jacob, and dissensions in Israel. "New England also, in some former times, has done something of this aspect, which would not now be so well approved of ; in which, if the Brethren in whose house we are now convened, met with anything too unbrotherly, they now with satisfaction, hear us expressing our dislike of every thing which looked like persecution in the days that have passed over us."

Cotton Mather wishes Posterity to understand, that he saw, "cursed bloody stains, in John Cotton's Bloody Tenet, washed white" — "cursed be the anger of the General Court who passed the sentence of Banishment against Roger Williams, approved by all the ministers of the Bay; *save one*" (who was ashamed of it) — "cursed be the anger of John Wilson, who struck Obadiah Holmes before the judgment seat, and said — 'the curse of God, or Jesus go with thee'" — "cursed be the anger of the General Court, who nailed-up the Meeting House, of the Brethren, where we are now convened" — In short, he would have Posterity understand him to say — "cursed be Theocracy, it is good for nothing, but only to make divisions in Jacob, and dissensions in Israel." And Posterity says — AMEN.

In review then of all this ; and of Gov. John Winthrop's refusal ; to sign any more sentences of Banishment — John Winthrop, Jr.'s "signing not as an act, but as a quere" — in view of Roger Williams' success, and renown among Posterity — well may we thank God, for Religious Liberty !

> "Mooshausick, quick with future glories, hears,
> Rolls up a brighter wave, and downward pours,
> To Narragansett's Bay the shout he rears,
> The Bay resounds it to echoing shores ;

> Coweset's wilds repeat the rejoicing cheers,
>   Pocasset answers from her mountain bowers;
>   Wild o'er the joyous isles the rapture roves,
>   And fair Aquidnay smiles, and waves her blooming groves."
>
> DURFEE.

Thus, by 1720, inside of 100 years from the Landing of the Pilgrims — the Puritans had tried their questionable measures, in the service of their Church and State policy; and with the Policy — of the "Magistrates and Elders;" sunk into Oblivion. This done — even Cotton Mather, boasted of the harmony in which various religious sects lived together in Boston: and stigmatized religious persecution, as an "Obsolete Blunder."

SECTION 2. — SYNODS DECLARED ILLEGAL.

The Ministers of the "Standing Order," organized a meeting, which bro't them together informally, once a year in Boston; but without any special end in view, and having no Ecclesiastical authority. This however did not prove to be very interesting; especially as they remembered the days, when the Elders of the Churches, enjoyed the special privilege, of acting as advisers of the General Court on all important occasions, in matters of Church; and State.

Weary of this "marching up the hill, and marching down again," they petitioned the General Court in 1725, to issue a call for a Synod; after the example of former times. Their request was referred to the English Lawyers, and after due consideration, they gave it as their opinion, that — "the holding of any such Synod would be illegal, without the express sanction of the King."

This decision was evidently, based upon the fact that,

no provision of the kind, was made in the Charter — and the common rule prevailed, that "all rights not mentioned, are reserved until granted." If therefore this decision were correct, all previous Synods, were also illegal; as the former Charter from Chas. 1st, was silent, on the subject of Religion. It follows also, that the calling, of previous Synods, by the General Court was likewise, illegal. Hence the whole Code of Theocratic Ecclesiasticalities; "Cambridge-Platform," "Half-way-Covenant;" "Public taxes for support of Religion," — were all illegal! So also was the Banishment of Roger Williams — illegal.

Thus the friends of Religious Liberty were helped, to triumph over the Theocracy, by having brought to their aid, unsolicited, the strong arm of the British King. This turn, of *Power*, against *Power*, was a just recompense upon the Puritans, for their conscientious assumption of civil coercion, over Roger Williams, and the Church of Salem; and for other interferings of the Court, against religion. And it was especially appropriate, and justly fitting, that the check on the Puritans should come from the king, inasmuch as their assumptions under the Charter, were in the name of the king, when he had not given them his name, for any such use. Similar aid was given Wickliffe in England, by the Duke of Lancaster, against those who opposed reform, in the king's name. Luther, was also helped, by Frederick the Wise, against those who opposed him, in the name of the Empire. William Prince of Orange, interposed his Princely Power, to stay the progress of the Inquisition in the Netherlands. Thus persecution in the Old World, and the New, was carried on in the

King's name — and declared illegal, and repelled, in the name of the King. And by *Conscientious* Puritans — finally interdicted as a "CURSED, OBSOLETE BLUNDER"!!

SECTION 3. — THE ECCLESIASTICAL TAXES REMITTED.

Limb by limb, of the Theocratic "Upas Tree," was taken, until root and branch, were annihilated. In 1727, the Episcopalians succeeded in getting the ministerial taxes assessed upon them, for the support of the Puritan Elders; turned over to them for the salaries of their own clergy. In 1728, the same justice, respecting ministerial taxes, was extended to Baptists, and Quakers. In 1729, Connecticut, and New Haven followed the same good example.

Thus the Four United Colonies, that would not admit Rhode Island to their Union, because "they followed Roger Williams in a different way from the rest of us, in matters of religion" — are brought around in the Providence of God, to do as they did; in R. I. So in the short space of 100 years; the Theocracy of the Puritans, had used up their conscientious blandishments, of FINES; PRISONS; WHIPPING-POSTS; BANISHMENTS; PLATFORMS; COVENANTS; SYNODS; and TAXES" — and come to see the meaning, of ROGER WILLIAMS' reply, to the call of the "unseparated, First church of Boston." In the same ratio as Theocracy died out by inches, and *decreased;* Religious Liberty *increased.*

Great variety existed in the several Colonies, as to the laws and regulations, on "religious concernments;" yet the main features were the same. Certain parties there were in each Colony, conscientiously clinging to the monopoly of State support of the churches; and others as strenuously opposed, to all State support whatever. The current of public opinion; was in the direction, of the sentiment that made Separatists, of the Pilgrims, and brought them to Plymouth; on towards, the once, "erroneous and very dangerous doctrine," that settled Roger Williams, in Providence; on towards, the doctrine that reduced persecution for conscience' sake, to an "Obsolete blunder;" on towards, the doctrine, that has given "Religious Liberty" to the United States; and which is, the Doctrine, "predestinated," to give Freedom of Conscience, to the WHOLE WORLD —and to lay all State and church establishments exceedingly low in the dust; yea to be "cast out and trodden under foot of men." Thus the "breath of the Lord Jesus, cast down," the Theocracy.

SECTION 4. — THE "HOLLIS" MINISTERIAL FUND.

Harvard College, which was conscientiously founded in 1638, for the purpose of higher education of youth, had already become famous. The "Hollis Fund," came from a family of that name in England. Thomas Hollis; was born in 1634, the year before the Banishment of Roger Williams; and 4 years before Harvard College was founded; he died in 1718, the year of the Ordination of Mr. Elisha Callander. His Son, Thomas Hollis 1st, died in 1731: (the year before the birth of Washington). Another Son, Nathaniel, died in 1738. Another Son, John, was partner with his brother, Thos. 1st. Thomas 3d, Son of Nathaniel, died in 1735.

Thomas Hollis 1st, was so called, because of his munificent donations to Harvard College; he was a wealthy merchant of London, and a Baptist. The occasion of his conscientious interest in Harvard College, was, that of the participation of Cotton Mather, and other Puritan ministers, in the Ordination of Mr. Elisha Callander, May 21, 1718; as pastor of the First Baptist Church, Boston. Altho' Liberty of Worship had been secured as early as 1680, in Massachusetts Bay, yet this Ordination service, "was so happy a demonstration," of the change in the conscientious opinions of the Puritans, concerning their Baptist brethren; that Mr. Hollis, conscientiously felt it to be his special privilege, to commemorate the event, by a special THANK-OFFERING TO GOD. This he did, by " placing in the hands of the Corporation of Harvard College, in Trust, a munificent sum of money, as a Fund; the interest only of which, was to be conscientiously used perpetually, and primarily, for the Education of young men for the Baptist Ministry."

His plan for carrying out this purpose, was; that, "The interest of his Fund should be conscientiously used for the salaries of two Professors — one of Divinity; and one of Mathematics, and Experimental Philosophy; and Ten Scholarships, for the education of pious young men of the Baptist persuasion." Besides this Fund, he sent from England, as a gift to Harvard; a Philosophical Apparatus, which cost £150; and 1,000 vols. to its Library.

Thomas Hollis 3d, was born in 1720. His donations to Harvard College, during his lifetime, exceeded £1,400, Sterling; $7,000. He died, in 1774. Timothy Hollis, gave £20, $100, to the Library. He died in 1791. Thomas Brand Hollis, the last of these Benefactors, was born in 1719. He died in 1804.

The entire Gifts of this Family, as a conscientious Thank Offering for "Good Men United," may be safely estimated at not less than £10,000 Sterling. Of this sum as much as £8,000=$40,000; have been on interest, at least 100 years; and some of it, 150 years. So that, the amount of the "HOLLIS FUND;" is large. Has it been conscientiously applied according to the purpose of the Donors? If therefore legitimately entitled to interest it cannot be less than from $500,000, to $1,000,000 — and now in the hands of the Corporation of Harvard College; "for the education of pious Young Men of the Baptist persuasion."

Surely an offering so munificent in amount; conscientiously, and piously given, as an offering of gratitude to God, for the triumph of Religious Liberty, over Irreligious Bigotry, and intolerance; specifically set apart to the sole, exclusive, and noble purpose, of educating living agents, for preaching the glorious Gospel of the Lord Jesus Christ, for all time — all these considerations carry with them a weight of sacred responsibility; which ought to keep this Fund, devoted to the purpose, for which it was laid upon God's Altar — yea *very* CONSCIENTIOUSLY!

Of this noble benefaction, known as the "Hollis Fund, of Harvard College" — it is recorded, that — "THE DISINTERESTED SPIRIT BY WHICH THE CHARITIES OF THE MESSRS. HOLLIS WERE PROMPTED, CONSTITUTES ONE OF THE MOST REMARKABLE INSTANCES OF CONTINUED BENEVOLENCE ON RECORD."

Mr. Hollis, upon hearing of the earnest efforts, of the Philadelphia Baptist Association, and their early endeavors in 1722, to start the Rhode Island College —

now Brown University — for the education of their rising ministry — corresponded with them on the subject. As the result of this correspondence, he conscientiously made known to them, what he had done, in providing for Professorships, and Scholarships, at Harvard College; and authorized them fully to avail themselves of all the advantages his benefactions had secured at Harvard; for the end they were so earnestly seeking.

Are those Benefactions available at the present day — and are they being practically applied, to the particular, and noble purposes had in view, by the conscientious and generous Founders? Can any good excuse be found, why Posterity should not be able promptly, and conscientiously, to answer these questions? Can we prove ourselves worthy, of the confidence reposed in us by the Messrs. Hollis — can we repel the accusation of being delinquents, and Defaulters, at the Bar of Public Opinion — Can we confidently expect of our Divine Master, His approval; which is to be given to such only as deserve it, — "WELL DONE GOOD AND FAITHFUL SERVANTS;" unless we can say, "THE HOLLIS FUND, OF HARVARD COLLEGE is *faithfully kept and applied?*"

SECTION 5.— RELIGIOUS AND CIVIL LIBERTY RELATED.

Just about 100 years after the subject of Soul Liberty began to be agitated in the American Colonies; the questions of Civil Liberty began to attract and absorb public attention. The providence of God was such, that the School of Christ in Soul Freedom, prepared the way for desiring, defining, and securing, Civil Rights.

So well had the Subject of Liberty of Conscience become understood, before the struggle for American Independence came on; that it called for very little attention, until after the Revolutionary War. But in the "Ordinance of 1787," before the Constitution was adopted; and before Washington, was President; it was conscientiously provided and stipulated, in — Article 1. "No person demeaning himself in a peaceable, and orderly manner, shall ever be molested on account of his mode of Worship, or religious sentiments in the Territory."

In August 1789, a Committee presented an address to President Washington, wherein they conscientiously expressed their high regard for his person, and appreciation of his eminent services — "but a fear, that our Religious Rights, were not well secured in our New Constitution of Government." Washington conscientiously replied — "That the religious Society, of which they were members, had conscientiously been thro'out America, uniformly the persevering promoters of the glorious Revolution — and assured them of his readiness to use his influence to make those rights indisputable." Accordingly in the following month, Sept. 1789, the First Clause, of the First Amendment, to the Constitution, was conscientiously passed; declaring, that — "Congress shall make no law respecting any Establishment of Religion, or prohibiting the Free Exercise, thereof."

The above conscientious opinion of Washington, upon the Baptists, differs very materially from the conscientious opinion of the Puritans, in their Law against them passed in 1644.

SECTION 6. — THE END OF THEOCRACY.

The foregoing End of Theocracy, suggests the like event, in the Reformation, known as the "Peace of Religion" — Concluded between the Protestant and Catholic Powers, Sept. 25, 1555. This grand end for which MARTIN LUTHER earnestly toiled; was not achieved until 9 years after his death. WILLIAM PRINCE OF ORANGE, achieved the like result for his country, — Holland in 1582; two years before his death. JOHN SMYTH and his compeers secured Toleration for England in 1688. ROGER WILLIAMS, lived to see the day, when — "As for the Anabaptists, they are now subject to no other pœnal statutes than those of the Theocratic way" — in 1682; one year before his death.

Thus from Sept. 1555, to the Amendment, to the Constitution under Washington, Sept. 1789; Religious Liberty conscientiously went marching on to Victory — "St. Bartholomew Massacre," in Aug. 1572 ; the Assassination of Prince of Orange, in July 1584 — the rigors of the British Star Chamber, from 1550-1650 — and the Banishment of Roger Williams, by the Massachusetts Bay Theocracy — all to the contrary notwithstanding!

But the last lingering roots of the old Theocracy, were not all conscientiously plucked up, until 200 years, after the time the General Court, interdicted the Ordination of Roger Williams; over the church in Salem. This conscientious uprooting was finally done in 1834, when the Amendment to the 3d Article of the Massachusetts Bill of Rights; put an end, to that "Obsolete Blunder."

All lovers of the truth who live in this 19th century, may look forward with confident expectation to the times when Religious Liberty shall conscientiously become the Fundamental Ecclesiastical Law of all Christendom — and that wherever the Gospel of Christ is preached in all the world ; men may learn to " Render unto Cæsar the things that are Cæsar's ; and to God the things that are God's."

SECTION 7. — JUSTICE TO ROGER WILLIAMS, YET TO BE DONE.

Unjust as that Sentence of Banishment against Roger Williams now seems, still it remains, Unrevoked ; just as it fell from the lips of the Court. Notwithstanding Gov. Winthrop, expressed his conviction, that it ought to be revoked, still it remains. Great as are the advantages Posterity has reaped from his vindication of Soul Freedom, still that Sentence remains. Even so recently as 1870, Hon. R. C. Winthrop ; said, in his Address at the 250th Anniversary of the " Landing of the Pilgrims " — " I palliate not a particle of the persecution he [Roger Williams] suffered, from whomever it came." The Great Protector — Cromwell, muzzled it'— yet it remains.

But nothing had been done to this end, until 1875, when a Petition from Citizens in the Town of Sturbridge Massachusetts, was presented to the Legislature ; Asking that — " The Sentence of Banishment passed in 1635, by the General Court of Massachusetts Bay, against Roger Williams, be revoked ; as an Act of Historical Justice." It was not acted upon until 1876, Jan. 19 ; when the Judiciary Committee conscientiously reported, that — "The Petitioners have leave to withdraw." Thus, the Massachusetts Legislature of that year conscientiously sustained the unglorified edict of the Court, of 241 years before; and this, in the light of the Civilization of the 19th Century!

Whether this act of justice be presently done, or be long postponed; it will not prevent the spreading forth of the Doctrine of Soul Liberty — as defended by Roger Williams — nor will it prevent the erection of Statues to his memory; nor check the flow of blessings upon his name; as they conscientiously fall from the lips of the Myriads of Posterity.

Nor will his memory suffer disgrace; from some stillborn efforts, at his "inculpation;" and the justification of the wrong-doings of the Puritans; by modern apologists, — especially, if they are read in the light of Historical Truth; and the rebukes of the Winthrops; and Washington; shining upon their unfounded, "persistent reiterations." The fame of Roger Williams' great name, will increase, while that of his vilifiers will decrease.

### SECTION 8. — THE TRUE SUCCESSION.

Theocracy is no more — has no succession — nor Successors. The true church is that whole family of the Faithful, who accept only Christ, as Master, and "all ye are Brethren." The interests of that church are best served, by a conscientious total "Separation" from the State; in polity; and support. The Spiritual interests of this Household of Faith, are best conserved by the grouping together, as circumstances require, into small independent bodies, or "Churches," according to the New Testament plan; all under Law to Christ; but no one or more, of said Churches, having any prerogative, over any one or more, of the others; beyond what good mutual conscientious Christian fellowship may suggest for the best good of all.

Towards the attainment of this end, the Gospel of Christ acts as leaven hid in the meal; nor is this end to be sought by the cry — " Lo here or lo there " in some great Ecclesiasticism; but, "the Kingdom is within you."

The Pilgrim Fathers of New England, more nearly, than any other class of the early Colonists, represented the germ, and scope, of the Gospel plan; and has gradually gained its present great and growing ascendency over the conscience, judgment, and public opinion, of American Christians: while the muddled system of the Puritans fell into the pit of their own contempt; and was by themselves pronounced, and abandoned, as an "Obsolete Blunder."

Cheerfully therefore do we ascribe to God's grace; that thro' the faith of His honored servants; Roger Williams — being one of them; he has begotten in the minds of Posterity, a just respect for Christ's injunction — " Render therefore unto Cæsar the things that are Cæsar's — and to God the things that are God's." And now that it has become the conscientious Fundamental Ecclesiastical Law, of the United States of America; may it "cover the Earth as the waters cover the Sea."

# PART SECOND.

## REASONS WHY THE SENTENCE OF BANISHMENT PASSED AGAINST ROGER WILLIAMS SHOULD BE REVOKED.

POSTERITY are requested to note — that in matters between Roger Williams, and the Puritans, we have preferred another, than the usual course of Histories, on this Subject; by not giving a cumbersome account of all that was done in Massachusetts Bay — in Church, and State; and on all occasions; ordinary, and extraordinary, Commingled.

Our aim is to disentangle such matters as expressly pertain, to the *issue* — between Roger Williams, and the Puritans — on the vital question of Religious Liberty; — so that his case, may not be confusedly confounded, with all the nondescripts of New England wilderness life, as tho' he, were one of them.

In Part First — of this writing, we have collected and adjusted certain plain authenticated facts — which are reliable, and without contradiction; and are open to the inspection of all Students of the times, about the struggle between the Puritans and Roger Williams — upon the vital question of Religious Liberty. Whatever future historians may discover to give us more light, will be most acceptable.

## CHAPTER I.

*JESUS CHRIST, AND HIS APOSTLES, TAUGHT THE DOCTRINE OF RELIGIOUS LIBERTY — WHICH ROGER WILLIAMS MAINTAINED — THEREFORE, THAT SENTENCE OF BANISHMENT PASSED AGAINST HIM OUGHT TO BE REVOKED.*

I. — CHRIST'S FUNDAMENTAL INSTRUCTIONS ON THE SUBJECT OF SEPARATION OF CHURCH AND STATE.

"THEN the Chief Priests and Scribes sent out unto Jesus, certain of the Pharisees, and Herodians, to catch Him in His words, and entangle Him in His Doctrine; That they might deliver Him to the power and authority of the Governor. And they sent forth Spies, who should feign themselves just men — Saying — Master — we know that Thou art true — and teachest the way of God in Truth — For thou regardest not the person of men. Tell us therefore, what thinkest, Thou; Is it Lawful to give tribute unto Cæsar, or no? Shall we give or shall we not give?

"But Jesus perceived their Craftiness, and wickedness, and said; Why tempt ye Me; hypocrites: Show Me the tribute-money. And they brought unto Him a penny. And Jesus answering, said unto them, whose image and Superscription, hath it? They answered and said unto Him; Cæsar's. Then Jesus answering, said unto them; Render therefore unto Cæsar the things which are Cæsar's; and, unto God, the things which are God's."

"And straightway in the morning the Chief Priests held a consultation with the Elders, and scribes, and the whole Council, and bound Jesus; and the whole multitude of them arose and led Him away and delivered Him to Pontius Pilate, the Governor. And they began to accuse Him, saying — We found perverting the Nation, and forbidding to give tribute to Cæsar; saying — that He Himself, is Christ — a King.

"Then Pilate entered into the Judgment-hall again and called Jesus. And when he was set down in the judgment-seat, his wife sent unto him, saying — have thou nothing to do with that just Man; for I have suffered many things this day in a dream, because of Him.

"And Jesus stood before the Governor, and the Governor asked Him, saying; Art thou the King of the Jews? Jesus answered him; Sayest thou this thing of thyself, or did others tell it thee, of Me? Jesus answered — My Kingdom is not of this World; if My Kingdom were of this World, then would My Servants fight; that I should not be delivered to the Jews : but now is My Kingdom not from hence.

"Pilate saith unto them, Shall I crucify your King? The chief priests answered — we have no King but Cæsar. And Pilate wrote a Title and put it over His Head on the Cross — and it was written in letters of Greek, and Latin, and Hebrew. And the superscription of His accusation was — This is JESUS of NAZARETH, the KING of the JEWS."

Here we have Christ's Doctrine, that He is Head of the Church — but not a temporal King — and yet we are to pay tribute to Cæsar; in civil things only. Hence Christ has not left in His place, any person or persons, as His Vicegerent on Earth — representing Him as Universal, Spiritual — and Temporal Prince.

### 2. — CHRIST IN HIS INSTRUCTION TO HIS DISCIPLES DISCOURAGED POLITICAL AMBITION.

"Then came to Him the Mother of Zebedee's children, with her two Sons — James, and John — worshipping, and desiring certain things of Him. Saying — Master we would that thou shouldest do for us whatsoever we shall desire. And there was also a strife among them, which of them should be accounted the greatest.

"And He said, what would ye that I should do for you? She said unto Him — Grant that these my two Sons may sit, the one on Thy right hand, and the other on Thy left hand, in Thy Kingdom — in Thy Glory. But Jesus answered and said unto them — Ye know not what ye ask.

"And when the Ten heard it, they were moved with indignation, and began to be much displeased, with the two Brethren — James, and John.

"But Jesus called them, and said unto them; Ye know that they which are accounted to rule over the Gentiles, and their Kings, and their princes, exercise dominion and lordship over them — and their great ones exercise authority upon them, and are called Benefactors.

"But it shall not be so among you — But whosoever will be greatest among you — let him be as the younger; and he that is chief, as he that doth serve.

"And I appoint unto you a Kingdom, as My Father

hath appointed unto Me ;—That ye may eat and drink at My tables in My Kingdom ; and sit on thrones judging the Twelve Tribes of Israel."

According to Christ's instructions to His Disciples — Ecclesiastics — even of the Apostolic Succession ; need not ape the function, Ex Officio — of bearing the Civil Sword. "Then said Jesus unto Peter — Put up thy Sword, into the Sheath."

3. — CHRIST'S APOSTLES REPRODUCED HIS DOCTRINE OF RELIGIOUS LIBERTY, IN THEIR TEACHINGS.

"Now when the Rulers of the People, and Elders of Israel saw the boldness of Peter and John, and perceived that they were unlearned and ignorant men they commanded them not to speak at all, nor teach in the Name of Jesus. But Peter and John answered and said unto them — Whether it be right in the sight of God, to hearken to you more than unto God: judge ye.

"Then went the Captain with the officers, and brought them before the Council ; and the High Priest asked them, saying: Did not we straitly command you that ye should not teach in this Name? Then Peter and the Apostles answered, and said — We ought to obey God rather than men.

"Then stood there up one in the Council, a Pharisee, named Gamaliel, a Doctor of the Law — And said unto them; Ye men of Israel, take heed to yourselves what ye intend to do as touching these men. And now I say unto you, Refrain from these men, and let them alone : for, if this counsel, or this work be of men, it will come to naught ; but if it be of God, ye cannot overthrow it: lest haply ye be found to fight against

God. And to him they agreed; and when they had beaten the Apostles, they let them go.

"And when it was day, the Magistrates sent the Sergeants, saying: Let those men go. But Paul, said unto them; They have beaten us openly uncondemned, being Romans — and cast us into prison; and now do they thrust us out privily? Nay, verily; but let them come themselves and fetch us out.

"And the High Priest, Ananias, commanded them that stood by him, to smite him on the mouth. Then said Paul unto him, God shall smite thee, whited wall; for sittest thou to judge me after the Law; and commandest me to be smitten, contrary to the Law?

"I appeal unto Cæsar. But when Paul had appealed, to be reserved unto the judgment of Augustus, I commanded him to be kept, till I might send him to Cæsar. . . . But when the Jews spake against — I was constrained to appeal unto Cæsar; not that I had aught to accuse my Nation of.

"For Rulers are not a terror to good works but to evil. For he is the Minister of God to thee for good. For he beareth not the sword in vain; for he is the Minister of God, a revenger to wrath upon him that doeth evil. Wherefore we must needs be subject, not only for wrath, but also for conscience' sake. Render therefore to all their dues; tribute to whom tribute; custom to whom custom.

"Submit yourselves to every ordinance of Man for the Lord's Sake: Whether it be to the King Supreme; or to Governors, as unto them sent by him, for the punishment of evil-doers, and for the praise of them that do well. Honor all. Love the Brotherhood. Fear God. Honor the King.

"For the Kingdom of God, is not meat and drink, but righteousness, and peace, and joy, in the Holy Ghost."

Roger Williams, need not have been troubled about the verity of the Apostolic Succession — as he is said to have been ; slightly — had he but recalled the facts, that the like things, suffered by Christ and His Apostles — he also had in his day, for Christ's Sake, had encountered similar things.

4. — CHRIST'S CHURCH FOR MORE THAN 1,000 YEARS, WAS DANDLED IN THE LAP OF THE STATE — CHURCH OF CONSTANTINE BUT EVER THE FIRE OF APOSTOLIC ZEAL, CONTINUED TO BURN, ON THE ALTARS, OF RELIGIOUS LIBERTY.

The Lord's valiant ones, in the fearful times, from the 6th to the 13th centuries, who dared to contend for Liberty of Conscience ; usually did it, amid perils — *perils* — PERILS.

Among them was a New Testament Bishop — CLAUDE — of Turin, in the 9th century. He was shielded from violence, by the Sword of the Lord, and of Louis I. of France. Claude belabored the Man of Sin, in his preaching against the Corruptions, of the Popish Idolatry.

Another was PETER WALDO — a wealthy merchant of Lyons — in the 12th century, who with his fortune accomplished a great work in the translation of the Scriptures. Papal persecution scattered his followers.

JOHN WICKLIFFE — of Yorkshire Eng., in the 13th Century made the First Translation of the whole Bible into English. God covered his head with the Sword and Shield, of the Duke of Lancaster. His bones were dug up and burnt.

JOHN HUSS — of the true Apostolic Succession — was Chaplain to the Queen of Bohemia — Rector of the University of Prague, in the 15th century. By the treachery of the Emperor Sigismund, he was betrayed to the Popish Council of Constance — and burnt alive.

MARTIN LUTHER — a converted Romish priest — in 1520 publicly burnt the Pope's Bull. He broke the Yoke of the Papal Civil Power in Europe. He was protected from violence under God — by Frederick the Wise — Elector of Saxony.

ADMIRAL COLIGNY — a brave Officer in the French Army — a Tower of Strength to the persecuted Huguenots — was fatally shot by Chas. IX., instigated by his mother — Early in the St. Bartholomew Massacre; Aug. 24, 1572.

WILLIAM PRINCE OF ORANGE — utterly overwhelmed the Army of Philip II. of Spain — under the bloody duke of Alva — delivered the Netherlands from the Spanish Inquisition. Assassinated July 10, 1584 — because he was a Christian, and defended Religious Liberty.

JOHN SMYTH — a Puritan *Separatist* — fled from Eng. to Holland, the Land of Religious Liberty — returned with his followers to Eng., and entered the Conflict against King and Parliament — and obtained Toleration for Dissenters, in 1688.

ROGER WILLIAMS — completes the special list of the Apostolic Heroes, and Martyrs for the *Separation* of Church and State. The last Battle for Religious Liberty was fought in the First Meeting House, on the

Corner of Dunster and Mill Sts. — Cambridge, Mass.— Oct. 19, 1635, between ROGER WILLIAMS and the GENERALL COURT — of Mass. Bay. Like the Battle of Bunker Hill — The Royalists held the Fort — but the Victory, was with the Vanquished. The Court said to Roger Williams — " DEPETE — to return no more without license." They afterwards invited him back without license — to accept Concessions from them.

" In the Name of Our God will we Set up Banners." In our Historical Panorama Behold Certain Cities — not of " Refuge " — not of welcome, to " Him, who cometh in the Name of the Lord " — nor to His Followers, but of repulse; of the most repulsive sort. These Cities, which have thrust from them — " Freedom to Worship God " — of which Jesus Christ, was the Author and Teacher — are Jerusalem — Rome — Paris — London — Boston. The Authorities who did so — were, the Sanhedrim — the Inquisition — the Star-Chamber — and the Court. The Instruments; were the Crucifix — the Rack — the Block — the Massacre — and the Whipping-Post. The Parties; Pharisees — Papists — Prelates — and Puritans.

But a Great Change has come. In Providence — the City of Roger Williams — is his " *Refuge for all Persons distressed for Conscience.*" This City, was never "drunk with the Blood of the Saints of the Lord Jesus." In PROVIDENCE ; is a Pillow without thorns — where JESUS might " lay His head."

Hence the Doctrine of CHRIST — on RELIGIOUS LIBERTY — was the same Doctrine, taught by His Apostles — by His Martyrs — by His Reformers — and by His Faithful Servant — Roger Williams.

Therefore the Sentence of Banishment, by a Civil Court — still an offensive innuendo against his good name; and by implication; against all — who like him, back to the beginning of Christianity — have taught this Doctrine of CHRIST.

Yet it Stands; with ill grace on the RECORDS of the GREAT COMMONWEALTH of MASSACHUSETTS — in the 19th Century of our Christian Civilization : and cannot be too Soon — REVOKED !!!

## CHAPTER II.

*ROGER WILLIAMS, AND THE PURITANS, HAD EQUAL RIGHTS— TO LIFE, LIBERTY AND THE PURSUIT OF HAPPINESS, IN MASSACHUSETTS BAY— THEREFORE — THEIR SENTENCE OF BANISHMENT AGAINST HIM OUGHT TO BE*
REVOKED.

WE venture unfearfully to predict, that the Golden Age has so far advanced upon the World — as to warrant a new departure — in the treatment of the absorbing Subject, concerning ROGER WILLIAMS, and the PURITANS. During the long Period of 250 years, very slight progress has been made, towards a harmonious public Sentiment, on this Greatest of New England, Ecclesiastical Historical questions.

Two leading causes of this tardy progress have been; misapprehension; and misrepresentation. From these two fountains, flow always, and only, *bad* waters — which vitiate all other waters, into which they empty their foul Sediment. These morbid Fountains — must be clarified. Not by the method once suggested by the Puritans : that — "Nothing short of a Synod, is competent to compose the System" — but much nearer at hand — than any human device — for all troubled waters — is Christ's Panacea — " A *new* commandment I give unto you — that ye love one another, as I have loved you."

In this light — Posterity may discover that the Puritans, and Roger Williams were Brethren, in Christ — and our Brethren, also. "And be ye kind one to another, tender-hearted, forgiving one another, even as God for Christ's sake hath forgiven you."

1. — LET US SUM UP THE CAUSE OF RELIGIOUS LIBERTY BETWEEN THE PURITANS, AND ROGER WILLIAMS — AS PLAINTIFFS, AND DEFENDANT.

We recognize both litigants as having *Equal Rights*, in Massachusetts Bay. Here are two parties represented — having two methods, diverse the one from the other — and an issue, pending; of no small import; about which both are equally, "conscientiously and contentiously," intent, to the end. Documents, and Books, are multitudinous — in which crimination and recrimination, have darkened the moral Heavens, as with the smoke from the bottomless Pit — and all that has come forth of it, is little else than reiterated inculpation and exculpation: like "frogs from the mouth of the Dragon." From this method, let us depart to a better one — precipitate into these turbid waters, an unmeasured quantity of that — "Charity which suffereth long and is kind."

We implore Posterity, to read the history of the Puritans and Roger Williams — under the direction of the Guardian Angel, Charity; on the basis that both parties were equally, conscientious, honest and sincere; and take it for granted, that both sides in all their measures, honestly hoped, and intended; thereby to accomplish the greatest good, to the greatest number, for the "Glory of God and the good of His churche."

It is to evolve this thought, and to exhibit it most conspicuously, and impressively, to the end that it may be taken in; and held — that we have *so often*, if not too often — in PART FIRST — used the word "CONSCIENTIOUSNESS."

Now let us advance upon this hitherto, hopelessly entangled, and agitated question, of the "Puritans and Roger Williams" with "olive-branch," in hand, and with the great "mantle of charity," upon our shoulders, and if need be; "Go backwards and spread it all over" that portion of the history of our Glorious New England.

Here let us *weigh well* — the importance of taking this ground — Here, "Stand still and see the Salvation of God" — for one all-sufficient reason — viz — that — The Standard church History of New England, has not yet, been written, and never can be written, — until the case of Roger Williams and the Puritans is correctly apprehended, and unhesitatingly indorsed, and adopted. Altercation, and imprecation, are but execrable bombshells filled with Satanic hate, and set on fire of hell — and hence are very unfit instruments for any two or more detachments, of the Lord's army to have, and to hurl at each other.

Let us be thoroughly and finally persuaded, that there will be countless, endless, merciless, useless, antagonism, between the friends of Christ, and the friends of the Puritans, and Roger Williams — until we all go upon the "Mount of Transfiguration" — and in that glistening light, take the correct and comprehensive view of this subject — and like the Disciples, in the presence of our Glorified Redeemer, — say — " Lord, it is good for us to be here — for One is our Master, and all we are Brethren."

The General Court of the Puritans, in Massachusetts Bay was, in its origin, an authorized Company of Colonists, with a charter from the King, and power of self-government, and self-perpetuation ; and subject to the King only so far, as — "Not to make any Laws repugnant to those of Eng."

The Court was not subject to election by the people — and yet they admitted to their aid, representatives from the Towns, but over these the Court held supreme veto power. According to the conscientious Theory, of the Puritans; this almost irresponsible civil power, assumed to be guardians, both of Church and State.

Notwithstanding this supremacy of the Court, over the civil affairs of the Massachusetts Bay Colony the King, and public, understood that the charter ; which was silent on the Subject of Religion, was intended to make New England a safe retreat for all consciences — which could not conscientiously conform to the ceremonials of the Church of England. Gov. John Winthrop states — "It was for this, that many came over to us." And yet John Cotton, states — that; "By the Patent we have Power to erect such a Government of the Church, as is most agreeable to the Word."

Wherefore it seemed wise, or otherwise, to the Puritans, to adopt conscientiously, a Restrictive Policy, upon the subject of Religion. Here then we meet the difference between the two Policies, of the Puritans, and Roger Williams. The Puritans, adopted *Restriction* in Religious opinions — *by the help*, of the Civil Magistrate. Roger Williams' Policy, was ; Conscientious *Liberty* — in Religious opinions, *without the help*, of the Civil Magistrate. As he stated — " True Civility, and Christianity, may both flourish in a State, or Kingdom; notwithstanding the permission of diverse and contrary consciences, either of Jews or Gentiles."

Notice; as we proceed, the developments, side by side, of these two diverse systems, or sentiments. Between these two points, the tussle is joined, and the issue depends.

Here then we may imagine the Puritans — and Roger Williams — brought face to face, in Boston, early in 1631. Both about to enter upon a conflict, surpassing far, in its moral influence, all other strifes in the history of the world — or, combining all others in this; as the outcome has proved.

The Conscientiousness of the Puritans; and Roger Williams' conscientiousness, ignited at their first touch; upon the Question of Liberty; or Restriction; in matters of Religious opinions.

The First Puritan Church of Boston, were anxious to maintain meetings for public worship, and so in the absence of their pastor, invited Roger Williams to preach for them. He responded to their call, by asking them the Question — " Whether they were separated, or unseparated, from the church of England?" Finding them "unseparated," he declined the call. Here the case of Plaintiffs, and Defendant, is fully opened.

This involved a declaration of opinion by him, upon the relation of Church and State; THE GREAT QUESTION OF THE AGES. His conscientious opinion was — that — " Magistrates ought not to intermeddle, in Religious opinions."

They on the other hand were conscientious in the *opinion* that — "The Civil Government was right, in rigidly ruling in spiritual things — and right in compelling men as to their Church Polity." Roger Williams, conscientiously believed, that the Puritan Policy of Restriction, would strangle true Religion — the Puritans conscientiously believed that his Policy of Liberty, would leave Religion to run wild. Here were two parties with Consciences, equally Conscientious ; — Roger Williams, and his Friends ; and the Generall Court, and their Friends. Both sincere before God, — " for the greatest good to the Churche " of Our Lord Jesus Christ, and the Commonwealth.

What could be done? neither Plaintiffs nor Defendants, would yield their Conscientious opinions. The Court, held the civil jurisdiction, of Boston. Roger Williams was not a Member of the Court, nor Citizen voter, and could not be, unless he were a Member of the Boston Church, and their Call, he had declined. Yet, tho' not a Member of the Puritan Court, he had as good and free a right to inhabit in Massachusetts Bay, under the King's Charter ; as had Gov. Winthrop or any other Member of the Court.

But deliverance soon arose from this dilemma ; in a call from the Church in Salem, heartily given to Mr. Williams, to preach for them. With a view to accepting this call, he removed to Salem — as they were largely imbued with the Spirit of Separation.

Presently, however — Ex-Gov. Endicott, of Salem, was notified, that — " The Court having heard that the Church in Salem had invited Mr. Williams to be their Teacher, they hoped the Salem People would act cautiously and not proceed in this matter without due advisement — Inasmuch as Mr. Williams refused to fellowship the Boston Church ; and had broached novel Opinions — that the Magistrate should not intermeddle in religious matters.

Here again, it was found that the Court held the Situation, in Salem, as in all the Colony — and so by this friendly forewarning from the Court, against any possible danger from the novel opinions of their proposed Teacher — " The Church for the present forbore proceeding with him."

As Moses said — " Stand still and see the Salvation of God " — So in this case two doors, were closed against him ; but another was opened, and a call given — So that while "this interference prevented the ordination of Mr. Williams at Salem, he went to labor at Plymouth." This Church of the Pilgrims — were " SEPARATISTS of the SEPARATISTS," most "conscientiously" — While the Puritans, were "conscientiously, *unseparated.*" Here he remained, about 2 years — " Where he was friendly entertained, and his teaching well approved."

In 1633 Mr. Williams was again called to the Church in Salem, as assistant to pastor Skelton. Upon his return, it was noised abroad, that while in Plymouth he had, — at the request of Gov. Bradford — written a Treatise upon the King's Pattent — on which the Charters of the Colonies, were based. In this writing he took the high moral and equitable view — that if the lands of the Indians had been taken from them by force, in the name of the King — without justifiable consideration — then, neither the Pattent of the King was good; nor were their Charters — as against the Aborigines.

By request of the Boston Court he submitted his "Treatise" to them for inspection. Finding that it was attracting undue attention, he wrote to the Governor privately — and to him, and the Court officially — "that he had no intention of blazing abroad his views, on this — and offering his manuscript, or any part of it to be burnt." So the Gov. and Council, "agreed to pass it over — as its influence might not be so great as they had feared."

Before this time, while Mr. Williams was in Plymouth, the King had determined to take action against the Massachusetts Bay Charter — because of ordinances passed by the Boston Court, which he considered — "repugnant to the Laws of Eng." The Court not knowing what might come, took measures to sustain their authority, in case their Charter, was removed.

One of the measures, was, what they called, "The Resident's Oath." To this Roger Williams took no exception, as a civil measure. But he took issue with it, as a *civil* interference, in matters of conscience. He maintained that it is a PREROGATIVE of CHRIST — to have His Office Established by "OATH." Therefore — "Christ's Oath, should not be required to establish a Civill Office. An Oath — is a part of God's Worship — hence Church-Members, ought not to use God's Worship, to induct men into Civill Office — nor, can carnall men, use God's worship — to put mortall men in office."

Popular opinion was with Mr. Williams — "The people being many of them, much taken with apprehensions of his godliness, many especially of devout women, did embrace his opinions." John Cotton — states — "His positions were so well taken, as to threaten the authorities with serious embarrassment, and to force the Court to retrace their steps, and desist from that proceeding." Behold these Plaintiffs — and Defendant!

In the meantime Mr. Skelton, died Aug. 12, 1634. Whereupon the Court, knowing the attachment of the People of Salem, for Mr. Williams—and perhaps conscientiously "taken with something more than apprehensions of his godliness;" we learn that — "the Government again renewed their 'Advice' to the church at Salem, not to call him to office, but to forbear a thing of such evil consequence." Hence with their former advice, "renewed," there were two conscientious inhibitions from the Court hanging over the Salem People — forbidding them to ordain him as their Pastor.

Just at this critical juncture of affairs — while the Court had before their eyes, respect for the popular favor towards the minister at Salem — the People so far presumed upon the Conscientious Christian Clemency of the Court — that — "about May — June 1635, they conscientiously proceeded, to complete his thus far prospective relation to them, and ordained him as their Pastor."

Whereupon — Mr. Williams was presently cited; "to appear at the next Session of the Generall Court, on July 18 — to answer to complaints against him." Among these was the "head and front of his offending" — that — "The Magistrate should not intermeddle in matters of the First Table." At this Court, earnest debate, reigned Supreme. We can easily imagine Roger Williams, nothing daunted before the "face of clay" — was "Conscientiously Contentious" — for *Liberty* in Religion — while the undismayed Puritan Court — was "Conscientiously Contentious" — for civil *Restriction* in Religion.

The Court Conscientiously judged Mr. Williams' "opinions, to be erroneous and very dangerous" — and requested him and the Salem Church, to reconsider the whole matter until the next General Court in 8 weeks — with the understanding, that; "unless the causes of complaint should by that time be removed, the Court must be expected to take some final action thereon." The Elders also, "Conscientiously" advising the Court — "That he who should obstinately maintain such opinions (whereby a church might run into heresy, apostacy, or tyranny, and yet the Civil Magistrate could not intermedde,) was to be removed, and that the other churches ought to request the Magistrates so to do."

At this session of the Court, the People of Salem presented a petition, for the *Papers*, conveying to the Town a certain piece of Land — belonging to the town. But the Court "conscientiously" declined to grant the papers — until Salem People should make amends — for "Contempt of Authority" in ordaining Mr. Williams as their Pastor — contrary to the double Advice — of the Court — "not to do a thing of such ill Consequence."

Whereupon, Mr. Williams conscientiously brought this refusal of the Court, to grant those papers — to the attention of the Church in Salem — as a malfeasance in their office as Magistrates — and hence a moral delinquency, in their conduct, as Church-Members! The church and Pastor resolved at once to write letters to the churches of which the Magistrates were members, — asking them to deal with them by way of Admonition ; not for a civil misdeed — but as an act, unworthy of their standing in the Christian Church.

This climax created a conscientious consternation, in the Court, and churches of the entire Colony ! !

It was discovered " in the twinkling of an eye," that the Church and Pastor of Salem had gained an invincible, damaging "flank-movement" — on the Court, and the other churches. The Elders had conscientiously advised the other churches, "to ask the Magistrates to remove Roger Williams, for his opinions — and now the churches are asked to deal with the Magistrates, for their derelictions. The two horns of the dilemma were pointedly presented — Either the Magistrates must confess their blameworthy fault upon Admonition — or be subjected to Church Discipline. If they declined to recognize the authority of the church, over delinquent members — then the Magistrates would be chargeable with "Contempt of Divine Authority" — a greater offence, than that with which they were charging Roger Williams.

Christ's Rule is — "If they hear not the Church, let them be as a heathen man and a publican." Hence the Magistrates found themselves, in the Church trap of their own. This gave the Magistrates a Capital opportunity to show Roger Williams, the Grace of respect for "authority" — by submitting to their own Ecclesiastical Authority — themselves — while they wished him, to respect, Civil Authority, over the Church.

But more than this — if the Magistrates were to take their chances on excommunication — according to their Theocratic System, that would deprive them of Church-Membership — and without that, they would lose Citizenship — without Citizenship they could not be Magistrates — and that would leave as many Vacant Seats, in the General Court as there were contumacious Magistrates, who would not be Admonished! evidently, something must be done in a hurry.

In order to make an escape from this tight place, it was "conscientiously" resolved by the Elders, and the Court to inaugurate a "counter-labor; and retort in Kind." This was done by adroitly persuading a small major part of the Salem Church, to disapprove the matter of sending out the "Admonitory letters," about the Magistrates; and then Conscientiously, bring an Admonitory complaint, against their pastor, and so make him appear to be in the wrong, for suggesting Admonition against the Magistrates, for the wrong they had actually done against the Town. Through this "Breach in Zion," the Elders and Magistrates, made their escape.

Roger Williams; finding that a small major part of the church — had conscientiously by means wise or otherwise been induced to leave him alone, to the tender mercies of the Elders and the Court — Conscientiously, wrote them a farewell Letter as Pastor. In this letter he bore witness with great vehemence of Soul; "against the grievous wrong, of Magistrates, intermeddling with Religious opinions — and that the breath of the Lord Jesus was sounding forth in him — (a poor despised ram's-horn,) the blast, which in His own holy Season, should cast down the strength and confidence of all these inventions of men, in worshipping of the true and Living God."

The Session of the Court was at hand, when — "The Causes of Complaint, if not removed — the Court must take final action." And now the Court was Conscientiously ready for business — Roger Williams "was demanded, whether he were prepared to give satisfaction to the Court in these matters?" In response he no doubt in his "Conscientiously *Contentious*" manner, "Justified the Admonitory Letters, about the Magistrates — and maintained all his opinions — and declared he was not only ready to be bound, and banished, but to die in New England, for most Holy Truth of God in Christ Jesus."

The charges in the indictment were ready. We note only the one which contained the Head and front of his offending — that — "The Civil Magistrate's power extends only to the Bodies and Goods, and outward state of men — that the Magistrate ought not to punish the breach of the First Table, except when the Civil Peace, shall be endangered."

Whereupon the Court in the same "Conscientiously Contentious" Spirit — as usual — On October 19, 1635, passed the Following Sentence — All the Ministers in the Bay — "Save one" — approving the Sentence. —

"Whereas Mr. Roger Williams, one of the Elders of the Church of Salem, hath broached and dyvulged dyvers newe and dangerous opinions, against the authority of Magistrates, as also writt lres of defamacon, both of Magistrates and Churches here, and that before any onviction, and yet mainctaineth the same without retraccon — It is therefore ordered, that the said Mr. Williams shall depete out of this jurisdiccon, within sixe weekes nowe nexte ensuing; wch if hee neglect to pforme, it shalbe lawfull for the Gour and two of the Magistrates, to send him to some place out of this jurisdiccon, not to returne any more, without licence from the Court."

These "Sixe Weeks"— having more than expired, Capt. Underhill was Conscientiously ordered to take a force of men, in a pinnace — and proceed by way of Marblehead to Salem, and apprehend Mr. Williams, and place him on board a vessel lying at Nantasket, to be shipped to Eng. While this "argonautic expedition" was preparing our Conscientious Gov. John Winthrop — had *privately* given Mr. Williams, a "hint from God"— to "arise and flee into the country of the Narrohigansetts — free from English Pattents." When the dutiful Capt. Underhill came to Salem — our Brother Williams, had been 3 days gone!

Here we see the immediate issue, of the World-renowned conflict between Roger Williams — and the Puritans of Massachusetts Bay. The definite point of its beginning was when he declined the Call of the Boston Church — about Mar. 1631 — until his flight from Salem, in Jan. 1636 — covering a period of about 5 yrs. 10 mos.

As Plaintiffs, and Defendant — let us contrast the idiomatic methods; of the Puritans — and Roger Williams, and note — when, "weighed in the balances, if either is found wanting." John Quincy Adams' phrase about Roger Williams, as " Conscientiously Contentious " — suggested to me the query — whether or no — the Puritans were not also — "Conscientiously Contentious?" They ought to have been, if they contended at all. "Contending earnestly for the faith," is commended in the Scriptures. Whether Mr. Adams intended this as a compliment to Mr. Williams, or not; it is a Compliment, of the highest order — and we gladly place the methods of Roger Williams, and the Puritans in opposite sides of the scales; as equally "Conscientiously Contentious." This view also suggested the thought of harmonizing this great question — by extending to each of them, Cordially and fully — the "Olive Branch — and the Mantle of Charity."

With this view we can look upon the methods of both, with equal contemplation. If Mr. Williams did at any time blaze away with too much "Conscientious" FIRE — the Puritans no doubt, could match him, with an equal amount of "Conscientious" IRE. If he overflowed, with too much STENTORIAN; they could balance him, with the PRETORIAN. If he was too free to EULOGIZE — they by "ereccon of hands" — could as freely, STIGMATIZE. If he used too much EDGE — they could dull it, with the SLEDGE. If he was the "ARCH-INDIVIDUALIST" — they could pose, as "ARCH-IMPERIALISTS." If he was bound to STAY — they could bounce him AWAY. If he was PUGNACIOUS — they could be CONTUMACIOUS. If he used PRESUMPTION — it would meet PROSCRIPTION.

Earnest men of God they were, on both sides, "men after God's own heart," they were indeed. No grander men, or better men, and women; ever were the Founders of any Country, or Nation, than our New England Forefathers — who first settled, at Plymouth

Bay — and Massachusetts Bay — and Narrohigansett Bay.

If the time has not fully come for this charitable view to be taken, it hastens — and may it speed on rapidly — and let our prayer be — "Thy Kingdom come."

We prefer to look upon the Puritans — and Roger Williams, as both "Conscientiously Contentious" — Plaintiffs — and Defendant — and extend to both — the "Branch and the Mantle."

2. — ROGER WILLIAMS — AND THE PURITANS WERE MUTUALLY CORDIAL — HOLDING EACH OTHER IN HIGH ESTEEM — FOR CHRIST'S SAKE.

For this reason ; their *Sentence ;* passed in a heated term — by many of them afterwards deeply regretted ; should be by *Special Act* — Revoked by Posterity — wrapped in the "Mantle of Charity" — and laid in The Sepulchre.

Notwithstanding the wide divergence — and sharply distinguished lines of Separate Policies, between these conscientious contest-ants, and Protest-ants — they each regarded the other as Magnificent Opponents — thereby adding dignity to the contest — as never more so — than when "Greek meets Greek."

The Puritans stood in the Conflict with their backs, towards the church of England, yet inclined toward her Church and State Polity, in a greatly modified form — conscientiously seeking in that way, to do the very best thing for the Church and Posterity.

Roger Williams, fronting the other way, like Paul, who "withstood Peter to his face" — pointed out to his Puritan contemporaries, a more excellent way. Each found the other, invulnerable, invincible, and incorruptible: and to their dying days, held each other in esteem, and affection, for Christ's sake, and for each other's sake.

Professor Diman, quotes Lowell — " Let me premise that there were two men above all others for whom our respect is heightened by their letters — the elder John Winthrop, and Roger Williams." A recent Biographer of Milton, terms Mr. Williams — " A picturesque figure forever — in Early American history, and no man of that Age deserves more attention. . . . So winning that, while still a youth he so gained upon the regard of Sir Edward Coke, the greatest Master of English Law; that he took a deep interest in his education, and affectionately addressed him as '*my Son.*' It is interesting to know that the Founder of Rhode Island, taught that — ' *The Sovereign Power of all Civil authority, is in the People* ' — and that he had the honor of the personal friendship, of the illustrious Judge, who was sent to the Tower, for resisting the encroachments of arbitrary power." If the Puritan Forefathers, were worthy — *and they were* — Roger Williams was their Peer.

a. The Puritans Esteemed Roger Williams.

Gov. John Winthrop, notes his arrival, at Boston — Feb. 15, 1631 — as, "a godly minister " — (with his wife Mary), tho' he was a fugitive from bishop Laud — of the King's Church.

Of a visit with others, to Plymouth, Gov. Winthrop writes — "On the Lord's Day, in the afternoon — Mr. Roger Williams, propounded a question; to which Mr.

Ralph Smith, the pastor, spoke briefly; then Mr. Williams, prophesied; then Gov. Bradford of Plymouth spoke; after him, Elder Brewster; then the Gov. (Winthrop) of Mass. Bay spoke; last Mr. Wilson, pastor of Boston spoke. It was his pulpit Mr. Williams declined to occupy.

Gov. Bradford, writes — "Mr. Roger Williams, (a man godly and zealous, having many precious parts), came over first to Mass. Bay — and came hither, (where he was friendly entertained, according to their poor abilitie). After a time was admitted a Member of the Church; and his teaching well approved; for ye benefite whereof I still bless God; and am thankful to him even for his sharpest admonitions and reproufs."

Elder Brewster — " Professed he feared Mr. Williams, would run the same course of rigid Separation, and Anabaptistry, as did Mr. John Smyth, of Amsterdam." Mr. Smyth and his church, went back to England, and challenged King and Parliament for Religious Liberty — the Pilgrims came to Plymouth.

After two years the Church at Salem recalled him, from Plymouth — as their Teacher — " having abated none of their affection for him while away."

"The Gov. and Council of Boston, passed over his Treatise on the Pattent, as its influence might not be so great as they had feared."

Mr. John Cotton, writes — " For his preaching on the King's Pattent — I presented with the consent of my fellow Elders, and Brethren — a Serious excuse to the Magistrates, that his course did rather spring from Scruples of Conscience, than from Seditious Principle."

Mr. Williams' popularity, for his Opinions, on the

"Resident's Oath" — ran so high in Salem, as to hold the Generall court in check for a time — many devout Women adopting his Opinions. Such was the popular enthusiasm of the people of Salem — presuming that the Court had left the field ; they conscientiously ventured to ordain him as their pastor.

Ex-Gov. Endicott's conscientious esteem for Mr. Williams, was so pronounced, that it emboldened him to extemporize a vehement animadversion, upon the action of the Court, in summoning the Church and pastor to answer for "Contempt of Authority," in the ordination of him as pastor. Altho' one of the Assistants of the Court, and a prominent citizen in Salem — Mr. Endicott, received a sharp reprimand from the Court, for his impromptu ebullition.

After getting at his case, very conscientiously, *perhaps* prayerfully, carefully, and deliberately — and Mr. Williams had perhaps, "Conscientiously contentiously" — declared, he would abate none of his Opinions — nor ask clemency — rather than proceed at once — they *offered* him a month, for reflection, and to prepare a defence. This offer he promptly declined ; in face of Gov. — Deputies — Assistants — and Magistrates — and Elders — and proposed to answer, then. Yet an adjournment of the Court was taken for a night's rest, and reflection. Perhaps, on account of the *not* undistinguished, "Prisoner at the Barr."

Further delay being perilous, promptly on the next morning Oct. 19, 1635 — the Court conscientiously passed *Sentence*, in which all the ministers — "save one" — concurred — as for their own advice. This "save one" — proved to be the Great John Cotton —

"not the least part of N.E." who conscientiously, withdrew from the Court Room, "just at the moment, of Sentence-passing" — and so did not concur, with the rest of the Elders and whether out of self-respect — or respect for the Court — or respect for Mr. Williams — or respect for Posterity — depends.

Mr. Cotton, afterwards wrote to Mr. Williams — "Let not any prejudice against my person (I beseech you) forestall either your affection, or judgment, as if I had hastened forward the Sentence of your civill Banishment; for what was done by the Magistrates, in that kinde, was neither done by my counsell nor consent." This statement would seem to be made, out of respect to Mr. Williams.

We are informed — that — "Towards Mr. Williams, as a Christian, and Minister, there was a General Sentiment of respect." . . . "It is due to the principal actors in these scenes, to record the fact, of which ample evidence exists, that personal animosity, had little if any share, in producing his Sentence of Banishment." No wonder the Court hesitated.

Neal's History states — that — "That the Sentence of Banishment against Mr. Williams being read, the whole Town of Salem was in an uproar; for such was his Popularity — and such the Compassion of the People . . . that he would have carried off the greatest part of the inhabitants of the Town; if the Ministers of Boston had not interposed."

It is a marked, and most extraordinary display of respect and friendship for Mr. Williams, that Gov. Winthrop, *privately* gave him the alarm, to give Capt. Underhill the slip — and so elude the toils of the Boston Magistrates.

In their confidential business matters, we find Prudence Island in the Narrohigansett Bay — was purchased by Roger Williams, of Canonicus, for Gov. Winthrop.

In view of Mr. Williams' services in preventing; by his personal, persistent, heroic, "Conscientiously contentious," efforts; the massacre of the English Colonists, by the Pequots, and their allies — "Gov. Winthrop, and many worthy gentlemen in his Council and out of it, were anxious to recall him; REVOKE his *Sentence;* and show him some distinctive tokens of regard." Will the Gov. and Council of Massachusetts of over 250 years afterwards, rise to the dignity, of carrying out Gov. Winthrop's charitable suggestion — for what Roger Williams has done for our Nation — and the World?

Mr. Williams writes how he and Ousamaquin, (Massasoit), had been great friends while at Plymouth. "I was known by all the Wampanoags, and Narrohigansetts, to be a public Speaker at Plymouth, and Salem — and therefore with them, held as a Sachem."

Again we find — "they had banished one Master Roger Williams, a man of good report, both for life and doctrine (even amongst themselves), for dissenting from them in some points of their Church Government."

Further — "This child of Light, Roger Williams — an Eminent Preacher, noted for Piety in his life and conversation." . . . "Esteem such for their works' sake." "He was devout, the people many of them, being much taken with apprehension of his godliness."

Besides — "Roger Williams was personally most likeable, sincere to the core, and of a rich, glowing peculiarly affectionate nature, which yearned even towards those from whom he differed publicly, and won their esteem, in return."

And again — "There can be no doubt, that Mr. Williams, the earnest defender of the Doctrine of Religious Liberty, and its zealous and successful advocate — did much to favor and further it, in connection with civil affairs, in Rhode Island."

b. Roger Williams' Esteem for his Puritan Contemporaries.

We shall not find him wanting in responsive appreciation of the virtues of those who could appreciate him.

Note here once for all; if these testimonials are reliable, then any characterization of him that is contradictory to all this evidence — Posterity has a right, to ask for the motive, for such "very erroneous" — malediction.

In his letter to Mrs. Sadleir, daughter of Sir Edward Coke — he writes — "Truly it was as bitter as death to me when bishop Laud pursued me out of this land, and my conscience was persuaded against the National Church, and ceremonies, and bishops, beyond the conscience of your dear Father — when I rode Windsor way, to take Ship — and saw Stoke House, where the blessed man was; and durst not acquaint him with my conscience and my flight."

In a letter to Mr. John Cotton, Jr. — "Being unanimously chosen Teacher at Boston, before your *dear* Father came — divers years." . . .

In writing of his Banishment, Mr. Williams has it — "One of the most eminent Magistrates — the Chief Judge in Court — that *heavenly man* Mr. Haynes —

Governor of Connecticut — pronounced the Sentence of my long Banishment, against me at Cambridge." . . .

In writing of his life-long friend, Mr. Williams, has it — "That *ever-honored* Gov., Mr. John Winthrop privately wrote me to steer my course to the Narrohigansett — Bay and Indians." . . . [Note — As there is a beautiful statue of "ye Govorneur John Winthrop," at the head of Cornhill — Boston — So may there not be found some appropriate place, for a like statue of his life-long friend Roger Williams — in Boston?]

In writing to Mr. Endicott, of his Banishment — Mr. Williams states — " Let it not be offensive in your eyes — that I single out the Point — That the civill Magistrates; dealing in matters of Conscience and Religion, and also for hunting, and persecuting any, for *any* matter merely Spirituall, and Religious."

Within a year after his Banishment — we find him writing to Mr. Winthrop — " Much honored Sir; the frequent experience of your loving care, ready and open toward me (in what your conscience hath permitted), as also of that excellent spirit of wisdome and prudence, wherewith the Father of Light hath endued you, emboldened me to request of you a word of private advise. . . .

" I therefore now thankfully acknowledge your wisedome and gentleness in receiving so lovingly my late lines." . . .

Again — " Deare Sir — (Notwithstanding our *differences* concerning the worship of God, and the Ordinances ministered by Antichrist's power), you have bene alwayes pleased lovingly to answer my boldnes in civil things; let me once more find favor in your eyes." . . .

In Mr. Williams' later writings we find.

"This [Separation] (as before I hinted) was the Heavenly Principle, of those many precious Souls, and Gallant Worthies, the Leaders and Corner-Stones of these New England Colonies, viz. : They desired to worship God in purity according to those perswasions in their Consciences, which they believed God had lighted up. They desired such for their fellow-Worshippers, as they (upon a Christian account) could have evidence, that to be true and real Worshippers of God in Spirit and Truth also. And there was a large effusion of the Holy Spirit of God, upon so many precious Leaders and Followers, who ventured their All to New England upon many Heavenly Grounds:—

1. The enjoyment of God according to their consciences.

2. For holding out Light to Americans.

3. For advancing of the English Name and Plantations.

These three Ends the Most High and Holy God hath graciously helpt His poor Protestants in a Wilderness to Endeavor to promote." . . .

The Names and fame of the Puritan Fathers, and of Roger Williams, would have been much more savory in the History of New England — than now — had there been fewer volunteer defamers' pens, scribbling scandal. Roger Williams esteemed the Puritans of Massachusetts Bay much more than some who have lived 250 years since, who didn't know them so well as he did. Gov. John Winthrop had a much higher opinion of Roger Williams, than some off-hand Books of the 19th Century.

3. — LET POSTERITY ASSUME TOWARDS ROGER WILLIAMS AND THE PURITANS THE MOST LIBERAL AND CORDIAL USE OF THE "OLIVE BRANCH AND THE MANTLE OF CHARITY."

We have already found the Puritans and Roger Williams, historically and conscientiously arrayed, as Plaintiffs and Defendant; on opposite sides, of the great Question of the Ages.

We are happy also to find them — not enemies to each other — and both friends of the same cause, of the Blessed God — only differing as to the best way to make it the most permanent, and its blessing the most far-reaching.

With this — *new view;* we propose to embalm them in our Memories, as the friends of each other — and of all mankind, in the bonds of that " Charity, which hopeth all things — believeth all things — and thinketh no evil."

No one can fail to see, that the main point at issue between these two Policies was, *Liberty* in Religion; without the Magistrate — the other *Restriction* in Religion ; by the Magistrate. Both these policies were designed, by each of their advocates to conserve the best interests of the Church and the State — One by a Union, of Church and State — and the other by a Separation, of Church and State.

The Theocracy of the Puritans — aimed to shun the monstrosity of the State and Church of the Dark Ages — and only contemplated the promotion of Evangelical Religion, by the assistance of the Civil Power, to discourage the influx of " erroneous, and very dangerous opinions"—and so effectually, "pull up the tares, the enemy might sow among the wheat."

The Massachusetts Bay Theocracy: was the last experiment, with Constantinianism: extending from A.D. 300 — and was the mildest form of the *heresy;* and the final effort, to "gather grapes from thorns, or figs from thistles."

There was a mistake in the Theocracy, as we can see now — but it was made Conscientiously — and after it was adopted was Conscientiously adhered to — and — was as conscientiously abandoned — as fast as light broke in — until it died like a wave along the shore. That mistake did not seek to compel men by the civil power — to believe unto Salvation, but was used to check the influx of heresy — and impart vigor to discipline.

The kind of Conscience we suppose the Puritans and Mr. Williams to have had — was — A Christ-like *conscience* — that loves God supremely — and our neighbor as ourselves. Also a good moral conscience — one that spontaneously, and lovingly, intends to do whatever is according to the Golden Rule. A good conscience, even — may chance, without malicious intent — thro' mistake — to do what is not, according to the Golden Rule. Such may have been the weak point in the Puritan Policy. All Persons who Conscientiously intend, and spontaneously, and lovingly, do, what is according to the Golden Rule — are entitled to all the protection of the Civil Law — against all violence, to person, and estate — and have the inalienable right of Self-defence. All persons who under plea of conscientiousness — habitually persist in doing what is contrary to the Golden Rule — are to be judged, as intentionally, contumacious enemies of mankind, — and should be restrained by the Civil Law.

The Puritans complained of Roger Williams, as mainly offensive to them — because of his excessive vehemence — in advocating his opinions — while with the same vehemence, they confronted him. Instead of resting the conclusions of their debates with him, on the merits of the arguments — or of the case — they cautiously and precautiously — and of course Conscientiously — (if not, contumaciously) kept the Magistrate, near at hand, lest there be "Contempt of Court" — and all be lost. In this way Gov. Endicott, for conscientiously and vehemently defending the Church at Salem, for ordaining Mr. Williams, was conscientiously and vehemently, by "ereccon of hands," committed. The Magistrates' hand tipt the scale of debate. So, when Roger Williams was before the Court, and by "argument conscientiously defended all his opinions; and could not by argument, be reduced from any of his errors" — but the Magistrates, and all the Ministers "Save one" — reduced him — to Banishment. Later on Mr. Gould, who *conscientiously* founded the first Baptist Church of Boston, was conscientiously committed.

If all were *conscientious* — wave toward them the "Olive Branch" — and spread over them the "Mantle of Charity." If otherwise — let Cotton Mather — the Puritan Historian — pronounce the imprecation — "Cursed be the OBSOLETE BLUNDER of Persecution for conscience." If they were Conscientious — then must the Sentence Bounce. The Court had a moral right, to think his opinions — "Erroneous, and very dangerous" — in their opinion — but no conscientiousness of the Court, can *justify* them; in the opinion of Posterity — for violating the Golden Rule, by Banishing Roger Williams, for his opinions. We allow their sentence to be a Conscientious, *mistake;* and spread over it the "Mantle." Whoever therefore justifies the Sentence to Banishment — makes it a Contumacious Crime!

For e.g.; a Loyal trustworthy General — a veritable Havelock — following his best judgment, Conscientiously issues an Order for Battle: —

> "Charge, Chester, charge —
> And into the mouth of hell
> Rides the Six hundred."

The order of said General is afterwards adjudged a very great military *mistake* — but, as it was "conscientiously given — he is not held for murder — of his men. Killing in Self-defence is justified in Law — Killing in malice — is murder. So is the Banishment of Roger Williams — if it were a "*quere*" — if it were a conscientious, *mistake* — hold out to it the "*Branch;*" Cover it with the "*Mantle.*" But if either — Roger Williams, or the Puritans — were Conscientiously contumacious — the "Olive Branch — and Mantle" — will need to "lie on the table."

By this same rule are we to reconcile ourselves towards each other as Christian Churches, of different denominations. It is only an "Obsolete Blunder" — to pretend that we are all, right — because we conscientiously — differ. If two parties differ widely — and conscientiously — and contentiously, even — if *one* be right — the *other* must be wrong — perchance, *both* may be wrong. The plea of conscientiousness, on both sides, does not rectify the difference. Still it is our duty to be Charitable, towards each other — altho' we cannot walk together in Church Fellowship. What is to be done? Simply bear with each other, because there is between us a conscientious, *mistake*. It is thus we must look upon Roger Williams, and the Puritans. Be charitable towards their conscientious differences.

Few are the persons in all the walks of life, but will claim to be conscientious in what they do. And yet how few but look upon others, and wonder, what kind of a conscience it is, that lies behind their lives! Matrimonial infelicities, are all based on a "just cause." (?) It is well to live in a land, and in an Age, when no power in Church, nor in State — in Court, nor in Camp — is either authorized; or allowed, to assume, judgment upon others' opinions — especially conscientious, religious opinions.

Hence as we have found — Roger Williams, and the Puritans were Equals before the Law — with equal rights to life — liberty — and happiness — and to inhabit in Massachusetts Bay — and equally conscientious, in their Religious opinions — and inasmuch as their Sentence of Banishment against him, makes them appear to be unequals — it is imperative, to remove that inequality; that their Sentence be REVOKED. For while we grant, that their Sentence, was a conscientious *mistake* — yet the *act* involved in the *mistake*, when done in malice is a *crime;* for it is assuredly a violation of Christ's Golden Rule. It was for their malice in it, that Peter said to the Jews — "Ye have taken Jesus of Nazareth, and by wicked hands have crucified and slain."

The Golden Rule, requires the correction, of a mistake; under however much conscientiousness made; just as promptly, when it is discovered to be a *mistake* — as it does, the correction of a trespass. The refusal to correct a conscientious *mistake*, as far as may be, when it is revealed as such — turns it into a contumacious trespass. If therefore; Roger Williams, or the Puritans, made any conscientious *mistakes*, and "fell on Sleep," before they became aware of their deflection; cover them, with the great "Mantle."

But the Apologist, who rises 200 years, or any number of years, afterward, and justifies the Puritans in their treatment of Roger Williams; as a righteous vindictiveness of the Court, on him; for his "conscientious contentiousness;" upsets everything. He makes Roger Williams, a disturber of the civil peace without cause — and makes the Puritans' conscientiousness, doubtful; and their act of Banishment against him, one of contumacious vindictiveness. Of this, thank the Lord, we've had enough, from; apologists.

It is good luck for modern scribblers about the Puritans that they did not live in those days; for they, and Roger Williams tho't more of each other, than they would of such men as busy themselves in representing either Roger Williams, or the Puritans — "as sinners above all men." And even in our own day such writers might well hide their diminished heads — when we recall the noble words of the Hon. R. C. Winthrop, now living — a lineal descendant of "ye noble Governour" — in his Oration at the 250th anniversary of the

Landing of the Pilgrims, delivered at Plymouth, Mass., 1870.

"I have an hereditary disposition, to be not only just, but tender toward his memory, for Williams and the Winthrops, of old, in spite of all differences, were most loving friends, from first to last. I would palliate not a particle of the persecution, or cruelty, which he suffered — from whatever source it came." . . .

In the very same line, of the foregoing words of Hon. R. C. Winthrop — For the Puritans' sake, for Christianity's sake, for humanity's sake — we venture — we presume — yea, we unhesitatingly, and conscientiously — and insistently ; claim, the right to use the Branch and Mantle of Christ's Charity, to be spread over all the conscientious *mistakes*, of the Puritan Fathers, whatever they were ; committed without malice ; so far as they were without malice. But let it be remembered, that the conscientious *mistakes* of the Puritans, or of Roger Williams, are not an inheritance, to Posterity, to be perpetuated, nor reperpetrated, cherished, nor even to be apologized for, separate, from conscientiousness. A *mistake* made thro' conscientiousness, or ignorance, is not a *crime*, in him who makes it — and yet that same act perpetrated with *malicious* intent, is a *crime*.

Hence the Generall Court of Mass. Bay, in 1635, Banished Roger Williams for his Religious opinions, thro' a conscientious *mistake* — and are not held for crime, in so doing — but if the General Court of Massachusetts should Banish a man out of *"ye lymitts"* — in 1890 — for his Religious opinions — they would be held for crime!

"The times of that ignorance God winked at — but now," etc. . . .

Therefore we fancy we have reached the immovable conclusion — that the Puritans — and Roger Williams, were Equals in their God given rights to life — liberty — and the pursuit of happiness — equally to be respected for their devout Christian *Conscientiousness* — equally entitled to the full benefits of the "Olive Branch" — and of Christ's "Mantle of Charity," for all their conscientious *mistakes* — and equally to be honored for their undiminished esteem for each other — while engaged on opposite sides — in working out the solution of the great, momentous, imperishable problems of Civil and Religious Liberty — in the Kingdoms of Christ and Cæsar — for the good of the whole world!!

## CHAPTER III.

*THE DOCTRINE OF RELIGIOUS LIBERTY AS ADVO-
CATED BY ROGER WILLIAMS, SURVIVES:—WHILE
THE THEOCRATIC SYSTEM OF THE PURITANS HAS
DISSOLVED AWAY, THEREFORE, THEIR SENTENCE OF
BANISHMENT AGAINST HIM, OUGHT TO BE*

REVOKED.

In this matter we may find an illustrious example of the "Survival of the Fittest." At least it survives. Nothing succeeds like success.

We will now stroll into Chapter III., to discover as we may — the success or failure, in public opinion, of the two Policies — as advocated, by the Puritans, *versus*, Roger Williams. It is said ; "a Town is a hard thing to fight." Public opinion —*vox populi*— is a mighty Town. If public opinion, is fortunate enough to get on the Lord's side —*vox Dei*— then, it is an Almighty Town. One with the Lord is the majority. "Who is on the Lord's ? Let him come to me."

The direct issue between Roger Williams and the Puritans — in Massachusetts Bay — culminated in his Banishment from "ye lymitts."

After the decision of the General Court of the Bay, on his case — the question involved, then went to the World. That "Almighty Town." Has the verdict of the "Town " — indorsed, or reversed, that of the Court?

If either of them proposed a system ; of Church and

State — or State and Church — or the Church by itself — and the State by itself — if either system, had its Foundation in the sand — and its walls made of hay, or wood — or stubble — or if it were as the "Colossus," of Rhodes — or an "Image of Gold, of Silver, of Brass, of Iron, and of Clay" — standing with one foot on "Land's End" — and one on "Cape Ann;" "Every man's work must be tried, so as by Fire."

If in our search for the "increase, or decrease" — of the two Policies ; of the Puritans — and Roger Williams — we find either of them — "Conscientiously Contentious" — in the RIGHT — or, either of them — "Conscientiously Contentious" in a MISTAKE — the result, can be prognosticated, if it be not predestinated. We have already committed ourselves to the Charitable Conclusion ; that neither of them intended to do anything, Criminally wrong. But inasmuch as their Theories, differed widely — and inasmuch as the practical results of their Theories differ still more widely — it is to be feared — that somewhere, somehow, somebody — has made a *mistake.*

A. The Decline and Fall of the Puritan Theocracy — was Predestinated, upon the conscientious mistakes of its Friends.

1. It appears now, that it must have been a *conscientious mistake* — in the Puritans, to accept a Charter, for their Colony, from King Charles I. — without any clause in it, concerning liberty, or Conformity, in Religion — and then to provide, in their System of Theocracy — for the Magistrate — and Court, to intermeddle in matters of Conscience and Religion.

2. It was a *mistake* — however conscientious — for

the Puritans in England to bind Mr. Ralph Smith, because he was a "Separatist"—by promise; not to preach in Massachusetts Bay—on his arrival there—without permission from Gov. Endicott—and then to send an order, by the same ship, in which Smith came, to Gov. Endicott—"not to permit him to remain in 'ye lymitts.'"

3. It looks now like a great *mistake*, in Gov. Endicott, to Ship the Brownes home; for "Separating" from the Church at Salem, and setting up Church of England Service. The more, as the Brownes were persons of consequence; Assistants in the Gov.'s Council; and above all to ship back members of the King's Church, after the King had given them a Charter, silent, on liberty in religion. This was setting the Brownes free in England to stir up "repugnance," in the mind of the King—towards the Massachusetts Bay Colony.

4. The Puritans might have avoided the *Mistake* of issuing their Farewell address, in 1630—from on board the Ship Arbella—of fraternal assurance, that they were still in loving membership with their brethren in and of the Church of England; and as soon as here, set up their Theocratic Churches, wholly omitting the Prayer Book.

5. It must have been an intensely conscientious *mistake*—as soon as the Puritans were anchored in Massachusetts Bay—before they had left the Ship Arbella—to order that houses be built for the Elders; and for their salaries to be paid out of the public treasury—under their Charter, from the King—*silent*, on liberty in religion.

6. Posterity can but wish—that our Puritan Fathers

had avoided the *mistake*, of ordering; that the right of Citizenship, and voting, should depend upon being a Church-member, in some Church of the Theocracy. This would be used, as "repugnant to the Laws of England."

7. It is a question for Posterity to consider whether or not it was a *mistake*, when pursued by bishop Laud, for Roger Williams to flee his Country Bristol way — and take ship, with his wife — to Boston? And also — whether it was a *mistake*, or not in him; when asked to preach for the first Puritan Church in Boston; to decline their Call, and give as his conscientious reason, that — they were an "unseparated people?"

8. Was it, or was it not, a *mistake* — after the Puritans had gladly left England, to get from under the burdens of the State Church there — for the Court at Boston, to warn the Church at Salem, not to employ Mr. Williams as their Teacher — because he had declined the Boston Call " — etc. ? Was it wise for them to lay burdens on the Salem Church, which they themselves would not bear in England?

9. What kind of a *mistake* was it, if it was one; for Roger Williams to accept a Second Call, to the Salem Church, and return there from Plymouth — while as yet the " Serious advice of the Boston Court " — was not withdrawn — inhibiting his installation over them as Teacher?

10. Was it a wise *mistake;* or otherwise; for the Court to issue a Second, " Serious Advice to the Church in Salem, not to call Mr. Williams to office, as a thing of such ill-consequence " — with the First advice still among the notices, " By Authority"?

11. Was it a prudent *mistake*— in Mr. Williams, to continue to teach; that "the Magistrate has no right by his Civill Office, to intermeddle in matters of Religion" — while he was aware that the Court held the opposite opinion; as tenaciously, and Conscientiously as he held his opinion? This was the Castle, to be held or taken.

12. Was it an imprudent *mistake*— and "Contempt of Authority"— or— an inalienable right— for the People of Salem, to proceed to the public Ordination of Mr. Williams— as their Teacher— with the double advice of the Court *not*— to do So— "without due advisement?"

13. It must have been, a conscientious, *Mistake*— and to be tolerated; as nothing worse than a mistake— for the Court to issue a peremptory summons to Roger Williams and the Salem Church, to appear before them to answer for "Contempt of authority"— in the important justifiable matter of his ordination, as their Pastor.

14. Was it a hasty or tardy *Mistake*— when the Court seemed to "be angry and sin not"— by "generall ereccon of hands, ordered Mr. Endicott committed" — for his conscientiously vehement protestation; because of their Magisterial intermeddling, in the question of the Ordination of Mr. Williams as Pastor by the Church at Salem?

15. Was it a timely, or untimely *Mistake*, in Pastor Williams, to write letters to the Churches where the Magistrates were Members, advising their admonition; for their malfeasance, as officers of justice?

16. Was it a commendable *Mistake*— for the Elders of Massachusetts Bay, Conscientiously even— to Com-

bine against a Brother Elder — and advise the Court to Banish Roger Williams, for Conscientiously contending against the right of *civill* Magistrates — to intermeddle in Religion?

17. Was it, or was it not — a *Mistake* — for Roger Williams to "maintain all his opinions" — in face of the Court — while the prospect of Banishment was before him tho' he declared himself "ready to be Banished, or die in New England"?

18. Was it else than a *Mistake*, as seen by Posterity — for the Court, to pass the Sentence of Civill Banishment, against him for *conscientiously* maintaining, that Magistrates ought not to intermeddle in Religion?

19. What kind of a *Mistake* was it — for Mr. Williams to preach in his *own house* — to those who desired to hear him, after his Sentence was promulgated — altho' he had been only restricted on " going *about*, to draw people to his opinions?"

20. If it were not a *Mistake* — it was a collapse — when the Court sent Capt. Underhill to arrest Roger Williams and Ship him to England.

21. Was it a *Mistake*, or not; for Gov. Winthrop, gamesomely, to send Roger Williams a "hint from God," that "he better not be there, when Capt. Underhill got there?" — and *he wasn't*.

22. How was it for a *Mistake* — when Gov. Winslow, conscientiously advised Roger Williams, to canoe over the river, from Seekonk; listening as he went to the kindly note — " Wha-cheer " — and was *welcomed* to the Wigwams of Miantonomo — and Canonicus — at Mooslausick?

From this point in their History, Roger Williams,

and the Puritans become equals, again — EACH HAD A COUNTRY. Their case is now in the hands of the Grand Jury — known as Posterity, who will have all the time to make up their verdict, from now until the "appearing of our Lord and Master — when he comes to judge the world in Righteousness."

Let the "Charge to the Jury" — be, that the *mistakes* of the Puritans towards him — are not Crimes — neither are the accusations laid to his charge, in their Sentence; *Crimes*. All their *Mistakes*, were *Conscientious* mistakes.

B. Symptoms of the Decrease of Theocracy — and the Increase of Religious Liberty — *before* — Roger Williams' Banishment.

1. The primary rebuff — from which Theocracy in Massachusetts Bay never recovered — was his refusal of their Call — Because they were "Unseparated." It pierced them, to the Core. That "wet-sheet" — fixed public attention, on that single point, and the more it was studied, the more the world saw it to be, the *Very Virus*, of Constantinianism. That "ill-egg" — which Dudley feared was in Toleration ; "hatched a cockatrice" — in Theocracy — to its Ruin.

2. The next blow under which Theocracy continued to reel and stagger, was the loss of their Charter. Almost within four years, after it was granted, the King had occasion, or took occasion, to listen to complaints, — well-founded, or ill-founded something — "repugnant," to the King, if not to the Laws of England. And let it be remembered, that all this was brought about — and the Charter "*reassumed*" — very soon after Roger Williams returned from Plymouth — so that

the "charge, that he undermined the foundations of the Colony " — is without any foundation.

3. Then came the beaching wave of public opinion, dashing against the Church-and-State-ship of the General Court, in the vigorous conscientious protest from Salem — against the "Magistrates meddling," with the Church for ordaining the man of their choice, as their Pastor. This Earthquake, shook "Colossus" — and shook it again ; and shook it down — in 100 years.

4. A still mightier washing of the sand from under the Theocracy, was the "infeccon of Mr. Williams' Opinions " — which had not only "filled all Salem " — but had very greatly leavened the Colony, as against the "Magistrates meddling in matters of Religion." "Many being taken with apprehensions of his godliness, and of the weaker sex, not a few." Before these demonstrations of the Consciences of Public Opinion the ; "Court desisted."

5. Another weakening in the Theocracy — was the revelation of the incoherent elements, in the Generall Court itself. The restful pillow on which the Court had "breathed its life out sweetly there " — was the strengthening and vivifying " *Advice* of the Elders." In the very act of " Sentence-passing " — against Roger Williams, the key-stone of the Theocratic Arch — fell out — in the Greatest Elder of the Elders, withdrawing from the Court.

Other eminent gentlemen were in sympathy with him, against the Sentence. This act of flinching at a critical point — was not an open protest — but suggestive of the presence of untempered mortar, in the wall. Roger Williams stood alone ; undaunted ; with the

Court, and Elders, against him,— while Mr. Cotton, with the Civil and Ecclesiastical Powers of the Colony behind him ; felt a weakness.

6. All that Roger Williams — and the cause of Religious Liberty suffered, in this "shock of Battle, and wreck of worlds"— was his *eviction*, from Massachusetts Bay, and Plymouth Bay Colonies — and his *induction*, into Narrohigansett Bay Colony. He to *increase* — the Court to *decrease*.

Up to this time, the Theocracy had received five telling blows ; and from the demolishing effect of each one of them, it never recovered — while all these, and many more followed, one after another, giving it no time to recover. And every blow that weakened Theocracy — strengthened Religious Liberty. Let Posterity cover the conscientious mistake of the Forefathers, with the "Mantle of Charity:" but correct the *mistake* of Banishing Roger Williams, by *Revoking* the Sentence.

Upon this principle, if the Pope of Rome — will in this 19th century apologize to Christendom ; for the questionable acts of his predecessors in office — as "Conscientious" *Mistakes* — we will make a pilgrimage to the Eternal City, bearing the "Olive Branch" — and cover his Infallibility, with the "Mantle of Charity" — as the God-father of all the Papal Fathers — and so POPERY — and PROTESTANTISM, be one — to-day !

C. Theocracy — Keeps on in Decline, from, and after, the Banishment of Roger Williams — Oct. 19, 1635.

We have seen, that the foundations for the overthrow of the Theocratic System were laid, and well advanced in the "repugnance felt in England about the Charter"

—*before*, Mr. Williams returned to Salem, from Plymouth — and hence the too modern slanders, too well indorsed, that ROGER WILLIAMS — "undermined the foundations of the Massachusetts Bay Colony;" are equally base, as baseless.

The decaying, and doomed, Theocracy, hastened to its fall, from internal disintegration — and blows from external demolition — the latter, mainly from England.

1. The hardest back-set to Theocracy, was the proposition of Gov. John Winthrop — "To recall Roger Williams — Revoke his Sentence — and show him some special marks of honor." Many of his council were in favor of doing it — but there was Conscientiousness enough among the rest — to make another, great *mistake*.

The English language cannot be framed into a paragraph to express a more damaging Criticism; derogatory of the action of the Court, in passing that *Sentence*. No wonder Mr. Cotton was sick, and wanted to go out. Evidently Mr. Winthrop esteemed his lifetime friend, Mr. Williams — more than he did the "Advice of the Elders." This suggestion of Mr. Winthrop, was as a "consuming fire," against Theocracy. At the same time Roger Williams was in Narrohigansett Country, sowing "the infeccon of his opinions."

When Posterity becomes sufficiently imbued with a sense of the Historical justice, contained in Gov. Winthrop's humane and Christian suggestion, they will, "draw forth from its dread abode" — the Sentence of the Court — and REVOKE it.

2. Then came the Mrs. Hutchinson Episode — as if it were "the Seed of the Woman, to bruise the head"

of Theocracy. This crusher took effect on the great Elder John Cotton, who inclined off from the more stable ones of the first Boston church, and favored her views. He however afterward apologized to the Church, and "thereby recovered his fame throughout all New England." But he was never so great after he dodged fire — at Sentence-passing, against Roger Williams — and after his return from scouting with the Hutchinsons. What he recovered, Theocracy lost.

3. The first New England Synod was called to prop up the crumbling walls of Theocracy. The number of "false, heretical, and very dangerous opinions" — reported was so great, that it was proposed not to entertain them before the Synod — as it would be a reproach to the Colony. Others were for ferreting out the heretics, and exposing them. Some confusion arose when the Synod called upon the "Magistrates to *intermeddle*" — at this some of the Delegates withdrew. The Synod managed to Sentence a few to "depete" to Rhode Island. The Synod closed, in something of the plight of Pharaoh's grain-fields, after the hail-storm.

4. About this time Roger Williams, with the People of Providence, had organized themselves into a voluntary civil Government — limited to "civil things only" — whereby Magistrates, were excused from "intermeddling" in religious opinions. This laid the foundation for the "Separation of Church and State." This the Elders and Court of Massachusetts Bay *Conscientiously* feared, as an "erroneous and very dangerous" Doctrine. Mr. John Cotton "considered Democracy, fit for neither Church nor State" — Mr. Williams considered it fit for either — and so fit for both.

5. About 1639 — Roger Williams became a Baptist.
As Elder Brewster thought he saw Anabaptist tendencies in him — like John Smyth of Holland. He was reported as "filling all Salem with Anabaptistry and rigid Separation" — and so it came to pass, in Providence — also. He was of no particular Denominational Confession before his Banishment — but is now well-known as founder of the First Baptist Church of Providence, Rhode Island, and in America. Verily he was like John Smyth of Holland; and the Baptists of England who published a Confession of Faith in 1611 — the year of the King James Version of the Bible. In this Confession we find — "The Magistrate is not to *meddle*, with Religion, nor matters of Conscience — nor to compel men to this or that form of Religion — because Christ is the King and Lawgiver of the Conscience." Roger Williams' idea of Separation of Church and State has grown and increased greatly — while the Great John Cotton's idea of Theocracy — has followed his example — " I withdrew myself."

6. Roger Williams obtains a charter — while the Bay Charter is reassumed. In going to England for this Charter, he could not pass thro' Massachusetts without license from the Court. He went by way of Manhattan (N. Y.). On his return, he was authorized to land at Boston, and pass to Providence. The Sentence of the Court was not recognized by the British Parliament.

7. In 1643 — the Colonies of the Massachusetts Bay — Connecticut — New Haven, and Plymouth, formed a Union   Rhode Island being conscientiously left out, "because the people followed Mr. Williams' religious

opinions." The Commissioners of this Union, offered their services "to suppress the influx of error under the deceitful Color of Liberty of Conscience." In 1646, these Commissioners called the Second N. E. Synod "to compose a Platform of Church Discipline." Still blind to their Conscientious *mistakes* — this Synod ordered — "if any Church shall walk obstinately in any corrupt way of their own — the Magistrate is to put forth his coercive power" — for their correction. This was in the "Cambridge Platform" — which slumped, and let the Theocracy through.

8. A very severe law was passed by the General Court in 1644, against some that walked in their own way. The next year divers merchants and others asked for a change in it.

9. In 1646, a petition was sent to the Court, complaining of the exclusive limitation of civil privileges to members of the Theocratic Churches — and asking for the enjoyment of the civil rights of English Subjects. Theocracy was not popular.

10. In 1649 — the Mass. Bay Court requested the Plymouth Bay Court to enforce their Law of 1644, in the Old Colony. Plymouth, more than declined — thereby dealing a moral and mortal blow against Theocracy. On his death-bed, Gov. Winthrop refused to sign a decree of Banishment, saying — " I have done too much of that already."

11. About this time, the Bay Court, asked the "Commissioners of the United Colonies" — for aid in subduing Warwick to prevent its being absorbed into R. I. as an additional field, for Roger Williams' opinions. A meeting of the Commissioners was held in Plymouth,

to consider the subject. Plymouth refused the aid — and the meeting broke up in what is sometimes called a Row — or something like that. So — Theocracy came tumbling down.

12. In 1651, occurred the public whipping of Mr. Obadiah Holmes, by order of the Court, on Boston Common. When this was heard of in England — Sir Richard Saltonstall wrote Messrs. Cotton and Wilson, Ministers of Boston — " Rev. and Dear Sirs — whom I unfeignedly love and respect — it doth not a little grieve my Spirit, to hear that — in N. E. you fine, whip, and imprison men, for their Consciences. . . . These rigid ways have laid you very low in the hearts of Saints. . . .

Theocracy — still grew unpopular.

13. In 1651 — Messrs. Williams, and Clarke, were sent by Rhode Island People, to England — by way of Manhattan again — to obtain a renewal and improvement of their Charter. This they did very easily.

Upon Mr. Williams' return — Oliver Cromwell gave him a passport, not only to land at Boston and go direct to Providence, as Parliament had done before — but an unlimited pass, "to go throughout all the United Colonies at all times without molestation, and *without, a 'license from the Court.'*"

We may imagine the estimate, in which John Winthrop — and Oliver Cromwell, held the Sentence of Banishment against Roger Williams — by the Massachusetts Bay Court. Mr. Winthrop wanted it REVOKED — Cromwell, authorized him to trample it under foot. Alas Theocracy!

14. The Government of Rhode Island having been

reorganized on the basis of the new Charter, at the General Election, May 22, 1655 — Roger Williams was re-elected Governor. A letter was duly received from Oliver Cromwell — "Confirming the Government as now established." Congratulations from England, and the Colonies were showered upon him, as "The ram's-horn of the Lord Jesus Christ, that was blowing the blast, that was to lay low" — such as the Theocracy. Roger Williams was not long after invited to Boston — without "license from this Courte " — on Business.

Professor Diman, in his Oration, says — " Thus for the first time in History, a form of Government was adopted which drew a clear and unmistakable line between the temporal and Spiritual power, which was an anomaly among the Nations. . . . The Covenant subscribed by the Settlers of Providence, was the first embodiment, in an actual experiment, of the great principles of an unrestricted Religious Liberty. . . . The unusual circumstances under which we came into being, only intensifies the gratitude with which we hail the Apostle of Religious Liberty as the Founder of Rhode Island."

15. In 1659 — the Court adopted such severe measures against the Quakers — that the popular indignation became so intense — that the Court however conscientious to protect themselves from annoyance were forced again — as in Salem — to desist. No such tumult in Roger Williams' land — for such cause. This use made of the Magistrates, in matters of religious opinion, by the Theocracy — grew more and more unpopular and unbearable — as the system died away.

16. Still heavier blows awaited the Theocracy. Dur-

ing the Protectorate of Cromwell, Toleration had a Sunny Season, so far as he could protect. But upon his death in 1658 — the way was open for the crown to pass to the head of Charles II. He at once ordered the suspension of capital punishment against Quakers — complete toleration for the Church of England — The repeal of the Law, requiring all Voters to be Church-Members — Also, that all persons of civil behavior, he admitted to the ordinances of Baptism, and the Lord's Supper. Chas. did not meddle with the conscientiousness, of the Theocratic System — but dealt crushing blows, upon its *Mistakes*. These he dealt with all the more summarily — as they were among the "repugnant" things, against his father's Charter.

17. In 1662 — the 4th N. E. Synod was called. Among its "canons," was; that — "It is the most to be abhorred maxim, that any Church should exempt themselves from giving account to any other church like themselves — or christian Magistrate above them." In due time however, the "Cambridge Platform" — and this *annex* broke apart and tumbled down. The noise thereof was Theocracy's Dirge.

18. The Orders of Chas. II. — struck the Church and State system of the Puritans, fore and aft. In front he demolished their breastworks — and supposed, strong points. Behind them, were the increasing population — and the rapidly growing Sentiment in favor of freedom in religion — and akin to it, a growing relish for civil liberty. Hence every breach made by the King was followed up by new — more urgent and increasing demands for popular Freedom.

19. King Charles sent royal Commissioners, to

inspect the doings of the Commissioners of the 4 Colonies. His agents did not hesitate to display in the face of the Puritans, the ceremonials of the church of Eng. — notwithstanding they were to them ever so distasteful. This was in part, amends for Endicott's shipping home the Brownes from Salem — for setting up Episcopal Service there.

20. In 1667 — a letter was received in Rhode Island intimating non-intercourse — if they did not conform to the policy of the United Colonies. Rhode Island replied — "It is much in our hearts to hold forth a lively experiment — of a prosperous Civil State, in which there is liberty in religious concernments."

21. In 1668 — Chas. sent an order to Massachusetts Bay — for — "Toleration to all Sects but Papists — and the suspension, of the church-member's vote. This blow struck the Theocracy hard, in the back-bone.

22. In 1669 — the First Church of the Puritans in Boston — the identical "*unseparated*" church whose call Roger Williams declined, was taken with a schism, and *separated*, among themselves. Out of this rupture came the "Old South Church." An appeal was made to the Generall Court — and the Separatists, were Sustained. This same Court, 34 years before — Banished out of the Colony Roger Williams — that "Arch-Individual Separatist." *Mistake*, or no *Mistake* — somewhere!

23. The fifth N. E. Synod, scarcely made their voice heard, or influence felt — beyond the hall — where their meeting was held. "Gently, oh, gently lead us."

24. About 1680 the Doors of the First Baptist Meeting House were nailed-up by a Authority. They were

found soon after (unostentatiously) unnailed. The *Court*, was more intimidated than the Church.

25. During the reigns of Chas. I.; Cromwell; and Chas II. — the whole Puritan Theocracy became very badly demoralized. Religious liberty, in the mean time waxed stronger and stronger.

26. On May 12, 1680 — the Sixth, and Last N. E. Synod was called. In its Decree on LIBERTY of CONSCIENCE — Chap. xxiv. sec. 3, was "Yet in such — differences about the Doctrine of the Gospel, or ways of the Worship of God, as may befal men, exercising a good Conscience . . . there is no warrant, for the Magistrate, to abridge them of their liberty."

This was Roger Williams' Doctrine, precisely in 1631, when he declined the call of the First Church of the Puritans, in Boston. And just within 50 years from the time he declared in Boston, that "Magistrates ought not to *abridge* Liberty of Conscience" — this 6th and Last Synod of the N. E. Theocracy promulgated what the "Elders" of Boston denounced — as Roger Williams' — "erroneous and very dangerous doctrine."

Verily the "blast of the ram's-horn" — by Roger Williams, blown for Jesus Christ, laid the walls of the Boston Theocracy — where the "walls of Jericho lay."

Roger Williams was yet alive, to see that Day!

Finis Theocracy. SELAH.

D. The continued and demolishing blows that fell upon Theocracy after the Death of Roger Williams.

1. It is not definitely Known, what is the exact Date of his Death. But, that he had attained to an honorable good old age, of about fourscore years, is known, and the time of his Death is supposed to have been during

March — April — 1683. Besides his world-wide imperishable renown, as the Apostle of Religious Liberty in New England — he is held in the highest esteem, by the good citizens of the State — as the Founder of Rhode Island. He was repeatedly chosen by the people to the Office of President — or Governor, of the Colony. "His Death occurred in 1683 — in the City of Providence — and he was buried under arms, in his Family Burial-ground ; with every testimony of respect, which the Colony could manifest."

The Christian Civilization of the whole World, will forever honor ROGER WILLIAMS. But with however much honor they may honor him — "To Whom Honor is due "—*all*— will not be done, which ought to be done ; until — The Sentence of Banishment, passed against him is Revoked — by Authority — and a Suitable Monument erected to his Memory — in Boston — Massachusetts.

2. Under James II. — 1685, Gov. Andros — the King's governor of the Colony — to the utter disgust of the Boston, *Puritan Separatists* — Ordered the church of England service, performed in their "Old South Meeting House." Yet its doors, were neither nailed-up, nor unnailed.

3. New Charter for Massachusetts.

The original Charter from Chas. Ist. — for Massachusetts Bay, had been a poor staff to lean upon after his reassumption of it in 1633. In 1692 — Sir Wm. Phipps arrived in New England as King's Governor of the Colonies. He brought the new Charter, which united Massachusetts and Plymouth Bay Colonies in one, under the name of Massachusetts. On the subject of Religious Liberty, it provided — "Toleration for all sects but Papists." No very low bow to Theocracy.

4. First Sermon under the New Charter.

At the first meeting of the General Court — after the Union of the two Colonies, in the Sermon on the Occasion — we find — "Things will not go well, when . . . the Civil Magistrate, with civil penalties, compels men to this or that way of worship which they are Conscientiously indisposed unto . . . when did fines and gaols ever cure heretics? . . . I would put in a barr against the persecution of any that may Conscientiously dissent from our way. . . . Nor would I desire myself to suffer persecution upon a clearer cause, than that of testifying against persecution of other Christians, who are not of my opinion."

Had the General Court accepted this Doctrine as it was preached to them 55 years before by the renowned Salem Pastor — whom Endicott was Committed for Conscientiously, vehemently, and contentiously defending — Roger Williams never would have been Banished.

5. A marvel at the Ordination of Mr. Elisha Callander, in 1718, as Pastor of the First Baptist Church of Boston.

By request — Mr. Cotton Mather, grandson of Mr. John Cotton — (the "save one" of the Elders), who withdrew, when the Court sentenced Mr. Williams; consented to preach the Sermon. Mr. John Cotton, would hardly have preached Mr. Williams' Ordination Sermon, at Salem, even if he had been requested. But Mr. Mather the grandson — had lived to see Theocracy fade away. Mr. Mather, was also the Puritan

*Historian*, and hence his words have weight; on *liberty* in Religion.

His Text, was Gen. 49: 7. Subject — "Good Men United." In it he said — " If our Brethren in whose house we are now convened, met with anything too unbrotherly, in former times; they now with Satisfaction, hear us expressing our dislike of everything which looked like persecution." He denounced the anger of persecution, as *Cursed:* and persecution itself, an "Obsolete Blunder." Mr. Increase Mather, also assisted at this Ordination.

This was a more quiet time than when Mr. Williams' Ordination, was a "Great Contempt of authority" — over 83 years before. It was a great improvement upon the Conscientious Mistakes — of former days. Posterity will respond — Amen, and Amen. Selah.

6. The Hollis Thank-offering, for "Good Men United."

The joyful event of "Good Men United" — So inspired one Mr. Thomas Hollis 1st., (or Jr.), of England with gratitude to God — for the glorious triumph (not of "Conscientious mistakes" — ) but Religious Liberty in New England that he celebrated the Event, by making a Thank-offering to God. This Act of Worship, took the tangible Form of a large bequest, to the Corporation of Harvard College — as a permanent Fund, for the Education of Young Men, for the Ministry of the Gospel of Christ — the "Hollis Fund" of Harvard by bequests of that Family.

7. Request for another Synod.

In 1725 — the General Court was requested to issue a call for another N. E. Synod. It was found to be judicious, to refer the matter to the English Lawyers; — who gave it as their Opinion — that "Such Synods were illegal, without express sanction of the King." This was a Summary disposal of the Theocratic Synods — and all their Conscientious mistakes. This opinion, would, by retroaction, make the Banishment of Roger Williams — illegal. Thus was Theocracy torn into Shreds by Public Opinion.

8. Rhode Island's example followed.

By the year 1729 — all State Taxes, for the support of the Theocracy, were abrogated.

9. Religious Liberty guaranteed, by the Constitution of the United States.

So thoroughly, and blessedly had Freedom in Religion, leavened public Opinion in the American Colonies, that it prepared the way, for Civil Liberty and National Independence. General Washington, was specially interested, and immensely helpful to its Friends — in getting Roger Williams' doctrine of Soul Freedom incorporated into the First Amendment of the Constitution of the U.S. in 1789.

How long will Posterity take National and Christian pride in indorsing the Amendment to the Constitution, placed there by Washington's helpfulness — and which pours such glory upon the great labors of Roger Williams — and not be keenly awake to some endeavor; even if it be a "Conscientiously contentious" one; to remove that *cobweb* Sentence, from the Records of the Commonwealth of the great State of Massachusetts — by asking our Legislature to REVOKE it?

E. The Sentence against Roger Williams should be Revoked — tho' Theocracy is gone.

1. Because John Winthrop, the First Governour of Massachusetts Bay — proposed to have it Revoked, in his day. This *Sentence*, is the last *Bone*, of the beast — let Posterity, grind it to powder.

How far Gov. Winthrop was in favor of the Sentence we may never know — if in favor of it at all. Gov. Haines of Connecticut presided at the time of Sentence-passing. Mr. Winthrop was one of the Deputies — and doubtless one of those, "divers worthy gentlemen, who would not have voted for the *Sentence*, but for Mr. Cotton's private advice and counsel." He was at least very silent in the matter.

But, call to mind that of so prominent a man in Massachusetts Bay; as John Winthrop, *privately* informing Mr. Williams, (Pochahontas did the whites, on a time), to "play hop at a skip," with Capt. Underhill, of the Court. Wo'ld he be likely to help a bad rogue, escape the clutches of the Law? Not he! But here we find John Winthrop, *secretly* helping Roger Williams to elude the Sentence of the Great and Generall Court, approved by *all* the *Ministers* of the Bay — "save one." Mr. Winthrop stood alone between Roger Williams, and all the Ministers — to prevent, all the Ministers from *doing* wrong; to *shield*, Mr. Williams from *suffering* wrong, from them! "I palliate not a particle, he suffered." . . .

Nor did Mr. Winthrop hesitate to help him privately — thro' any fear that the Court might find it out — and accuse him of "contempt of authority." He feared not, to disregard the Order of the Court — to fulfil the Golden Rule to his friend!

Allowing that Mr. Winthrop had been persuaded to

coalesce in the Sentence — Yet he acted independently in his private "hint from God" — in time for him to escape. He acted independently, when he requested his Council to revoke the Sentence and honor, Mr. Williams. But his Council, "gave him leave to withdraw." He made the request out of the burning consideration, of Mr. Williams' services, in saving the whites from a massacre by the Pequots — in which he had rendered good for evil, to his conscientious Massachusetts Brethren.

Has not Posterity some *good reasons* in consideration of the Services of Roger Williams — if not in the Pequot War — yet in the War for Religious Liberty — that we can do his Memory the justice, and ourselves the credit — by "Revoking his Sentence, and showing him some marks of esteem"? Tho' years of forgetfulness have flown — and pages of Records have grown — let's correct the Record — "It's never too late to mend a wrong."

Roger Williams, was as much a Boston man — as John Winthrop — "they were loving friends." He was the one man, the Court could not make "yield to truth" like Mr. Endicott. He was the only "young stripling stranger, who could sit in judgment on his Elders." Roger Williams is the *only* man we know of — to whom Massachusetts ever knuckled. Geo. III. could not sit on Massachusetts.

Gov. Winthrop's Bill, presented for services of Roger Williams in the Pequot War has not yet been paid. Massachusetts still owes him this, and interest, for 260 years: besides; for his services, in "Blowing the Ram's-horn, of the Lord Jesus," that has prostrated the walls of the Massachusetts Bay Theocracy. These Bills are imperative — over-due — and can only be cancelled, with the securities named by Gov. Winthrop. Not in gold — United States Bonds — "fiat money" — nor ".50 on the dollar." But by "Recalling Roger Williams' Sentence — Revoking it — and showing him some distinguished marks of esteem."

2. However *conscientious* the Court may have been in passing it — the Sentence against Roger Williams was *always* unpopular.

Justice — only sleeps, until either the offender relents, or until the jury brings in the verdict, "Vengeance is mine I will repay saith the Lord." No voice of the Public Conscience, was *ever* heard in approval of that Sentence, but often low, and loud, denunciations of it have filled the air.

The calling of him back from Plymouth, to Salem, was not complimentary, of the advice of the Court; "not to employ him as Teacher." The *protest* from Salem about the "Resident's Oath" — was not flattery, in the face of the Court — for "the Court *desisted* from that proceeding." The scheme to divide the church after Mr. Williams' ordination, and then to order the church and pastor into Court, (however *conscientiously*), for "contempt of authority" — was met by a storm of Public disapprobation — and whether wise or otherwise, was vehemently denounced by Mr. Endicott. This was before the Sentence, but did not pave the way to make it popular — but contrariwise. Mr. Cotton, before the Sentence, said — "The Court is so incensed, that neither your voice, nor any two voices, will prevent the Sentence." It was held in contempt in advance.

"Divers worthy gentlemen," had to be dragooned into voting for it — by Mr. Cotton's "advice and counsel." But the most utterly prodigious farce of all, was, the Great Cotton — Elder, of the Elders — to get up, and go out, at Sentence-time: as tho' that would save the fat from the fire. Was it not "Contempt of Court," contempt of himself — and contempt of the Sentence?

Why did the reading of the Sentence, fill Salem with a tornado of PUBLIC INDIGNATION — if it were popular? Why did Mr. Cotton the "save one" — implore Mr. Williams not to remember it unkindly against him if he were not ashamed of it? Roger Williams *never apologized* to Mr. Cotton, nor tip-toed out of Court — for "Blowing the Ram's-horn!! And the good John Winthrop, acknowledged his chagrin, by asking his Council to "REVOKE it!!"

Even Gov. Haines was almost persuaded — that — "Perhaps God had designed this country as a home for all consciences." Roger Williams invited to Providence — "all oppressed for conscience." Ah, the *Sentence* of the Court, was the Serpent the Elders didn't kill at the Synod — and needs to be set at "Swallowing itself."

Gov. Winthrop had the sagacity to comprehend clearly the status of that, Sentence, as wholly illegal. Even if the Charter of the Massachusetts Bay Company, from Chas. Ist had been in full force, at the time of the Sentence, 1635, it gave no authority for any such Sentence. But we find the Charter had been "reassumed" about a year before Mr. Williams' Ordination at Salem. Hence, a sentence based either on an illegal use of a charter; or on that charter after it had been *dead* a *year* — would seem to guarantee the Sentence — as illegal. This Gov. Winthrop knew.

The last fossil of the Theocracy, that remains, is this Sentence of the Court. Let it be "dragged forth from its dread abode "—and formally disposed of. The Massachusetts Bill of Rights, in 1834 — made a very thorough end of the Theocratic System — but why should this obnoxious old keepsake, as a bone of the idol our Fathers did allow — be retained? Let it be cremated.

3. Gov. Winthrop's Proposal Revived.

In the 240th year after the Banishment of Roger Williams — It seemed good to the People of Sturbridge, Massachusetts, upon the solicitation of the Pastor of the Baptist Church in that Town, to Memorialize the General Court as follows : —

" To the Honorable Senate, and House of Representatives of the State of Massachusetts.

A petition —

From Citizens of the Town of Sturbridge, Mass.

Whereas — It is a sentiment of honest pride in every good Citizen to render honor to whom honor is due — and a commendable ambition to revive and preserve the memory of the virtuous, godly, and useful, who have passed from Earth to Heaven — to whom we are greatly indebted, for special blessings, which have come to posterity thro' their labors and trials : —

Whereas — It has become a national sentiment — that, the Separation of Church and State, has been of incalculable advantage to the United States, in securing to us our present Civil and Religious Liberties ; and that our National History points out the name of

Roger Williams as the foremost man in our early Colonial times, who advocated the Separation of Church and State;—and who founded the Colony of Rhode Island, introducing into its Charter a proviso for such Separation:—it being the first instance of the kind, in a Civil State, within the range of human knowledge :—

Whereas—Our National History contains the unwelcome fact, that the agitation of the subject of Separation of Church and State, by Roger Williams, gave offence to the General Court of Massachusetts Bay: —that for this agitation he was arraigned, and tried:— and that on Oct. 19, 1635, Said Court passed against Mr. Williams late Pastor of the First Church in Salem, Massachusetts, a Sentence of Banishment; that he 'depete out of their jurisdiccon within sixe weekes;' all the Ministers of the Bay being present, and 'save one,' approved the sentence : —

Whereas,—the lapse of time has matured a better judgment, upon the subject of Separation of Church and State; even Gov. John Winthrop, a Member of the Court afterward proposed to his Council, that, in consideration of eminent services rendered Massachusetts Bay, by Mr. Williams in the Pequot War, his Sentence of Banishment ought to be Revoked;—that in the Charter of 1692, for the Union of Massachusetts Bay, and Plymouth Bay Colonies, under the name Massachusetts; toleration in Religious matters was provided for : — now that perfect Religious Liberty as advocated by Roger Williams, has become the fundamental sentiment throughout all Christendom :—also the Congress of the United States, having publicly honored the memory of Roger Williams, by accepting his statue, as a gift from the State of Rhode Island, and placing it in the National Capitol at Washington, D.C., therefore —

Resolved — That we, citizens of the Town of Sturbridge Massachusetts; deem it our duty, and honor; To Petition the Honorable Legislature of Massachusetts; as an act of Historical Justice to the State; and to the memory of Roger Williams; and to place the Record of the Generall Court, in harmony with the Spirit of the Age; to pass an 'ACT' during its session in 1875 — REVOKING the aforesaid Sentence of Banishment against Roger Williams.

And your Petitioners will ever pray.

T. M. Merriman.   J. R. Reading.   J. F. Reading.
                  T. E. Arnold.    E. T. Brooks.
N. A. P. Rhodes.  Mark Currier.    Rev. M. L. Richardson.
E. M. Gifford.    J. Mcdonald.     Hon. H. Haynes.
Hon. S. F. Marsh. Rev. C. Fowler.  Dea. Cas. Fuller.
David Wright.     T. Charles.      N. Bennett.
Rev. S. Boyer.    S. F. Andrews.   Marvin Clarke.
J. Montgomery.    W. J. Oatley.    N. D. Ladd.
Hon. G. T. Lincoln. B. S. Chase.   Hon. E. L. Bates.
Dea. T. Snell."

In the Records of the Massachusetts Legislature, is the following — Mar. 18, 1875 : —

Hon. G. T. Lincoln — presented the Petition of Rev. T. M. Merriman, and others for Revoking the Sentence of Banishment against

ROGER WILLIAMS.

This Petition came in too late for action at this session — and so was laid over to the next Legislature.

In the same Records, we find, Jan 13, 1876 : —

On Motion of Hon. Mr. Mackintosh of Newton, this Petition was taken from the Files — and referred to the Judiciary Committee.

On Jan. 18, Mr. John Washburn — of Worcester — chairman of the Committee — Reported —

"That the Petitioners have leave to withdraw."

In the presence of the House in Session — and of the Spectators — we heard him say —

" Roger Williams was an enemy to the Government of the Colony. That he was Banished for Sedition against the Government of Massachusetts Bay — and not for his Doctrine of Religious Liberty. That Liberty of Conscience would have prospered, better without his help than with it. That Roger Williams was a Bumptious good fellow — but deserved Banishment. That he thought well of him — but was anxious for the reputation of the Fathers also."

ORDERS OF THE DAY — JAN. 19, 1876.

"Inexpedient to Legislate."

Whereupon — we see — That neither the Council of the Governor of 240 years before — nor the Council of the Governor of 1876, could coax their consciences, to relax an uncharitable, unpopular, and illegal civil decree, against a "godly minister" — who for Conscience' Sake had maintained the Doctrine of Freedom of Conscience from being "intermeddled with by the Civil Magistrate."

So ; upon the report of Chairman Washburn — the gentlemanly, humane Proposal of Gov. Winthrop ; is again politely (?) — " Passed by on the other side."

It was a very grave Custom in Pilate's time, to release some Criminal, on the Feast-day — as a sign of Magisterial Clemency — and so Pilate to show himself worthy of his high office, "released Barabbas, who had been cast into prison for murder — and delivered Jesus to be crucified."

A semblance of that custom survives in the good old Commonwealth of Massachusetts — that is, in so far; that a murderer, for good behavior, can be credited one month off each year, of a sentence of twenty years.

But when Gov. Winthrop; and the Sturbridge Petitioners — ask, that, for saving the Massachusetts Bay Colonists, from having their heads split with *Tomahawks* — and being "conscientiously contentious" — in saving Massachusetts clergymen, from being conscientiously "shipped to England as factious and evil-conditioned " — Roger Williams, "deserves high tokens of regard " — " No " — says Chairman Washburn — " he deserved to be Banished ! ! "

"Roger Williams, was a Bumptious good fellow — but it's not expedient to Legislate." No — Mr. John Winthrop — we can't release him, he didn't *kill* anybody. No time off his Sentence for good behavior — during the fourscore years he lived, and 200 years since : No; he didn't KILL anybody.

True Roger Williams, was ahead of his Age in proposing liberty of conscience — but the Mountain has since come to him — and not he, gone back, to the Mountain.  Gov. Winthrop — was ahead of his Age — but it has come to Posterity, to move the Mountain to the front.  Much that was begun by the Fathers has come to us to push on — "that they without us should not be made perfect." Christ's Commission has come to us, not yet completed.

But while we wonder that Gov. Winthrop's Council, did not Revoke the Sentence — we wonder more and more, that it was ever passed — but we cease not to wonder, — after it was overlooked 240 years — that when bro't to the attention of the Massachusetts Legislature, in 1876 — they, like Gov. Winthrop's Council — " passed it by on the other side."

The occasion is not forgotten when a record of censure was made, on Beacon Hill, against the imperishable name of Charles Sumner — and how soon after, like "the snake that crawled into the Elder's seat in Sermon-time it was despatched." So mote it be. Let Massachusetts carry out the suggestion of Governour John Winthrop, concerning Roger Williams, and REVOKE, that ignominious Sentence. So, mote it be.

4. Gov. Winthrop's Proposal, severely criticised.

Whosoever wishes — can take note — that — the "Sturbridge Petition" — was not presented to the Mass. Legislature, until Mar. 18, 1875 — and did not receive its "Sentence of Banishment" — from the State House in Boston, until Jan. 18, 1876 — 10 months. But lo! on Jan. 15, 1876 — there issued an intended rebutter to the Sturbridge Petition in the form of — a Book — entitled ; "As to Roger Williams and his Banishment," etc. Observe — *three days* before ; the Proposal of Gov. John Winthrop, First Governor of Mass. Bay ; was Conscientiously bowed out of the State House, on Beacon Hill.

The book, is a marvel of erudition. So, in its magic

preparation. How such an amount of literary labor — in the midst of other pressing cares, could have come from one pen — in less than 10 months — is well nigh incredible. The immense collection of important Historical foot-notes — in so convenient a form, is well nigh invaluable. But — the astounding *use* made of those facts, must have been born of a zeal, worthy of a better cause.

The book, provides for itself — an "open-top," helmet — in the Style of a highly complimentary Dedication — as tho' that ; would atone for what follows.

"To the Honorable Robert C. Winthrop, LL.D. . . . Posterity is indebted to the candid pen of your noble and illustrious ancestor" — "ye Governour."

Scarcely could a more worthy name have been selected ; and scarcely could a more unworthy use, been made of it.

Look at it — the iconoclastic object of the book, is to pillory Roger Williams as a "bumptious good fellow" — then condemn him, and justify his Banishment.

Now note — it was "ye Governour, John Winthrop" — who first proposed, that this "Sentence be Revoked" — 240 years, before this much Dedicated book, appeared.

Surely the Hon. R. C. Winthrop, LL.D. might have been amused, or otherwise ; at the Dedication of this book, to him ; 5 years after his "Oration, at the 250th Anniversary of the Landing of the Pilgrims " — in which he said — " I palliate *not* a particle of the persecution against Roger Williams ! " Then comes, a discharge from the whole broadside — of the book, at — " A few excellent — if not erudite — people, residents of the

Town of Sturbridge, Massachusetts, petitioned the Massachusetts Legislature of 1875 — to Revoke the Sentence of Banishment, against Roger Williams."
. . . Again — "It seems suitable to avail of the Occasion . . . of any possible Public interest growing out of this remarkable procedure, to make a clear authentic statement of facts. . . . I must be allowed to think ; that any historian who shall reproduce the former slanders, in the face of the demonstration herein offered, must be condemned, as paying better fealty to indolence or prejudice, than to truth." . . .

In that fashion the "Sturbridge Petitioners" are disposed of. The *absence* of *candor;* in these utterances, *precludes* all *labored*, reply. They were "excellent if not erudite." And yet it necessitated, a plethoric volume of 140 pages — containing citations many — from "papers, registers — treatises — documents — records — and books carefully collated" — and all this travail, by a pen adorned with over a dozen, ERUDITE TITLES — to construct a rebuttal — to the "remarkable procedure" — of a few "Sturbridge illiterates."!! Altogether too much powder for the game.

All future historians, are interdicted, from making any other representations of "facts" — than this book, lays down — on pain of being "condemned, as lazy or prejudiced." Where is liberty of opinion ; speech ; or pen ; if *one book*, is to button the door of knowledge?! Indeed — but the "representation of facts" — in that book — were not born of laziness ; nor "Brotherly Kindness."

Gov. Winthrop's critic — still further declares — that — "The Denomination of Christians, known as Baptists, having canonized Roger Williams, as their pet hero — Seem to prefer without regard to facts, to re-utter the old denunciations; as if an inadequate statement could, by persistent reiteration be made a whole truth."

Note this statement, of the book; that, "Baptists have *canonized*, Roger Williams." Is it true; or false? Baptists, have never "canonized," anybody. The term "pet hero" — can hardly be taken as a conscientious compliment. We regret, for Somebody's sake, that book was ever written — ever printed — ever published. Spread over it, the mantle.

As to "reiterating what is not according to facts, until it becomes a whole truth" — is philosophically impossible. As impossible as to stir the Atlantic Ocean with a teaspoon, until it turns to butter. Hon. R. C. Winthrop, to whom this book, is obsequiously ascribed, don't believe Baptists are " reiteration " LIARS!

The next; criticised in the book, is Roger Williams — whom Gov. Winthrop wished recalled. After Mr. Winthrop had reported him a "godly minister," the book, of Jan. 15, 1876 — Styles him — "a curt, stripling stranger of scarce a score and a half of years, who was assuming to sit in judgment on his Elders."

Gov. Winthrop; and the "Stripling, were loving friends." . . . Hon. R. C. — "I palliate not a particle," of calling him names.

The style in which Roger Williams, "assumed to sit on his Elders" — was copied somewhat by Adoniram Judson — when he, "assumed to sit," on the American Board of Commissioners for Foreign Missions. Alas for the book, cover it with the mantle.

That literary — (not illiterate), venture — "As to Roger Williams " . . . charges him with, "undermining the Foundation of the Colony, by writing against the King's Pattent." In a few lines further on, strange to say, it informs us, that "The Gov. and Council agreed to *pass over*, the offence, as its influence, might not be so evil as they feared." It was a mild blast of the " Ram's-horn."

The book, charges him with — " Endangering the Stability of the Government, by his opposition to the Resident's Oath."

Mr. John Cotton says ; " Mr. Williams' positions were so well taken that the Court desisted from that proceeding." The book, tells he had "a fervid female following " — because the First Ladies of Salem, were with him in the popular favor. Has the book, "As to Roger Williams," any remarkable, "fervid following," of any kind ?

Both the book — and chairman Washburn say — " He deserved to be Banished." Aye — but Mr. Cotton dodged for all that — and tried to dodge, for what he had done in it.

The most remarkable ellipsis in the whole book, is ; no criticism, on Gov. Winthrop for aiding and abetting Mr. Williams, to escape Capt. Underhill, and the Court. It is as well *not*, to criticise him, so long as "ye" book, is so happily dedicated to one of "ye" Governour's " Hon. Posterity."

Not a single *point*, is *made ;* in the book, thus far ; against Roger Williams. The agony of the book, over the "Sturbridge Petition ; " is just as much against Gov. Winthrop's proposal. The Massachusetts Legislature of 1875-6, gave Hon. John Winthrop, First Governor of Massachusetts Bay — and "the excellent if not Erudite " — Sturbridgers — *both* — " Leave to withdraw."

Further on, in the book, a mighty plunge is made — at the vital point — thus saith it — " I cannot help thinking that the weight of evidence is conclusive, to the point, that his exclusion from the Colony, took place for reasons *purely political* — and having no relation to his notions on toleration." . . . Now on the next page — see how clear the book, makes it — i. e., as clear as a point-blank Contradiction can make it — " For the most grievous thing about him and that which clearly most exasperated his enemies — was ; that he was so *intensely* rigid, in his principles of *Separation.*"

What does the book, mean ? It leaves us in the dark. Hear its dictum ! " It was *this* — it was *that* — for which he was excluded." No — " It was *not this* — it was *not that*" — " As to Rogers Williams." . . . Alas — Alas — that book, must be dazed !

But, whatever the cause of the exclusion — it caused no abatement of the " loving friendship, from first to last" — between Williams, and Winthrop. Besides — " His eminent Worthiness — Hon. R. C. Winthrop LL.D." (to whom the book, is so dexterously ascribed —) " Conscientiously, and Contentiously" declares — of Roger Williams' exclusion, " I palliate not a *particle* of it."

Good-by, book. Thou hast " leave to withdraw."

And then, as tho' this extreme of absurdity, were not extreme enough — the book, proceeds — " It seems fair notwithstanding all, to claim for our [ Puritan] Fathers, a Course of procedure towards the Baptists, which was liberal, for that time ; as it was far more humane than that which the professors of the same faith received in the Fatherland."

What ails the book? It starts, with the preconceived determination to "go over all the Records and *fix it* — so that no lazy, prejudiced, historian can make it other than is declared in, this book." It says they didn't Persecute — that even "Banishment was enlargement" — of a Comfortable Sort.

Further on, the book, admits, what it began to deny ; yes, "they did *persecute* — but it was liberal, humane persecution." Thus the book, Brands the Puritans, as Persecutors !! Alas ; what in other parts of the work is often and stoutly repudiated.

" Humane, persecution " — yes indeed — in so far as the Boston, " Whipping-post " may be more " humane," than the " Rack of the Inquisition "! ! Good-by, — book, — spread over it, the " mantle of Christ's, Charity " — and set the " Olive Branch," by it.

After all that has been uttered, in looking over the Criticisms of Gov. Winthrop's proposal to Revoke — the Sentence, against Roger Williams — we find the climax of self-stultification — on page 140.

" If Massachusetts, as Colony ; or Commonwealth ; — failed, to abolish all lingering Union between Church, and State — until within the memory of the middle-aged men of to-day — it is by no means sure, when the mother-Country — to say nothing of the rest of the world — will stand on this question ; where the Bay State has been standing for the last 40 years ! ! ! "

The proud position where the Bay State now stands

— is — the very position to which the State was called, by the blast of Roger Williams' "Ram's-horn" — 240 years before.  Had the Bay State stood where it does now, on freedom of Conscience — when Roger Williams declined the call of the "unseparated" church of Boston, he never would have been Banished.  Gov. Winthrop would never have proposed to have him recalled.  That book, would never have charged the Puritans, with "*mild*, humane, persecution."  That book, would never have been written ; if the Puritans of 240 years ago, had adopted Roger Williams' *Opinions* — as the descendants of the Puritans in the *Old Bay State*, have done, 240 years after.

If Roger Williams was wrong — then Massachusetts is wrong to-day ; for catching the "infeccon of his opinions " — but if Roger Williams was right, and Massachusetts is right, "for the last 40 years ;" then the Puritans were wrong 240 years ago.

Farewell thou book : written in haste, to condemn Roger Williams ; and commend the Puritans — turns a summerset — and commends Roger Williams, and condemns the Puritans !

F. Finally — let Massachusetts do herself the immortal honor First ; to REVOKE that Sentence of Banishment.  Then place the name of Roger Williams, on the list with her honored Citizens — to whose Memory a Suitable Memorial shall be erected, in the City of Boston.

The Universe, is Jehovah's Monument.  God's Seventh Day on which He rested — is a Memorial Day — that the Creator, Created, Creation, for His Creature Man.  The Rainbow, is a Covenant Memorial.

Mount Moriah — is Memorable, for Abraham's faith — the site of Solomon's Temple — and the visit of God's Well-Beloved Son. The Hebrew Passover — a Type of Christ — is memorialized in the Lord's Supper. Twelve Memorial Stones were taken from the Bed of the Jordan. The Old Testament, and the New Testament — are the Memorial Tables of Law — and the Gospel. Let Roger Williams have a Memorial in Boston!

The University of Leyden, Holland — founded by William, Prince of Orange — is a Memorial Thank-Offering to God, for the Gift, of Religious Liberty to his Country. The Hollis Fund — of Harvard College, is a Thank-Offering to God for the Gift of Religious Liberty to New England — from the Hollis Family. The First Amendment to the Constitution of the United States, is a Memorial guarantee — of Religious Liberty — to all the People of this Nation.

Rhode Island — has shown herself truly grateful to God, for Religious Liberty — by placing a Statue of Roger Williams in the National Capitol at Washington, D. C.

As a further tribute, to the Memory of the Man whom — Gov. Winthrop was anxious to honor — is the Roger Williams; Park, Providence, R. I.

On Oct. 16, 1877 — 242 years lacking 3 days, from the Banishment of Roger Williams, and 194 years after his Death — an immense concourse of people, thronged from the City of Providence, to the spot where the ceremonies were to occur. Col. Dexter, manager — announced the unveiling, which was done by Mr. Franklin Simmons, the Architect. Immense applause greeted the magnificent work of Art — the Band playing — and children singing the Original Hymn; by Mrs. Sarah Helen Whitman. Col. Dexter, addressing Mayor Doyle said — "I now deliver this monument of Roger Williams — to the city." The Mayor fittingly responded.

A few extracts from the Oration of Prof. Diman, on the Occasion of the Consecration of the Park — and the Unveiling of the Statue of Roger Williams; may be useful, by way of suggestions.

"In settling upon the shores of the Narragansett, nothing was farther from Roger Williams' thoughts than to become the Founder of a new Colony. . . . Mr. Williams says — It was not price, nor money, that could have purchased Rhode Island. It was purchased by the love and favor, which that Honorable Gentleman Sir HARRY VANE, and myself, had with the great Sachem Miantonomo. . . . In obtaining these lands, Mr. Williams acted upon the principle he had so earnestly avowed — as to the King's Pattent — that the Indians were the rightful proprietors of the lands they occupied — and that no English potentate could convey a complete title to them. . . .

"The land was conveyed to him by formal Deed from Canonicus — and Miantonomo — and was as much his as any man's coat on his back. . . . Let it be borne in mind that this statue of Roger Williams, stands in the midst of fields which he received as a free gift from these great Sachems — in grateful recognition of the many kind services he had continually rendered them. And these lands have for more than two centuries, remained in the uninterrupted possession of his posterity, and which have only passed from their hands to the City of Providence, to be forever preserved as a Public Park. What more fitting Site could have been Selected, than the spot which thus recalls the estimate in which he was held by the original possessors of the soil? . . .

"We are now upon land once owned by Roger Williams — which has been recently bequeathed to the City of Providence, by MISS BETSEY WILLIAMS — his Great-Great-Granddaughter. The love she bore the City her great Ancestor Founded — and her reverence for his Memory — prompted this bequest — by which she provided, that this tract of land — which contains about 100 acres, might be forever kept as a Public Park — and be known — as 'ROGER WILLIAMS PARK.'

"In these ceremonies of setting up with solemn religious rite this Memorial tribute, whose enduring bronze and granite, shall attest to coming generations, our estimate of Roger Williams, we owe it to ourselves, we owe those who shall gaze upon it with respectful interest, after we are gone — a deliberate statement of the grounds on which that estimate is based. . . .

"But Roger Williams, not only merits our admiration for his personal qualities, his intellectual culture was generous, and broad. By the favor of Sir Edward Coke, that greatest Master of English Law, he was sent to one of the most famous of the great Schools of England. On the roll of Students, in which his name ranks among the Earliest, are the names of Barrow, Addison — Steele — John Wesley, Blackstone. At Cambridge he took his degree of Bachelor of Arts, in 1627.

"We find him enjoying the highest regard of Sir

Harry Vane — like himself, an enthusiast for Ideal truth — a spirit touched to the finest issues ; a man of extraordinary parts, and whom Milton extolled, as a Senator unsurpassed in Roman story. At the country-seat of Sir Vane, Mr. Williams, when in England, was always a welcome guest.

"But in the circle of Roger Williams' friends, was one more famous than Sir Vane. During his second visit to England we find him instructing John Milton in Dutch; who in return read him many more languages. They stood side by side in the great battle of freedom of thought ; tho' even Milton did not advocate a Liberty of Conscience, so complete and absolute, as that claimed by Roger Williams.

"With the great Protector, too, he was sometimes admitted to close discourse. I need not comment on the kind of man Roger Williams must have been, who was permitted even the occasional companionship of Sir Vane — of Milton — and of Cromwell.

"We find Gov. John Winthrop, writing to him in language that does equal honor to both — 'Sir, we have often tried your patience, but could never conquer it.' . . . The recent biographer of Milton, terms him a 'picturesque figure forever in early American History, and no Man of the Age deserves more attention.' . . . Thro' life his most trusted counsellor was the wise, the discriminating, the magnanimous, Gov. Winthrop — who he declares — 'tenderly loved me to his last breath.' . . .

"Roger Williams, was a sturdy, uncompromising separatist, when he renounced the Communion of the Church of England ; and such he remained to the day of his death. Warmly as he denied the Theocratic Policy — of the churches of the Bay — he always cordially approved, their 'Heavenly Doctrines.'

"As we recall the remarkable circumstances under which we came into existence as a State — they only intensify the gratitude we owe to God, while we hail the APOSTLE of RELIGIOUS LIBERTY, as the FOUNDER of RHODE ISLAND. . . .

"Here, we have placed our Statue of ROGER WILLIAMS. Here let it stand: here in a seclusion the thoughtful study challenged by its various excellences; here — amid the fields which he accepted as gifts of friendship from CANONICUS and MIANTONOMO — here; in silent companionship with kindred dust. . . .

"Here, let it stand; Here, let returning Seasons greet it; here, let Men as they rest from their toil; here let the Women of America, bless the Fathers and Mothers of the Man; and his Wife; who rocked the cradle of Soul Liberty, in the City of Providence: nor forget, 'BETSEY WILLIAMS;' who modestly outdid Canonicus and Miantonomo — by giving back to the Memory of Roger Williams — land they gave to *him;* here, let children, as they pause in their play — gaze with delight upon this splendid Statue of a *Man* — who chose to suffer persecution, as bitter as death — rather — than to act with a doubting Conscience."

# INDEX.

Title, I.
To Posterity, III.
Prefatory, V, VII.
Contents, VIII, IX.
Ages, Dark, 1, 247.
Ainsworth, 9.
America, 2, 37, 126, 208, 246, 297.
   Separatists look to, 10.
   Pilgrims in, 21.
Ann, Cape, 31, 36.
Apostles, 1, 217.
Arbella, Flagship, 48.
   Address on, 48, 257.
   Arrival of, 49.
   Compact, and Order on, 49.

Banishment
   of Ralph Smith, 39, 58, 74.
   of Brownes, 41, 59.
   of Lynn, 60.
   of 14 persons, 61.
   of Roger Williams, 104, 116.
   of John Clarke, 147, 121.
   of Wheelwright, 121.
   of Mrs. Hutchinson, 121.
   Edict of, 144.
   Ship to England, 152.
   Mary Dyer, 161.
   Quakers, 162.
   Gould, etc., 175.
   Revoke, of Roger Williams, 116, 210, 213.
Baptist,
   John Smyth, a, 9, 10, 124.
   Roger Williams, a, 116, 125, 266.
   1st Church of, in America, 126.
   Edict against, 129, 135, 144.
   Clarke John, a, 144, 149.
   A Sermon on, 150, 174.
   Dunster, and Chauncey, 154.
   Thomas Gould, a, 171, 175.
   1st Church in Colony of Mass., 171, 176.
   Meeting House of, in Boston, 181, 182.
   Charged with Idolatry, 182.
   Doors of, Nailed-up, 182.
   Edict against, gone, 182, 5, 209.
   1st Church Ordination, 199, 204, 5.
   Concessions to, 200.
   Hollis Fund, 205.
   Washington, on, 208.

Bay,
   Cape Cod, 15,
   Pilgrims in, 18, 21.
   New Plymouth, 22, 31, 33.
   of Massachusetts, 36, 127, 8.
   of Narragansett, 24, 109, 115, 122,3,128.
   the Three unlike, 115.
   of Mass. and Plym., unite, 192.
Bible,
   1st English, Printed, 4.
   Authority of, 4, 9, 133.
   Robinson's Advice, 12, 77.
   on Religious Liberty, 214, 221.
Born, 1st Child in New England, 18.
Boston,
   Founded, 49.
   Church taxes, 53.
   Roger Williams comes to, 67.
   Roger Williams called to 1st Church of, 71.
   Magistrates of, 73.
   Pastor in, 102.
   Roger Williams ordered to, 108.
   Importance of, 115.
   1st Church of, 118.
   Elders of, 124.
   Roger Williams goes thro', 128.
   2d Synod in, 136, 9.
   Jail in, 148.
   Wilson of, 150.
   Puritans of, 150.
   Whipping-post in, 151.
   Not sail from, 152.
   Roger Williams in, 155.
   Roger Williams invited to, 158.
   3d Synod in, 159.
   Quakers in, 161.
   Church and State in, 160.
   4th Synod in, 166.
   Prayer Book in, 172.
   Religious Liberty in, 173.
   Debate in, 175, 9.
   "Separation" in, 177.
   5th Synod in, 178.
   Baptists in, 180.
   6th Synod in, 183.
   Roger Williams' decline of call, 71, 186.
   Governor Andros in, 189.
   Episcopacy in, 190.
   To honor Roger Williams (as she has John Winthrop), 273, 279, 293.

Bradford, Wm., 13.
  Mrs., 21.
  Sickness of, 23.
  Chosen Governor, 24.
  Canonicus' present to, 26.
  Exposes Lyford, 28, 9, 31.
  Commends Roger Williams, 74, 5.
  Treatise for, 76, 82, 229, 240.
  Did not put the Vote, 133.
Brewster, Wm., Elder, 8.
  Goes with the Pilgrims, 11.
  Favored by Governor Bradford, 28.
  In Plymouth, 32, 115.
  On Roger Williams, 77, 116, 125, 190, 240.
Brownes,
  Displeased, 41.
  Separate worship, 41.
  Shipped to England, 41.
  Sympathy for, 42.
  Agitation by, 50, 1, 9, 61.
  Reaction, 63.
  A Mistake, 165, 172, 7, 9.

Callendar, Elisha,
  Ordination of, 199, 274.
  Sermon by Mather, 199.
  Hollis Fund, 205.
Cambridge (New Town),
  Court at, 97, 100, 3.
  Hooker, pastor at, 103.
  Meeting House at, 103.
  1st Synod in, 119.
  2d Synod in, 136, 8.
  Platform of, 139, 142, 166.
  Schools to fit for, 145.
  Presidents of, 154, 5.
  Harvard College at, 204.
Canonicus.
  Bundle of Arrows, 26.
  Lands to Roger Williams, 113, 260, 295, 8.
Carver, John.
  In England, 11.
  Chosen Governor, 16.
  Looked for landing, 19.
  Sickness of, 23.
  And Massasoit, 24.
  Death of, 24.
Chauncey, Charles.
  Prest. Ilr'vd Col., 155.
Charter — Mass. Bay,
  Date of, 36.
  Confirmed, 45, 226.
  Silent on Religion, 46, 57, 73, 128, 165.
  King could annul, 56.
  Endangered, 59, 84.
  Exceeded, 61, 230.
  Plea for, 62.
  Demanded, 63.
  Reassumed, 63, 84.
  Superseded, 63, 4, 87, 152.
  Communion, 65.
  Cotton's opinion of, 66, 226.

Charter, *continued.*
  Not undermined by Roger Williams, 78, 84, 5, 7, 147, 170.
  Gone, 79, 88, 96.
  Assumed power, 65, 105, 108.
  Restored, and overrode, 165, 9, 170, 4, 182, 3.
  Reissued, and reassumed, 189, 191.
  New-given, 192.
  Sermon on, 194.
  Retaliation, 202.
Christ,
  The Story of, III.
  Taught by, V.
  Head of the Church, 1, 33.
  Church planted by, 1.
  Gospel of, 2.
  Church Independent, 2, 34, 40.
  Supper of, 3.
  Faith in, 5.
  Follower of, 12.
  Light of, 15.
  Under Law to, 22, 33, 40.
  Things of, and Cæsar, 48.
  Magna Charta of, 74.
  Prerogative of, 86.
  "Ram's-horn" of, 95, 109, 272, 278, 280, 293, 272, 8, 280.
  Fundamental text of, 95.
  Need of faith in, 120.
  King and Lawgiver, 124.
  Platform of, 136.
  Kingdom of, 140, 9.
  to Suffer with, 150.
  Peace and Order of, 185.
  on Church and State, 214, 216.
  Taught His Apostles, 217.
  Suffered for, 219.
  Panacea of, 223.
  Good of the Church of, 228.
  a Conscience like, 248.
  Mantle of, 253, 4.
Church,
  History of, V.
  Head of, 1.
  of Christ, 2.
  Independence of, 2, 32, 33, 34, 40.
  the true, 5.
  King's, 5, 35.
  of Rome, 6.
  Separatists from, 7.
  in Amsterdam, 9, 266.
  of Eng., 9.
  of Leyden, 10, 17, 22, 31, 32.
  of the State, 10.
  no Union of, and State, 17.
  of Scrooby, 18.
  a, in New England, 22.
  Management of, 32.
  no Rule but the Word of God, 33.
  Smith, Pastor, 257, 33.
  of Eng., 38.
  1st, formed in N. E., 40.
  Skelton, Pastor, 40.
  Mixed, 40, 43.

# INDEX. 301

Church, *continued.*
1st, of Salem, 41.
Brownes "Separate," 41, 257.
of the Puritans, 44, 49, 52.
not "Separatists," 38, 45, 59, 257.
the English, 48.
Taxes for Elders, 49.
Magistrates and Elders, 53, 226.
Holidays, 53.
Things mixed, 64.
John Cotton's Idea, 66, 226.
Sir Coke's Work, 244, 68.
Roger Williams in Church of Eng., 68.
Against the National, 258, 70.
1st Boston, unseparate, 71, 73, 227.
Call R. Williams, 71.
He declines Call of, 71, 261, 227, 258.
Salem call R. Williams, 72, 228.
at New Plymouth, 72.
in Salem warned, 73, 228, 258.
at Plymouth call R. W., 258.
Order of Service, 75.
in Salem recall R. Williams, 77, 258, 229, 240.
and State in Mass. Bay, 79.
Magistrates re-warn Salem, 81, 228, 258.
Skelton's death, 83.
Pastor of Salem watched, 83, 266, 264.
Cotton favors, R. W., 85.
in Salem face the Court, 87.
Magistrates subside, 87, 269, 231, 241.
in Salem ordain R. W., 259, 231, 87.
in Salem indicted, 88, 262, 232.
Admonish Magistrates, 90, 259.
Elders retort on the Salem, 91, 233.
in Salem, succumbs, 92.
in Salem Meeting House, 93.
R. W., farewell letter to, 93, 234.
and State question, 94.
R. W. firm for "Separation," 95, 235.
Elders of, vindictive, 96, 260.
the Salem, gone over, 96.
R. W. firm for liberty, 96, 237, 260.
and Pastor, called to Court, 97.
Held in contempt by the Court, 97.
Defended by Endicott, 241, 98, 259, 249, 278.
and Endicott, succumbs, 98.
and all excited, 99.
Court in Meeting House of the, 103.
Elders of, and Court pass *Sentence* against R. Williams, 104, 260, 241.
Cotton, Elder of, apologizes, 107, 262, 242, 271, 280.
Elders of, fear R. W., 108, 265, 260, 242, 264.
R. W. ordered to Boston to be shipped to Eng. by Elders of, and Court, 236, 108.
Gov. Winthrop of the, Boston, gives R. W. a "hint," 109, 260, 236, 242.
Elders of, lost their game, 109, 263.
Elders feared R. W. still, 110.
Salem Ex-Pastor in Exile, 111.

Church, *continued.*
Salem Ex-Pastor Peacemaker of the Indians, 112.
at Plymouth asks R. W. to go on, 260, 112.
R. W. Ex-Pastor settles in Providence, R. I., 114.
the, of N. E. drove R. W., 114.
of the Three "Bays," 115, 122.
Protected by R. W., 116.
Gov. Winthrop asked the Elders to recall R. W., 116, 277, 289, 264, 243.
no, or Court has yet, 281, 116, 293.
1st in Boston, not at peace, 118.
and Court, call 1st, Synod, 119, 265.
and Cotton, at one again, 120, 265.
Troublers of the, sent off, 121.
in Rhode Island, 122.
and State, no Union of, 122.
Under 3 "Compacts," 123.
Accepts Cotton's Excuse, 265, 123.
Confession of faith, in Eng., 124.
1st Baptist, of America, 126.
Elders and Court, Decree, 129.
Divines of Westminster, 130.
Elders and Court, stern, 132.
Eldsrs and Commissioners alert, 132.
Elders and Court smother, 267.
Toleration in Plymouth, 133.
and Cotton's Keys, 133.
Elders and Brethren to rule, 134.
in the, Women ruled out, 134.
Elders mighty — but the Brethren weak, 134.
Must have Ruling Synods, 135.
Elders, couldn't explain, 135.
Elders and Court, ask Commissioners of United Colonies, to call the 2d Synod, 136.
1st Boston, sends no delegates, 136.
Elders and Court, a soft Edict, 137.
Elders and Synod indorse the Westminster Creed, 138.
Elders, drop the Church of Eng., 138.
Elders, and the Snake, 139.
"Cambridge Platform," 139, 270.
in R. I. untrammelled, 141.
With two Platforms, 142.
at Rehoboth, 143.
Court, warning, 143.
in Rehoboth tolerated, 144.
in Newport, to Lynn, 147.
Cobbett, Pastor, 148.
Elders, and Mr. John Clarke, 146.
Elder Wilson and Holmes, 150.
in Boston and Providence, 152.
in Eng. grieved, 153.
Cotton and Wilson reproved, 153.
Unity in Doctrine, 154.
Elders, and Prest. Dunster, 154.
Roger Williams in Boston, 155.
in R. I. gets Religious Liberty, 157, 260.
R. W. explains, 157.
Elders invite R. W. to Boston, 158.

Church, *continued.*
   Elders and Court overruled, 159, 266, 268.
   Elder John Cotton's death, 159.
   3d Synod, 160.
   Who are Members, 160.
   Half-way Covenant, 160.
   of Puritans, splits half-way, 160.
   Decree on Quakers, 161.
   Elders and Court, halt a 2d time in Salem, 162, 269.
   Elders in Warwick, 162.
   Members' vote vetoed, 165.
   of the Puritans, crumbling, 165.
   in 3 parties, 166.
   Elders and Court dazed, 166.
   Calls a 4th Synod, 166.
   "Half-way Covenant," nowhere, 167.
   Independency vetoed, 167.
   Religious Liberty in R. I., 168.
   Elders alarmed, 170.
   1st Baptist of Boston, 171, 249.
   of Eng. Service in Boston, 172.
   of Puritans offended, 172, 271.
   in R. I. for Soul Liberty, 173.
   in Boston and Providence, 173.
   Taxes resisted, 174.
   Members' vote assailed by "Third Party," 174, 175.
   Elders try a debate, 175.
   Court helps the Elders, 176.
   at Noddle's Island, 176.
   1st of Boston, a Schism, 176.
   Old South formed, 177, 271.
   Puritans, Separate, 271.
   Court calls 5th Synod, 178.
   Puritans grow Independent, 178.
   Platform and Covenant, 179.
   Plantation Edict, 179.
   at Noddle's Isle, build a Meeting House in Boston, 180.
   Elders' Edict against building Meeting Houses, 180.
   the, hold a Meeting, 181.
   Court, NAIL the DOOR, 181.
   Elders pulled the nails, 181, 271.
   Mather's Divine Right, 182.
   Baptists, equal rights, 182.
   Court sentenced nailed-up, 182.
   This for that, 183.
   Elders, 6th and last Synod, 183.
   R. W. Sees the "holy Season," 183.
   Winthrop's lament, 184, 267.
   Elders, Liberty of Conscience, 184.
   Success at last, 185, 272.
   Death of R. Williams, 186, 272.
   Great achievement for, 186.
   Bancroft's Eulogy, 187.
   R. W. honored in R. I., 188.
   a, Conscience, 188.
   has more Honors for R. W., 188, 273.
   of the Theocracy, torn, 189.
   of England service ordered in "Old South," 189, 273.

Church, *continued.*
   Worse had been before, 190.
   Toleration never slept, 190.
   Episcopal Meeting House, 190.
   Elders face the King, 191.
   Toleration in Eng., 191.
   Elders, of N. E. take it, 192.
   Puritans, blame the Elders, 192.
   Gets rid of Theocracy by the New Charter, 192, 274.
   Elders, final cruelty, 193.
   Sermon, on New Charter, 194, 272.
   Pastors for life, 197.
   and State demolish Church and State, 198.
   1st Baptist, ordain Elisha Callander, 199.
   Elders, Mathers, there, 199.
   "Good Men United," 199, 274.
   Evils of Theocracy seen and cursed, 249, 200.
   Harmony in Boston, 201, 275.
   Elders on a Vacation, 201.
   Synods illegal, 276, 201.
   Rough retrospect, 202.
   Taxes remitted, 203.
   "4 Colonies," follow and accept R. I., 203.
   What Roger Williams meant by "unseparated," 203.
   Reconstruction, 204.
   of Christ wins the day, 204.
   "Hollis Fund," 204, 7.
   Religious Liberty the root of Civil Liberty, 207.
   "Ordinance of 1787," 208.
   "Constitutional Amendment by Washington, 208, 276.
   "Peace of Religion 1555, to Mass, Bill of Rights, 1834," 207.
   Gov. Winthrop's Proposal to Revoke Roger Williams' Sentence, remains, 210, 109, 116, 243, 276, 8, 282, 287, 289.
   Brethren in Christ, 211, 153, 172, 195, 200, 214, 254.
   Triumph of Religious Liberty in the United States, 183, 212.
   History of N. E., 223, 5, V., 186.
   Reasons why the Sentence of Banishment against Roger Williams should be Revoked, Part II., 213, 298.
Cities, of persecution, 221.
Clarke,
   Buys Island, 122.
   Pastor at Newport, 144.
   Others go to Lynn, 149.
   Endicott Challenges, 149.
   Publishes "Ill News" Eng., 153.
   Tarries in Eng., 155.
Clark's Island, 20.
   Pulpit Rock, 20.
Cobbett, Thos.
   Discourse of, 148.

Cobbett, Thos., *continued*.
   Clarke, Holmes, and Crandall, at meeting, 150.
   Call to Ipswich, 174.
Coke, Sir Edward.
   Sees Roger Williams, 67, 8.
   Daughter of, 69.
   House of, 109, 186, 239, 244.
Coligny Admiral, 220.
Colonies, United.
   Four unite, 127.
   R. I. left out, 127.
   Decree of, 132.
   Call 2d Synod, 136.
   Refuse aid to, 145.
   Rectify R. I., 146.
   Roger Williams goes thro', 155.
   Accuse Plymouth, 159.
   Edict of, on Quakers, 160.
   Policy of renounced, 160.
Colossus, 256, 262.
Compact, of Pilgrims,
   Agreement of, 15.
   Names of Signers, 16.
   no Church and State Union, 17.
   See 40, 46, 49, 52, 64, 101, 2.
Congregational,
   Church order, 139.
   Order of, 141.
   Those of that way, 182, 209.
   the Orthodox, 160.
Conscience,
   of the Bishops, 4.
   of the "Separatists," 7.
   Liberty of, 11, 14, 34, 42, 3, 68.
   the Question involved, 71.
   Endicott warned, 73.
   Elder Brewster's advice, 78.
   Scruple of, 85.
   Christ Lord of, 40, 124, 5, 9.
   Oath is Christ's, 86, 89, 4, 103, 104.
   Shelter for, 114.
   Exiles for, 125.
   Under color of, 132.
   Freedom of, assured, 141.
   Public and Court, 159, 119, 125, 211, 212, 163, 183, 4, 187, 194, 5, 8, 203, 4, 284.
   Friends of, cheered, 129.
   Persecution for sake of, 139.
   Banner, 221.
   in Religious Opinions, 220.
   Decree on, 184, 272.
Cotton, John.
   Roger Williams meets, 68.
   Comes to N. E., 78.
   Settlement of, 80.
   Reports Magistrates, 81.
   Counsels the Court, 84.
   Sides with R. Williams, 85.
   Reports R. W., 86.
   on R. W., Sentence, 99.
   Lame apology, 107.
   Left the Court, 104, 6, 8, 280, 263, 266, 242.

Cotton, John, *continued*.
   Aristocratical, 110.
   With Hutchinsons, 118, 120.
   Apologizes, 123.
   Bloody Tenet, 127, 8.
   Keyes, 133, 5.
   Platform, 137,
   Sermon of, 148.
   Letter to, and reply, 153.
   Opinion of Charter, 66, 226.
   on Democracy, 141, 265.
   Death of, 159.
Court, Generall.
   Chartered, 45.
   Charter of, 46.
   by Charles I., 46.
   Silent on Religion, 46.
   of Assistants on Arbella, 48, 49.
   Houses for Elders, 49.
   Boston Founded, 49.
   1st Session of, 51.
   Morton shipped to Eng., 51.
   2d Session of, 52.
   Citizens to be Church Members, 52.
   Elders advisers of, 53, 201.
   King and Charter, 56.
   Exceed Parliament, 61.
   go beyond Charter, 61.
   Charter called for, 63.
   no Charter Basis, 64.
   Assume Military Power, 65.
   Beacon Hill, 65.
   no Charter Authority, 66.
   Caution Salem Church, 73.
   Winthrop at Plymouth, 75.
   Church and State, 79.
   Advice of Elders to, 80.
   Caution Salem again, 81, 83.
   Sit on "Treatise," 81.
   Pass it over, 83.
   Cotton to, 84.
   Charter, 84.
   and Roger Williams, 85, 6.
   "Resident's Oath," 85, 6.
   Double advice to Salem, 87.
   no Charter power, 88.
   Summons of, 88.
   Advice of Elders, 88.
   Refuse a Deed, 89, 232.
   Liable to Church Discipline, 89.
   Admonitory Letters, 90.
   Retort in Kind, 91.
   Push Williams, 92.
   Summons of, 96.
   had no Charter, 96.
   Elders advise, 96.
   Session of, 97.
   Stormed by Endicott, 98, 241.
   Deputies to return, 98.
   Adjourned, 99.
   Much Excitement, 99.
   the GREAT SESSION, 100.
   Indictment of R. W., 100.
   Composition of, 101.
   in a quandary, 102.

# INDEX.

Court, *continued.*
  Adjournment, 104.
  a bad job, 104.
  PASS SENTENCE, 104.
  no Charter Authority, 105.
  not Unanimous, 222, 106, 8.
  Sixe Weekes Extended, 108.
  Orders Williams' arrest, 108.
  Gov. Winthrop's hint, 109.
  Solicitous alarm, 110.
  not all for *Ostracism*, 112.
  Proposal of Gov. Winthrop, 116.
  1st N. E. Synod, 119.
  Gain Mr. Cotton, 120.
  Wheelwright and Hutchinsons ejected, 121.
  Edict on Anabaptists, 129.
  Claims Shawomet, 126, 131.
  R. Williams forbidden, 131.
  Without Charter, 131.
  Edict of, no change in, 132.
  2d N. E. Synod, 136.
  Deputies in doubt, 136.
  Desists the 2d time, 137.
  Protest to Plymouth, 143.
  Cruel Edict, 145.
  Demand of Plymouth, 146.
  Trial of Clarke and others, 148.
  in the two Bays, 152.
  Malden Church fined, 152.
  Cromwell sets the Sentence of R. Williams aside, 155.
  Invites R. W. to Boston, 158.
  Complain of Plymouth, 159.
  Calls 3d Synod, 160.
  Edict on Quakers, 160.
  Death of Cromwell, 164.
  Rebuked, 164.
  3 parties, 165.
  Changes, 166.
  Calls 4th Synod, 166.
  and Kings, Commissioners, 170.
  go pro and con, 170.
  Great Debate, 175.
  Letters to R. I., 173.
  Calls 5th Synod, 178.
  Trying Evils, 179.
  Edict on Meeting Houses, 180.
  " nailed-up," 181.
  Calls 6th Synod, 183.
  Decree on Religious Liberty, 185.
  Death of Roger Williams, 186.
  Havoc of James II., 189.
  bow to W. III., of Eng., 191.
  Mather yielded, 192.
  New Charter, 192.
  Sermon on, 194.
  Act of new, 196.
  Advocate Toleration, 197.
  Curses Persecution, 200.
  Eccl. taxes outlawed, 203.
  Religious Liberty the Law, 210.
  Petition to revoke Sentence against Roger Williams, 210.
  Spread the " Mantle of Charity," 225.

Covenants,
  of Separatists, 10.
  of Pilgrims, 16.
  of the Puritans, 40.
  Cambridge, 136, 9, 178, 183, 202.
  Half-way, 176, 7, 179.
  Providence, R. I., 269.
Coverdale's Bible, 4.
Cromwell, Oliver.
  Commonwealth under, 143.
  Protector, 155, 174.
  Congratulated, 158.
  Confirms R. I., Gov't., 160, 158, 269, 210.
  Intimate with Roger Williams, 297.
  Death of, 164.
Cushman, Robt.
  in Eng., 11, 13, 14.
  Sermon of, 25.
  Goes in Ship Fortune, 26.
  Agt. in Eng., 28.
  Death of, 31.

Dunster, Henry.
  President Harvard College, 154.
  Removed, 154.
  Succeeded by Chauncey, 154.
Duke of Lancaster, Protects Wickliffe, 2.

Elders, Puritans,
  Houses for, 49.
  Ruling, 77, 134, 139, 142, 167, 175, 8, 9.
  State Support, 49, 79.
  Advise the Court, 80, 83, 84, 96, 7, 9, 102, 124, 127, 132, 166.
  Stop Admonitory letters, 99, 1.
  Such as they, 144, 5, 150, 3, 162, 175, 6, 184, 193, 194, 199, 234.
  Advice defunct, 183, 201, 3, 212, 221, 223.
  Roger Williams an, 104.
  John Cotton an, 120, 280.
  J. C. not for Roger Williams' Sentence, 106, 8.
Endicott, Gov.
  Get Patent, 36.
  Sent to Salem, 37.
  Interested in Pilgrims, 39.
  Sends off Smith, 39, 257.
  Ships the Brownes, 41, 172, 271.
  Cautioned, 42.
  Example, 49.
  Warned by the Court, 73, 228.
  Storms the Court, 98, 241, 249, 279.
  Succumbs, 98, 278.
  Challenges Clarke, 149.
  Challenge accepted, 149, 175.

Forerunners, 1.
Frederick the Wise,
  Favors the, 3.
  Protects Luther, 3, 220.

Giddings, Geo., 174.

## INDEX.

Gould, Thos., 171.
   Dealt with for Schism, 171.
   Imprisoned, 171.
   Public debate, 175.
   at Noddles, 176.
   Builds a Meeting House, 179, 180, 1.

Harvard College,
   Founded [1638], 204.
   Schools to fit for, 145.
   Dunster and Chauncey Prests., 154.
   Hollis Fund of, 204, 7.
Higginson,
   Comes to Salem, 38.
   not a " Separatist," 38.
History, Eccl. of N. E., 246, 252.
   Prefatory, V., 186, 223, 5.
Holland,
   Prince of Orange in, 6.
   Pilgrims flee to, 8.
   Religious Liberty in, 43.
Hollis Fund,
   Founders of, 204.
   Occasion of it, 205.
   Thank-offering, 205.
   Philosophical Apparatus, 205.
   Specific objects, 206.
   Large amount, 206.
   Beneficiaries who, 206.
   to be Sacredly applied, 206.
Holmes, Obadiah,
   Pastor at Rehoboth, 143.
   Goes to Newport, 144.
   Goes to Lynn, 147.
   at Mr. Witter's, 148.
   Tried and imprisoned, 148.
   at Whipping-post Boston, 151.
Huss, John,
   Chaplain, 2.
   a Council, 3.
   Betrayed and burnt, 3, 220.

Independence,
   of Churches, 2.
   Pilgrims were, 22, 32.
   Synods opposed to, 139, 178.
   Puritans become, 178.
Inquisition, fell, 6.

Kepler, 187.
Kettle, copper, 18.

Lancaster Duke, Protected Wickliffe, 2, 220.
Landing of Pilgrims, 18.
   Date of whole Company, 21.
   (of Puritans, 49.)
Leyden,
   Separatists go to, 10.
   Smyth's influence, 10.
   Separatists Leave, 11.
   Farewell Sermon, 12.
   Church disbanded, 31.
   University, 204.

Louis I. Protects Claude, 219.
Luther, Martin,
   Helped by Frederick, 3.
   Peace of Religion, 6.
   at Worms, 7, 220.

Massachusetts Bay, Colony.
   Gov. & Co., 36.
   Boundaries of, 36.
   Patent for, 36.
   Endicott sent, 37.
   Many come to, 38.
   1st Church in, 40.
   Stately move, 43, 44, 56.
   Charter of, 46, 55.
   Emigration to, 48.
   Enemies of. 59.
   Apologists for, 62.
   Charter threatened, 63.
   Status of, 65.
   Charter of, 78.
   Roger Williams no underminer of, 78, 84, 87.
   Court of, 97.
   and Plymouth, 115.
   Claims Shawomet, 131.
   Claims Warwick, 146.
   Restriction in Religion, 152.
   Respects Cromwell, 155.
   non-intercourse with R. I., 173.
   Toleration Order in, 182.
   New Charter, 192.
   and Plymouth united, 192.
   Sermon on New Charter, 194.
   Accepts Religious Liberty, 197.
Massasoit, Chief.
   Friendship of, 24, 76.
   Gives Roger Williams land, 111.
Mather, Cotton.
   Advice of the Court, 81.
   of the Holy Flock, 91.
   Reports matters, 119, 139, 193, 199, 200, 1, 5, 205.
Mather, Increase, Divine Right of, 182, 191, 199, 275.
Mather, Richard, to prepare for a platform. 137.
Mayflower,
   to sail in, 13.
   Pilgrims on, 17.
   Compact on, 17, 114.
   at anchor, 21.
   on as a Church, 22.
   Land from the, 22.
   Returns to Eng., 24.
   Returns from Boston, 50.
   the, of Roger Williams, 113.
Meeting House,
   1st at Plymouth, 26.
   at Salem, 93.
   Cambridge, 103.
   Boston, 180, 1, 2.
   Decree on, 180, 192.
   Old South, 189, 271. 3.
   an Episcopal, in Boston, 190.

Miantonomo, Chief.
    Gifts to Roger Williams, 113, 260, 295, 298.
    is tomahawked, 127.
Mooshausick,
    Roger Williams settles at, 112.
    Meadows of, 113, 122.
Ministers' Lots,
    Set apart as, 79.
    Standing order, 197, 201.
Mosheim, 1.

Narrohigansetts Bay,
    Bay of, 24.
    Roger Williams to steer to, 109.
    Held back by R. Williams, 116.
    Providence Plantations on, 128.
    Clarke buys Aquidnay, 122.
    R. W. buys Prudence, 243.
    Separatists go to, 123.
Newton, 187.

Peace of Religion, 6.
Peasants, war of, 3.
Pilgrim Fathers,
    rise of, 2.
    "Separatists," 4.
    Spread of, 6.
    Depressed, 7.
    two Congregations of, 8.
    for Religious Liberty, 8.
    for in Holland, 9.
    for at Leyden, 10.
    for Hudson River, 11.
    for Liberty of Conscience, 11.
    Sermon of departure, 12.
    Left Leyden, and Delft Haven, 13.
    Sail in Mayflower, 14.
    Compact signed, 15.
    at Cape Cod, 15.
    Thanksgiving, 15.
    John Carver, Gov., 15.
    Miles Standish, Capt., 17.
    no Union of Church and State, 17.
    1st landing of, 18.
    2d landing, 18.
    Child born, 1st in N. E., 18.
    3d landing, 19.
    First encounter, 19.
    1st "Sabbath," in N. E., 20.
    Pulpit Rock, Motto on, 20.
    Mrs. Bradford drowned, 21.
    Final Landing, 22.
    Plymouth Rock, 22.
    Independents, 31, 32, 34, 22, 40.
    no Synods or Councils, 12, 22, 32.
    as a Church from Scrooby, 22
    Pilgrim Fathers, New Plymouth, 22.
    Settle in Families, 23.
    Leave the Mayflower, 23.
    Organize military, 23.
    Samoset, "Welcome Englishmen," 24.
    Friendship with Indians, 24.
    Good Title to Lands, 24.
    Severe sickness, 24.

Pilgrim Fathers, *continued.*
    Gov. Carver dies, 24.
    Mayflower returns, 24.
    Wm. Bradford, Gov., 24
    Ship Fortune arrives, 25.
    Joint Stock System, 25.
    Sermon by Mr. Cushman, 25.
    Build Meeting House, 26.
    Canonicus sends arrows, 26.
    Public Worship, 26.
    Pastor Robinson's Lament, 26.
    First Fast, 27.
    Great Thanksgiving, 27.
    5 Kernels of corn, 27.
    Lyford Case, 28.
    Independents, 32, 40.
    Form of Worship, 32.
    Collections taken, 32.
    Regard for the Holy Word, 33.
    Fellowship for Salem, 40.
    Ralph Smith, Pastor of, 40.
    Friends of Religious Liberty, 42.
    Call Roger Williams, 72.
    Visit of Gov. Winthrop to, 75.
    System of Church expenses, 53, 75.
    Roger Williams a "Sachem," 76.
    Roger Williams' friendship with Indians, 76.
    Roger Williams' writings, 76.
    Roger Williams coworker with Smith, 75.
    Roger Williams' daughter born at, 76
    Roger Williams recalled to Salem, 77.
    Elder Brewster's advice, 77, 125.
    Some go with Roger Williams, 77.
    Independents of Independents, 115.
    R. Williams reappears at Seekonk, 111, 2.
    Gov. Winslow's request, 111, 131, 141
    Gov. Bradford wavers, 133.
    Favor Mr. Holmes, 143.
    are chided, 144.
    Deny Commissioners' claim, 146, 267
    Complained of, 159.
    Reply to a Threat, 173.
    Plymouth Bay united with Mass. Bay, 194, 273.
Pope, 2.
    in Fear of Huss, 3.
    Paul III., 5.
    and Peace of Religion, 6, 263.
    Resisted by the Prince of Orange, 6.
    Luther and "Bull" of, 220.
    Independent of, 115.
Protestants,
    League of, 4.
    Compel Chas. V., 6.
    Reformers, 219, 221.
Providence, R. I.,
    Mooshausick, 112.
    Founded by Roger Williams, 114.
    Independent Church in, 115.
    well peopled, 172.
    Platform, 142.
    Roger Williams hurried on to, 155.

## INDEX. 307

Providence, *continued*.
  Statue of Roger Williams from, to Washington, D. C., 188.
  Throngs of its people, 294.
  Gift of Betsey to, 296.
Plummer Hall, Salem,
  in rear of Meeting House of 1634, 93.
  Shelters House Roger Williams preached in, 92, 93.
Puritans,
  Reformers, 5.
  Appeal to the Bible, 5.
  Why so called, 5.
  Timid and Bold, 7.
  3 Classes, 35.
  get a Charter, 36.
  Disliked, Separatists, 38.
  6 Ships of, sail, 38.
  not Separatists, 38.
  Style of, by Smith, 39.
  1st Church of, 40.
  Brownes Separate, 41.
  Brownes shipped, 41.
  Endicott cautioned, 42.
  New move, 44.
  Conscientious, 44.
  not for Religious Liberty, 44.
  Charter of, 45.
  Charter Silent on Religion, 46, 73, 128, 165.
  Letter to Church of Eng., 48.
  not Separatists, 48.
  Come to Mass. Bay, 49.
  Compact, Arbella and Mayflower, 49, 15, 17.
  Set up Churches, 49.
  Church and State, 49.
  Status Equivocal, 50.
  Some go back to Eng., 50.
  Vassal goes to Plymouth, 50.
  Stern rule, 51.
  Ship Lyon brings Roger Williams and Wife, 51.
  Theocratic Basis, 52.
  Church Polity of, 52.
  not Independents, 52.
  Elders and Magistrates, 53.
  Fast and Thanksgiving, 53.
  Ministers, Style of, 53.
  not Fathers of Religious Liberty, 54.
  a Mock Hearing, 55.
  get a Charter, 55.
  King glad they go, 56.
  a Veto on Charter, 56.
  Impolitic Devices, 57.
  not Separatists, 58.
  Chagrin of the Brownes, 59.
  Charter violated, 60.
  King offended, 60.
  Charter in danger, 60.
  Charter defended, 62.
  Called for, 63.
  Reassumed, 63.
  Commissioners appointed, 63.
  Were Charterless, 64.

Puritans, *continued*.
  Fortify Castle Island, 65.
  Light on Beacon Hill, 65.
  Mass. Bay Co. annulled, 65.
  Call Roger Williams, 71.
  He declines their Call, 72.
  Salem cautioned not to employ R. W., 73.
  R. W. goes to Plymouth, 74.
  Gov. of, at Plymouth, 75.
  Cotton and Hooker, 78.
  Church and State, 79.
  Settlement of Cotton, 80.
  Issue with R. W., 80.
  Salem warned again, 81.
  Charter trouble, 81.
  Challenge R, W., 82.
  Cotton and Wilson Calm, 83.
  Alarm for Charter, 83.
  Fast Sermon, 84.
  Cotton with Williams, 85.
  Cotton's testimony to, 86.
  Charter gone, 87.
  R. W. ordained, 87.
  Summoned to Court, 88.
  Elders' advice, 89.
  Salem send out letters, 90.
  Elders intercept letters, 90.
  Retort Discipline, 91.
  Hooker and Cotton troubled, 96.
  Magistrates ignore Church Discipline, 97.
  Gov. Endicott troubled, 98.
  Salem to back down, 98.
  Intense Excitement, 99.
  Court pass Sentence, 104.
  Mr. Cotton apologizes, 106.
  Court not Unanimous, 108.
  "Sixe Weekes," Extended, 108.
  R. W. cited to Boston to be shipped to Eng., 108.
  Gov. Winthrop's hint, 109.
  Capt. Underhill too late, 109.
  Dire chagrin, 110.
  R. W. in exile, 111.
  Massasoit a friend, 111.
  R. W. and Family at Seekonk, 111.
  Gov. Winslow's hint, 111.
  R. W. goes to Mooshausick, 112.
  Temporary triumph, 114.
  Bay not at peace, 117.
  Call a Synod, 119.
  Gain John Cotton, 120.
  Banish Hutchinsons, 121.
  Clarke and others go to R. I., 121.
  the 3 Colonies, 122.
  Arnolds submit, 126.
  Miantonomo tomahawked, 127.
  the 4 Colonies unite, 127.
  R. W. goes thro' Boston, 128.
  a Court Law, 129.
  Edict of "4 Colonies," 132.
  Cotton's Keys, 133.
  Complain of Aspersions, 135.
  ask 2d Synod, 136, 9, 194.

Puritans, *continued.*
　Warn Plymouth, 143.
　Warwick Sarcasm, 145, 162.
　Clarke arrested, 148.
　John Cotton's Sermon, 148.
　Holmes Whipped, 150.
　R. W. not sail out of Boston, 152.
　Cotton and Wilson reproved, 153.
　Prest. Dunster, resigns, 155.
　R. W. free pass, 155, 182.
　R. W. invited to Boston, 158.
　Plymouth reminded, 159.
　Quakers inhibited, 160.
　3d Synod, 160.
　Separate, 160.
　Decree of United Colonies, 161.
　John Winthrop Jr. quere, 161.
　Quakers hang, 161.
　King reaffirms, and overrides the Charter, 165.
　3 parties, 165.
　Say, not understood, 166.
　4th Synod, 166.
　Abhor Independency, 167.
　King's Commissioners, 169.
　Theocracy totters, 170.
　3d party hopeful, 170.
　Gould in prison, 171.
　Prayer Book in Boston, 172.
　Threat of non-intercourse, 173.
　Letter to R. Island, 173.
　Giddings' "pewter platters," 174.
　King hits Theocracy, 175.
　Great Debate, 175.
　"Unseparated," Separate, 177.
　5th Synod, 178.
　Independency, grows, 178.
　Platforms unsafe, 179.
　Meeting Houses inhibited, 180.
　Meeting Houses Nailed-up, 181.
　Mather's Divine Right, 182.
　Anabaptists tolerated, 182.
　King's, tit for tat, 183.
　6th Synod, 184.
　Williams, "Holy Season," 183.
　A. t of Toleration, 185.
　Self-Condemnation, 185.
　Death of Roger Williams, 186.
　Theocracy Revolutionized, 186.
　a Royal Governor, 189.
　Prayer Book in Boston, 189.
　Episcopal Meeting House, 190.
　in a Quandary, 191.
　Suppliants, 192.
　Witch hanging, 193.
　New Charter, 194.
　Mass. and Plym. Bays unite, 194.
　Sermon on New Charter, 194.
　Plea for Religious Liberty, 195.
　the "Standing Order," 196, 201.
　Elisha Callander ordained, 197.
　Sermon "Good Men United," 199.
　Church and State done, 201.
　Synods illegal, 202.
　Theocracy all illegal, 202.

Puritans, *continued.*
　Hollis Fund, 204.
　Thank-Offering, for Religious Liberty, 204.
　Church and State inhibited in the Northwest Territory, 208.
　Religious Liberty favored by Washington, 208.
　Roger Williams' *Sentence* still remains, 210.
　Petition of 1875 on Gov. Winthrop's Proposal, 210.
　Justice is waiting, 210.

Quakers, much wronged, 159, 160, 1, 2, 3, 190, 2, 5.
　Tolerated, 173, 175, 195.

Religious Liberty,
　Waldenses for, 2.
　Protestants for, 4.
　Prince of Orange for, 6.
　"Separatists" for, 7, 69.
　in Holland, 8.
　John Smyth for, 10, 69.
　Pilgrims, Fathers of, 22, 31, 42, 14, 54, 125.
　Roger Williams defends, 114, 115, 137, 183, 4, 7.
　in Rhode Island, 114, 141, 168.
　in England, 125.
　Success in New England, 152, 115, 183.
　Edict for, in Mass. Bay, 165, 189.
　and Civil related, 166, 207, 8.
　Sermons on, 194, 6, 200.
　Thank-Offering to God for, 205, 294.
　Eccl. Law of the United States, 212, 32.
　Religious Liberty in Mass. and Plym. Bays, 192.
　Opinions prevail, 198.
　Persecution an "Obsolete Blunder," 201.
　all Opposition to him illegal, 201, 2.
　Highly Esteemed, 151, 239, 214.
　Theocracy annihilated, 203.
　Hollis Thank-Offering for Religious Liberty, 205.
　Helps American Independence, 208.
　Washington Confirms Religious Liberty, 208.
　Toilers from 1555 to 1686, 209.
　Gov. Winthrop's proposal yet lingers, 210, 245.
　Cromwell, muzzled the Sentence, 210.
　Hon. R. C. Winthrop, "I palliate it not," 210.
　Sturbridge Petition, 210.
　Christ taught Religious Liberty, 214, 17.
　Christ's Apostles taught Religious Liberty, 217, 19.
　Christ's Reformers taught Religious Liberty, 119, 22.

## INDEX.                                                                309

Religious Liberty, *continued*.
  Christ's "Ram's-horn," Roger Williams, taught Religious Liberty, 224, 54, 99, 109, 110, 234, 278, 280, 290.
  Christ's DOCTRINE of RELIGIOUS LIBERTY, *Survives*, 255, 293.
  Christ's Disciples of the Nineteenth Century can suitably indorse Religious Liberty, by revoking Roger Williams' Sentence of Banishment, 293, 298.
Rhode Island,
  Gov. Winthrop suggests to Roger Williams the "Narrohigansett Country," 109.
  R. W. with 5 others leave Seekonk in the "Mayflower" Canoe, as the Pilgrim Fathers, of Rhode Island, landed at "Wha-Cheer" Cove, 113.
  Welcomed by the Indians to Mooshausick, 113.
  Land given him by Canonicus and Miantonomo, 113.
  Founded Providence for Religious Liberty, 114.
  Voluntary Gov't formed, 122.
  Shawomet claimed, 127.
  Roger Williams goes to Eng. for Charter, 127.
  Left out of United Colonies, 127.
  R. W. gets Charter of "Providence Plantations," 128.
  Refused help of "United Colonies," 145.
  Warwick claimed, 146.
  Goes by Manhattan, 152.
  R. I. Charter readily Confirmed, 152.
  Letter to Endicott, 154.
  Full Liberty thro' the Colonies, 155.
  R. I. Gov't confirmed, 156.
  Chosen President, 156.
  Defines Religious Liberty, 157.
  Cromwell confirms R. I. Gov't., 158.
  Rechosen Governor, 158.
  Invited to Boston, 158.
  Lived to see Power of Magistrates to meddle in Religion taken away, 185.
  Death of Roger Williams, 186.
  Whole life a triumph, 186.
  Sovereign Civil Authority in the People, 187.
  Bancroft's Eulogy, 187.
  Statue of, in Washington, 187.
  Park at Providence, 188, 294-298.
  to be honored more and more, 188, 116, 7, 183, 210, 224, 243, 7, 268, 276, 8, 281.
  R. I. Charter not given up, 189.
Robinson, John,
  Pastor in Leyden, 8.
  Bishop Hall tells, 9.
  Parting Sermon to Pilgrims, 12.
  Letter and regret, 26.
  Death of, 31.
  Family arrive at Salem, 39.

Robinson, John, *continued*.
  Family go to Plymouth, 31.
  Advice, 33.
  Rock, Pulpit, on Clark's Island, 20.
  Inscription on, 20.
  Fame of Plymouth, 21.
  What-cheer Cove, 113.
Sabbath, First kept in N. E., 20.
  How spent, 20.
  on the "Mayflower," 21.
Salem, N. E.,
  Covenant at, Naumkeag, 40.
  Endicott arrives at, 37.
  Higginson, Robinson family, and others arrive, 39.
  Ralph Smith sent away from, 39.
  Fast observed at, 39.
  Church organized, 40, 43.
  Brownes set up Church of Eng. Service, 41.
  Brownes shipped to Eng., 41, 51.
  Call Roger Williams, 72, 229.
  Endicott warned by the Court, 73.
  R. W. leaves, 73.
  R. W. recalled to, 77.
  Date of his return to, 78.
  Church again advised by the Court, 81.
  R. W. preaches at, 84.
  R. W. upheld by Public Opinion, 86.
  R. W. Ordained at, 87.
  R. W. and Church Summoned to Court, 88.
  Petition denied, 89.
  Church send Admonitory Letters, 90.
  Church bribed, 91.
  Build a Meeting-House, 93.
  People meet at his House, 95.
  Deputies sent Home from Court, 97.
  Endicott Storms the Court, 98.
  R. W. Sentenced to Banishment, 104.
  Uproar in, at Sentence of R. W., 242, 280.
  Underhill sent to, for R. W., 108.
  Gov. Winthrop telephones R. W. at, 109.
  R. W. departs from, 109.
  Deed and Deputies, where now? 99.
  Obadiah Holmes of, 143, 7.
  Witchcraft and Cotton Mather, 145, 162, 192, 3, 4.
Saltonstall, Sir Richard.
  of the Mass. Bay Co., 37.
  Returns to Eng., 51, 60.
  Defends the Charter, 62.
  Letter to Cotton and Wilson, 153, 268.
  School System, N. E., 145, 159.
Shawomet,
  Claimed by Mass., 127.
  Sought by Mass., 131.
  Included in R.I., 156.
  Redress for, 158.

Skelton,
    Minister from Eng., 38.
    Pastor at Salem, 40.
    with R. W., Teacher, 77.
    Death of, 83.
Smith, Ralph.
    Takes Ship in Eng., 38.
    Describes Puritans, 39.
    Sent off, 39.
    Call to Plymouth, 39.
    with Roger Williams, 75.
Smyth, John.
    Pastor in Eng., 8.
    Studies the Scriptures, 9.
    Bishop Hall of, 9.
    "Grandee of Separation," 10.
    for Religious Liberty in Eng., 10.
    a "Separatist," 38.
    Gains Toleration in Eng., 209, 220.
Standish, Miles.
    with the Pilgrims, 17.
    Chosen Military Capt. 17.
    Goes Ashore, 18,
    at the Encounter, 19.
    Goes to Eng., 31.
    Brings sad News, 31.
Standing Order, Ministers of, 197, 201.
Synods,
    Pilgrims none, 12, 22.
    1st called, 119.
    for Discipline, 119.
    2d opposed, 136, 9.
    Prepare a Platform, 137.
    Edict on Magistrates, 137.
    Vote Westminster Assembly, 138.
    Cambridge Platform, 139.
    None in R. I., 142.
    3d in Boston, 160.
    Half-way Covenant, 160.
    4th in Boston, 166.
    who Church Members, 167.
    Veto Independency, 167.
    5th in Boston, 178.
    Reforming, 178.
    6th Confession, 184.
    all declared illegal, 201.

University,
    of Oxford, 3.
    of Prague, 3; of Leyden, 294.
    of Wittenberg, 3.
    of Cambridge, Eng., 68, 186
    of Harvard, 145, 154, 159, 204, 5, 7.
    of Brown, 207.

Vane, Sir Harry.
    with Hutchinsons, 118.
    Receives R. W., 152.
    Letter to R. Island, 156.
    R. W. replies to, 157.
    R. W. intimate, 295.
    R. W. entertained, 297.
Waldenses, 1.
    Lancaster Friend to, 2.
    Lollard a, 2.

Waldenses, *continued*.
    Mosheim of, 1.
    Peter Waldo, 219.
Wampanoags, "Welcome, Englishmen," 24, 111.
Warwick,
    Opinions of, 145.
    Alarmed, 146.
    and Towns unite, 156.
    Disgusted, 162.
    not far wrong, 194.
Washington, Geo.
    Interviewed, 208.
    Petition to, 208.
    Reply of, 208.
    Opinion of Petitioners, 208.
    gets Const'l Am'd't, 208.
    Ordinance, 1787, 208.
Westminster Assembly, 138.
"Wha-cheer," 113.
White, John.
    Starts Cape Ann Colony, 36.
    gets a Charter, 36.
White, Peregrine, 19.
Winslow, Gov.
    his Report, 13.
    Letter to Roger Williams, 111.
Wickliffe, John.
    Protected by Duke, 2.
    Translates the Bible, 2.
    its Sufficiency of, 2.
    Writings, get to Huss, 2.
William, Prince of Orange.
    Immortal Reformer, 6.
    His is a Land of Refuge, 9, 10, 124, 43.
    Roger Williams goes by, 127.
    Roger Williams goes by Colony of Holland, 152.
    III. Prince of Orange, 191.
    Checks the Inquisition, 6, 209, 220.
Williams, Betsey.
    Gives Land to the City of Providence for a Roger Williams Park, 188, 296, 298.
Williams, Roger.
    Parentage, 67.
    when and where born, 67.
    Noticed by Sir Edward Coke, 67, 8, 70, 109, 186, 239, 244.
    Studies at Cambridge, Eng., 68.
    Beneficed in Church of Eng., 68.
    Studies Nonconformity, 68.
    Inclines to "Separation," 69.
    Meets Cotton and Hooker, 69.
    Flight from Eng., 70.
    Letter to Mrs. Sadlier, 70.
    and Mary his Wife in Boston, 71.
    for Religious Liberty, 71.
    Reported by Gov. Winthrop, 71.
    Call to 1st Church, Boston, 71.
    Declines the Call, 71, 227, 236, 258, 261, 289.
    Firm "Separatist," 72.
    Call to Salem, 72, 228, 9.
    Inhibited by the Court, 73.

INDEX. 311

Williams, Roger, *continued.*
 Call to Plymouth, 73.
 Reported by Gov. Bradford, 74.
 Associate with Ralph Smith, 74, 240.
 Gov. Winthrop visits Plymouth, 240, 75.
 Toils for the Indians, 75.
 Manual labors, 76.
 Names of Children, 76.
 Key of Indian Languages, 76.
 Held as a Sachem, 76.
 Treatise on Pattent, 76.
 Recalled to Salem, 77, 228.
 Brewster's Opinion of, 77.
 Return to Salem, 77.
 Teacher with Skelton, 77, 229.
 no enemy to Mass. Bay, 78, 84, 5, 87, 147, 170, 230.
 Fearless and Faithful, 80.
 Submits his Treatise, 81, 230, 240.
 no Enemy to Mass. Bay, 83.
 Preaching criticised, 84.
 Opposition subsides, 85.
 Preaching not dangerous, 85.
 on Resident's oath, 230, 241.
 Positions firm, 86.
 Sustained by Public Opinion, 86, 242.
 Ordained at Salem, 87.
 Summoned to Court, 88.
 Elders advice against, 88, 232, 241.
 Letters of Admonition, 90, 233.
 Elders in their own Trap, 90.
 Church bribed against, 91.
 Last Sabbath as Pastor, 92.
 Farewell Letter, 93, 234.
 Stood alone firmly, 94, 235.
 Opened his own House, 95.
 " Filled all Salem with his Opinions," 194, 262.
 Undismayed, 95.
 Wife joins in his Opinions, 95.
 Stood for Toleration, 96.
 not an Underminer, 96.
 Invulnerable Point, 92, 96.
 the Court invincible, 97.
 Endicott storms the Court, 98.
 Court assembles, 100.
 Indictment presented, 100.
 Justified all his opinions, 241, 103.
 Contest with Hooker, 103, 247.
 Court adjourned, 103.
 Sentence passed, 104.
 Ostracized, 106, 235, 241.
 Mr. Cotton apologizes, 106.
 Court not unanimous, 108.
 " Sixe weekes " extended, 108.
 Cited to Boston, 108.
 Gov. Winthrop's hint, 109, 236, 242, 5.
 Capt. Underhill too late, 109.
 Dire Chagrin, 110.
 R. W. in exile, 111.
 Massasoit a Friend, 111.
 Wife and Family at Seekonk, 111.
 Gov. Winslow's hint, 111.

Williams, Roger, *continued.*
 Goes to Mooshausick, 112.
 Lands given by Canonicus and Miantonomo, 113.
 and Wife give site for the City of Providence, 114.
 Faith in Religious Liberty, 115.
 Quiets the Pequots, 116.
 Gov. Winthrop's Proposal, 116, 210, 243, 264, 285, 6, 292.
 Proposal not yet carried out, 117.
 Buys Prudence Island, 243.
 Receives the Exiles, 122.
 the Name of " Rhode Island," 122.
 Founds Providence and a voluntary Civil Government, 122.
 and the three Colonies and Compacts, 122.
 Father of Religious Liberty, 124, 5.
 Anabaptistic Tendencies, 125.
 Founds 1st Baptist Church, Providence, 126, 266.
 Annoyed by Arnold, 126.
 goes to Eng. for a Charter, 126.
 Miantonomo tomahawked, 127.
 R. I. left out of the " Union of the four Colonies," 127.
 Publishes " Key " and " Tenet " in Eng., 127.
 Charter of " Providence Plantations," 128.
 Walks slow thro' Mass. Bay, 128.
 Case of Enchugsen, 129.
 Success of, Alarms the Bay, 129.
 Returning, meets opposition, 131.
 Religious Liberty grows, 137.
 Frames the new Government of R. I., 141.
 Freedom of Worship assured, 141.
 Warwick claimed by the Bay, 145.
 Plymouth opposes the Claim, 145.
 " Commissioners of United Colonies " pay double, 145.
 no Underminer, 146, 264.
 Plymouth refuses to take Warwick, 146.
 R. W. and Clarke go to Eng. for Charter, 146, 152.
 R. W. returns by Boston, 155.
 Cromwell confirms the Charter, 155.
 R. W. had the freedom of the Colonies, 155.
 Four towns unite under Charter, 156.
 R. W. chosen President, 156.
 R. W. explains Religious Liberty, 157.
 R. W. called to Boston, gets redress, 158.
 Religious Liberty secured, 168.
 Non-intercourse intimated, 173.
 Religious Liberty in Providence and Boston, 173.
 *Death* of Roger Williams, 186.
 Bancroft's Eulogy of R. W., 187.
 R. I. honors R. W. with a Statue in the National Capitol, Washington, D.C., 188.

Williams, Roger, *continued.*
  Providence has a Roger Williams Park, 188, 294-8.
  yet to be honored, 116, 117, 183, 207, 210, 224, 243, 247, 268, 276, 278, 281.
Winthrop, John, Gov.
  of the Mass. Bay Company, 37.
  Opinion of the enterprise, 44.
  Silence on Religion in the Charter, 46, 57, 236.
  John Cotton's opinion, 66, 226.
  Letter on Arbella, 48.
  Arrive in N. E., 49.
  Reports Roger Williams' arrival, 51.
  Parts with Sir Richard Saltonstall, 51.
  Visits Plymouth, 239, 75.
  Assistant of the General Court, 101.

Winthrop, John, Gov., *continued.*
  Gives Roger Williams a "hint," 109, 236, 242, 260, 277.
  Always friendly to R. Williams, 253, 112, 277.
  Proposed to recall R. Williams, 116, 210, 243, 264, 285, 6, 291, 2, 278.
  Buys Prudence Island, 243.
  Death-bed Regret, 183.
  Death, 143.
Winthrop, John, Jr., 161, 184, 200, 244.
Winthrop, Hon. R. C.
  Oration of, 110, 210.
  Roger Williams and Winthrops friends, 252, 3, 291.

Ziska of Bohemia, 3.

www.ingramcontent.com/pod-product-compliance
Lightning Source LLC
Chambersburg PA
CBHW030742230426
43667CB00007B/815